1973

The Mind of

INDIA

The Mind of
I N D I A

E D I T E D,

With an Introduction, Notes, & Bibliography by

W I L L I A M   G E R B E R

The Macmillan Company, NEW YORK

Collier-Macmillan Ltd., LONDON

Library of Congress Catalog Card Number: 67-13639

First Printing

The Mind of India is part of a series, Classics in the History of Thought, prepared under the general editorship of Crane Brinton and Paul Edwards.

The Macmillan Company, New York
Collier-Macmillan Canada Ltd., Toronto, Ontario

Printed in the United States of America

THE KIND PERMISSION of the following publishers and copyright owners to reprint passages from the books indicated is gratefully acknowledged:

Advaita Ashrama—*Selections from Swami Vivekananda.*

George Allen and Unwin—(1) S. Radhakrishnan, *An Idealist View of Life* (for rights everywhere except the United States); (2) Rabindranath Tagore, *The Religion of Man* (for rights everywhere except the United States).

Sri Aurobindo Ashram—Aurobindo Ghose, *Last Poems.*

Curtis Brown Ltd.—Ernest E. Wood, *The Glorious Presence* (for rights in the British Empire).

Central Jaina Publishing House—Ghuna-Bhadra, *Atmanushasana*, translated by J. L. Jaini.

Clarendon Press, Oxford—(1) Max A. Macauliffe, *The Sikh Religion;* (2) *Gaina Sutras* (volume 45 of *The Sacred Books of the East*, edited by F. Max Müller), translated by Hermann Jacobi.

E. P. Dutton & Co., Inc.—(1) Dwight Goddard (ed.), A *Buddhist*

CONTENTS

II. *The Road to Nirvana*: *Ancient Buddhism*

LATER DISCOURSES

III. *Reverence for Life*: *Ancient Jainism*

LATER DISCOURSES

Contents

V. *"The Life Divine"*: *Modern Mysticism*

VI. *"The Men of the Great Soul"*: *Twentieth-Century Popular Philosophy*

NOTE.—*The English spelling of words in Sanskrit and other Indian languages varies, as does also the use or nonuse of diacritical marks over or under certain letters in such words, showing, for example, some vowels to be long and some consonants as pronounced either far forward in the mouth or halfway between the front and the back of the mouth. In this book, the spelling conforms (as far as the editor's introductory statements are concerned) to the most widespread usage— for example, "Shiva" rather than "Siva"—and diacritical marks are omitted.*

PREFACE

Interest in Indian philosophy is increasing. In fact, with writers such as Aldous Huxley on the sympathetic side, and Arthur Koestler in the opposition, Indian thought has recently become a focus not only of attention but of controversy. Huxley, in one of his last lectures, cited the Indian "That art thou" as the consummate expression of the theology of mysticism. Koestler, in *The Yogi and the Commissar* and *The Lotus and the Robot*, came away from Indian philosophy with disgust.

As part of this tide of interest, popular editions are being published here and abroad of books presenting significant Indian efforts to understand the universe and man. The *Kama Sutra*, a frank philosophy of love, has been reissued, in Richard Burton's polished translation, with a foreword by the popular novelist and travel writer, Santha Rama Rau. Works on Buddhism have fed the Zen movement. Alan Watts, in his books, lectures, and broadcasts, has spread the word about pinnacles of self-realization as taught by Indian sages.

Nevertheless, despite these developments, the masterworks of Indian philosophy are for the most part not readily available in English or in other modern tongues. Of those which have been translated, some can be found only in rare volumes in the largest libraries, or in new books published in India and not widely noted or acquired in the Occident. Moreover, the pertinent sources are mainly scattered in multiple volumes interspersed with other material.

Where the sources are more readily available, as in the admirable volume entitled *A Source Book in Indian Philosophy*, edited by

xiii

Sarvepalli Radhakrishnan and Charles A. Moore (Princeton, 1957), the translations seem to have been chosen more for their scholarly literalness than for their meaningfulness and poignancy to Western readers. Indeed, the profusion of unfamiliar names and the scantily explained metaphysical complexities in many works on Indian philosophy tend to repel many Westerners.

What has been needed, therefore, is a compilation in a single volume, with translations in readable English, intended for the educated layman and with explanatory matter for that readership. Such a compilation should make the whole corpus of Indian reflective thought, with its enduring splendor, available to the non-specialist, through simple explanations of the pertinent facts, words, and principles. The present volume aims to fill this need.

In preparing this volume, I have perused not only the available single-volume and multi-volume histories and source collections of Indian and Eastern philosophy, including the source book compiled by Radhakrishnan and Moore, but also many monographic studies of single thinkers, single works, and general trends. Whenever I have found that an Indian philosopher, or an anonymous work in Indian philosophy, has been rated as important by subsequent Indian thinkers and by Western scholars familiar with the works in the original languages, I have searched for translations which would justify the centuries-old high evaluation.

In coverage, I have aimed at casting a wide net, i.e., at broad coverage of schools and movements, while at the same time giving, in the case of each work selected for inclusion, a large enough excerpt to be meaningful and revealing.

For a general justification of an anthology of this kind, we have the authority of John Milton that "as Wine and Oil are imported to us from abroad, soe must ripe understanding, and many Civill Vertues, be imported into our mindes from Foren Writings, and Examples of best Ages." Also pertinent is what Milton said in another connection (in his history of Muscovy), "What was scatter'd in many volumes . . . with no cursory pains I laid together, to save the Reader a far longer travaile."

WILLIAM GERBER

INTRODUCTION:

The Currents and Course of Indian Philosophy

THE MOST SIGNIFICANT, MOST PERSISTENT CURRENTS OF INDIAN philosophy may be expressed in eighteen theses, each of which leads into the next one. Many of the eighteen theses have noteworthy counterparts in the philosophy of the West. References to some of these counterparts are adduced in the following comments on the eighteen theses.

THESIS 1. *To live is to suffer.*

THIS IS NOT to say that living is without its pleasures and satisfactions. Indeed, the first two of the four standard values of Indian life (see thesis 13) are material possessions and psychological compensations. Nevertheless, suffering, according to the Hindu, is fundamental in life.

This first tenet of Indian philosophy, to live is to suffer, corresponds roughly to a basic tenet of existentialism: the agony of existence. The theme of the agony of existence, however, is an old and abiding one in Hellenic, Judeo-Christian civilization, long antedating existentialism. "Man," said Job's neighbor, "is born unto trouble, as the sparks fly upward." The Stoics recognized that suffering is a part of life, and they recommended enduring it. "Sunt lacrimae rerum" (weeping is a basic reality), sang the author of the *Aeneid.*

The agony of existence is a common theme in Western literature and art, perhaps more so today than in the past. Thus, in the great Western dramatic tragedies, defeat and destruction are inevitable. The lyrics of Western poets which touch us most are those of sadness and disillusion. Suffering is plain in the faces depicted in paintings with the deepest meaning.

THESIS 2. *That we suffer is, at least in large part, our own fault.*

THERE ARE TWO Indian interpretations of this tenet, the orthodox and the liberal. According to the orthodox interpretation, our suffering in this life is due to our misdeeds committed in an earlier life or in earlier lives. This is the theory of *karma*, the burden of the moral consequences of our former conduct. It entails the concept of *samsara*, the cycle of births and deaths (see thesis 10).

According to the liberal interpretation, our suffering is due to our failure to take advantage of the way to eliminate suffering (thesis 5). In this view, the suffering of those who fail to seek the way of deliverance from suffering is their own responsibility.

Thus, both orthodox and liberal Hindus hold that suffering is, at least in large part, man's own fault. But Western explanations of the existence of evil and suffering also commonly ascribe much if not all of it to man himself. Original sin and the general assignment to man rather than to God of responsibility for man's suffering constitute a conspicuous thread in the fabric of European thought.

THESIS 3. *There is a way to eliminate suffering.*

INDIAN THOUGHT is sometimes described as saying nay to life. This is not an accurate description. The Indian recognizes not only the pervasiveness of suffering, but also the availability of a way to a more abundant, blissful life, a life in which pain will not hurt. There is, he repeatedly asserts, a way to eliminate suffering.

In Western thought, this theme takes the form of emphasis on the reality of salvation. Suffering, yes; suffering without the possibility of redemption, no. There is, the West says, a way to salvation. The way is religious or secular, depending on the guide. Salvation is salvation of the soul, according to some teachers. Salvation is the betterment of material and cultural conditions, through improved social and economic forms and the progress of technology, according to others.

THESIS 4. *The way is open to all.*

ALTHOUGH SOME Indians expect only the members of the highest caste, Brahmins, to seek salvation, India's greatest thinkers teach that the way does not depend on predestination, caste, or the grace of God. It depends only on the initiative and persistence of the sufferer in following the prescribed way. No caste is excluded. Any human being can go the way which eliminates suffering.

The Hellenic, Judeo-Christian tradition is ambiguous on this issue. One strain of Western thought is spiritually equalitarian; another is exclusive. Stoicism is a way of life for all men; Platonism makes distinctions. The way, according to Boehme and other mystics, is open to all who are willing to submerge their individual egos; the turnstile, according to Calvin, however, will not work for everybody.

THESIS 5. *The way to eliminate suffering is to eliminate attachment.*

WE SUFFER because we badly want, and cannot always have, comfort for ourselves and pleasure for those we love. We are attached to comforts and pleasures. We are attached to family and friends. We are attached to life. But all these objects of attachment are subject to dissolution, and that is why we suffer. No attachment, no suffering, says the Hindu.

In the West, this corresponds to the philosophy of contentment. Stoicism teaches contentment by advocating *ataraxia*, non-attachment. Although Job was not contented, he was resigned to the will of God and thus willing to forego attachment: "The Lord hath given, and the Lord hath taken away; blessed be the name of the Lord." The Christian monastic tradition, prescribing poverty, chastity, and obedience, reflects a quest for spiritual contentment through self-denial—renunciation of attachment to property, family, and self-will.

Peace of mind, acceptance of yourself as you are without addiction or attachment to illusions, recognition of yourself as a worthy human being without attachment to fetishes or guilt complexes— this is the form in which thesis 5 of Indian philosophy is found in the popular philosophy and psychology of twentieth-century Europe and America. Western philosophers, however, are not unanimous in deprecating attachment. Nietzschean philosophy, for example, calls for vigorous pursuit of what one wants.

THESIS 6. *The way to eliminate attachment is to wake up from our slumber of largely unconscious habit action (unawareness or ignorance of self) and to become self-aware.*

TECHNICALLY, THIS is called, by the Indian, removing *avidya* (ignorance) or seeing through the veil of *maya* (illusion).

How can we wake up and become self-aware? Buddha gives the technique. In a passage presented in Chapter II of the present volume, he says that a sage, taking a short breath, is aware that he is taking a short breath; equally, in taking a long breath, the sage observes that he is taking a long breath; turning his head to the left to see something which has caught his eye, he is aware that he is turning his head to the left; hearing a sound, he observes that he is hearing a sound; taking a step in walking, he observes that he is taking a step; lifting a burden, he is aware that he is lifting a burden; speaking a word, he is aware that he is speaking a word; being seated, he is aware that he is seated.

In one of the Upanishads, a bird on a branch is described as watching another bird on a nearby branch. As the second bird moves, the first bird watches him move. As the second bird eats, the first bird watches him eat. As the second bird turns his head, the first bird watches him turn his head.

Be the first bird to yourself. As you stand, watch yourself stand. As you eat, watch yourself eat. As you turn your head, watch yourself turn your head. As you do anything at all, at any time, morning, noon, or night, while shaving, while walking, while becoming angry, while shouting, while feeling hurt by an insult, while feeling pain from a hurt finger, while feeling anxious, while feeling relieved, watch yourself doing or feeling, acting or being acted on, observe yourself being in a state, condition, or situation.

India originated this technique. Some Western mystics later discovered it independently. Socrates' injunction, γνῶθι σεαυτόν, know thyself (ascribed also to Thales and other early Greek thinkers), was in the tradition of self-awareness. However, Socrates did not spell it out as a technique, although from time to time he went into a trance in which his concentration on the inner life was so intense that he was oblivious of those around him.

Cicero viewed the precept "to know ourselves" as "the most difficult of all lessons" and also as "a precept so forcible and so comprehensive that it has been attributed not to a man, but to the god of Delphi himself."

The eleventh-century Islamic theologian al-Ghazzali, in his *Incoherence of the Philosophers*, referred to the self-aware man thus: "When his inattention ceases, he awakens to himself." Montaigne wrote: "Everyone looks before him; I look into myself. I have no other business except myself. I am constantly meditating about myself; I control and taste myself."

"My answer," said Tolstoy, "to the question whether one should try to attain complete consciousness in one's inner spiritual life, is that this is precisely the most needful and important business of our lives." And Maeterlinck said: "Without suspecting it, we are all living like somnambulists, performing the day's tasks mechanically, blindly . . . To wake us with a start . . . some brutal and extraordinary blow is needed: the revelation of an incurable malady, the loss of that which is dearest to us . . ." (Zen Buddhists of the past and present have used shock techniques to bring novitiates to a state of awakened awareness.)

Paul Tillich wrote that "no one can experience depth without stopping and becoming aware of himself."

THESIS 7. *There are degrees of intensity of self-awareness.*

CONSTANT PRACTICE of the exercise of self-awareness, over a period of a week, a month, a year, or many years, deepens the degree of self-awareness that one achieves. At first, one achieves a superficial level. Then one plumbs more deeply. At some levels a plateau is reached, which one finds it hard to better. The way to greater depth may, in fact, proceed by discernible steps and not continuously.

Modern Indian mystics, especially, recognize the degrees of intensity of self-awareness and preach it as a doctrine. In Western writers, particularly the medieval mystics, the degrees are often referred to as stages of contemplation or as rungs on the ladder of ascension.

THESIS 8. *In a high degree of intensity of self-awareness, one transcends—in knowledge and perhaps in actuality—the opposites of self and not-self.*

THIS MEANS that one senses oneself as united with the not-self. That is, one either *is* united with the not-self and one knows this, or at least one clearly *seems* to be united with the not-self, and the seeming is so vivid that nothing else that seems at all seems more vividly. In other words, one feels then that if one ever knew anything to be true or real, then one knows this union to be true or real.

The not-self with which one feels united in this experience is either (a) "all things" or (b) "the all-soul, the world soul."

In the terminology of Western mystics, that which one is then united with, and clearly feels oneself to be united with, is God, or, in Plotinus's word, "the One" or "the Alone" (the flight of the alone to the Alone). In Indian philosophy, the experience is sometimes called the merging of the self with the Self.

Two English poets have provided descriptions of this experience. According to Shelley, "Those who are subject to the state called reverie, feel as if their nature were dissolved into the surrounding universe, or as if the surrounding universe were absorbed into their being. They are conscious of no distinction." Tennyson reported, of a particular reverie: "All at once . . . individuality itself seemed to fade away into the boundless being, the loss of personality (if so it were) seeming no extinction but the only true life."

THESIS 9. *The achievement of this state of conscious immersion in and identification with "the all" results in unspeakable bliss.*

THE STATE is called nirvana. The achievement of it is *moksha* (liberation). Its psychological aspect is called *samadhi* (a mystic trance characterized by a sense of union with "the all"). It is evidenced by a feeling of *bodhi* (enlightenment). *Samadhi* is thought of as a temporary state; *moksha* and nirvana, as enduring states.

Western mystics uniformly characterize the mystic union as a state of indescribable bliss. Women mystics, such as St. Catherine of Siena (fourteenth century) and St. Theresa of Avila in Spain (sixteenth century), have written of the joy of their marriage with the One.

THESIS 10. *The achievement of "moksha" not only results in immediate bliss, per se. It also sustains the bliss by ending the dreaded cycle of births and deaths.*

THE CYCLE of births and deaths, that is, the preexistence in another human or animal body of every man now living, and his fated rebirth in another form after the death of his present body, is generally taken for granted in Indian philosophy, which also assumes that termination of the cycle through absorption in "the all" is a good thing. It is a further assumption that if *moksha*, liberation, is sustained, rather than merely achieved for a brief time, then the cycle is broken.

Thinkers west of India who have entertained at least the idea of the cycle of births and deaths (usually referred to as "the transmigration of souls")—if not also the idea of the breaking of the chain when one achieves *moksha*—include Pythagoras, Empedocles, Plato, Cicero, Jesus (who said that John the Baptist was a reincarnation of Elijah; Matthew, xvii, 12–13), Plutarch, Origen, Plotinus, Bruno, Hume, Goethe, Novalis, Kant, Fichte, Schopenhauer, Wordsworth ("Our birth is but a sleep and a forgetting"), Emerson, Thoreau, Nietzsche, Tolstoy, Charles Renouvier, C. D. Broad, and C. J. Ducasse.

Present-day Western analysts of mysticism have found that self-awareness, deep enough to provide a sense of union, if it does not actually confer eternal nirvana, at least affords a unique sense of timelessness. But timelessness is not universally admired in the West; an important Western attitude (Bergsonism, pragmatism, process philosophy) extols or emphasizes change, duration, dynamism.

THESIS 11. *Every man should seek "moksha" at the appropriate stage of his life, namely, the fourth stage.*

THE FOUR STAGES of man's life are enumerated in thesis 12. In the first three stages, one may or may not seek *moksha*, according to one's inclinations. But after completing the first three, one is obligated to devote the fourth to this objective.

In Western thought, those thinkers who discuss salvation at all say that the obligation to be saved is not confined to a special period in life. The youth, the mature man, and the old man are equally urged to choose the way of salvation.

THESIS 12. *The stages of a man's life are, first, childhood, youth, and education; second, manhood and family responsibility; third, retirement from public responsibility, with continued residence at home, in preparation for the period of intense seeking of "moksha"; and, fourth, retirement to the forest, for a life of begging of one's bread, of concentrated meditation, and of intense seeking of "moksha."*

IN THE FIRST STAGE, studentship, an Indian is expected to practice celibacy. In the second, that of a householder, he is expected to beget a son, perform the religious rituals, and entertain ascetics and other guests. In the third stage, that of an anchorite, he prepares, through penances and austerities, for complete renunciation of worldly interests. In the fourth stage, as an ascetic, he seeks *moksha.*

In Western thought, the stages of life have no special standing in serious philosophical, religious, or anthropological discussions.

THESIS 13. *The values of a man's life, culminating in "moksha," are four in number, namely, first, "artha" (material possessions and comforts); second, "kama" (the enjoyment of pleasures, the satisfaction of desires); third, "dharma" (the doing of one's duty, the rendering of justice); and, fourth, "moksha."*

THE FIRST THREE of these values apply especially to the first two stages of a man's life, but partly also to the third stage. *Moksha* applies especially to the fourth stage and in a lesser degree to the third.

The values of life, like the stages of life, are not so definitely standardized in Hellenic, Judeo-Christian civilization. Plato set up a pyramid with wisdom, courage, and prudence at the bottom and justice at the top. Sometimes the good, the beautiful, and the true are taken to be the basic values. Some writers classify values as instrumental or intrinsic; others classify them as relative or absolute. But generally, the classifying of values in Western thought is extremely varied.

THESIS 14. *The effort to achieve "moksha," especially in the fourth stage of life, is aided by ethical discipline practiced in the first three stages and carried over to the fourth.*

THUS, SALVATION is virtually reserved for the upright. This is not, however, a strict requirement; it is rather a prop, an adjunct.

This thesis has its parallel in the more rigid dogma of Western religious thought in general that heaven is only for the righteous. However, Western mystics, as a specific group, lay little stress on moral conduct as an aid to achieving union with the One.

THESIS 15. *Ethical discipline includes, first, conformity to conventions of caste; second, adherence to ideals of non-injury and non-violence; and, third, the practice of telling the truth.*

CONVENTIONS OF CASTE include the injunction to marry in one's own group. The four groups, not counting the outcasts, are, first, the *Brahmins*, the priestly class; second, the *kshatriyas*, warriors and rulers; third, the *vaishyas*, merchants; and fourth, the *sudras*, servants. The outcasts, a fifth group, are thought to be the descendants of the less-civilized aborigines whom the invading Aryans encountered on entering India some 3,500 years ago (as distinguished from the civilized Dravidians whom they also encountered and who are the ancestors of today's Tamils of southern India).

Non-injury and non-violence, though especially stressed by Jainism, are virtues in all the philosophies of India. Truth-telling is stressed in the best-known Indian epic—*Mahabharata*—and elsewhere.

Western ethics, while acknowledging non-injury, non-violence, and truth-telling as meritorious ideals, usually downgrades conventions of social stratification. Plato and Aristotle, however, said that certain social classifications conform to the different kinds of human nature.

THESIS 16. *Ethical discipline is dependent upon religion.*

THIS DICTUM refers not to a particular religion, but rather to religion in general. It is closely related to thesis 17, on universal religion.

In Western thought, this issue has caused a cleavage between religiously oriented moralists, who espouse thesis 16, and secular moralists, who reject it. Within the school of religious moralists, some hold that the rightness of a morally right action is inherent, but the impulsion to do it must come from religion, while others say that the rightness of a right action consists solely in God's commandment of it.

The earliest secular moralist who denied that ethical discipline is in any way based upon religion was Socrates. In his conversation with Euthyphro, as reported by Plato, he asked the provocative question whether an action is holy because it is favored by the gods, or whether it is favored by the gods because it is holy. He did not categorically defend either answer, but his sympathy with the secular answer, that the gods favor an action because it is holy, is clear from the context.

THESIS 17. *(a) The religion of every people and every locality reflects a core of universal religion. (b) Specific religions should therefore not be dogmatic.*

ACKNOWLEDGMENT of the core of universal religion is implicit in the Hindus' recognition that a man may reasonably worship now one god as supreme and now another. It is actually explicit in the writings of Ramakrishna and other mystics of the nineteenth and twentieth centuries, who recognize that the basic truths of religion are found in Christianity, Judaism, and Islam, as well as in Hinduism and other faiths.

In Western thought, the core of universal religion is adumbrated, for example, in the universalistic hymn of Cleanthes to Zeus (third century B.C.), and is fully explicit in such apostrophes as Pope's:

> "Father of all, in every age,
>   In every clime adored
> By saint, by savage, or by sage,
>   Jehovah, Jove, or Lord."

That specific religions should not be exclusive or dogmatic follows from the premise of a core of truth in all religions.

In the Hindu religion, recognition is accorded to gods on four levels:

(a) There are three gods, each of whom is sometimes worshiped as the sole God; first, Brahma, the World Soul, the Self which includes all selves, the impersonal divine principle (or logos); second, Purusha, creator and lord of the world (analogous to Plato's Demiurge); and third, Prajapati, father or progenitor of gods and men, spirit of procreation.

(b) There are gods who are sometimes joined in a trinity. In earlier periods, a widely worshiped trinity consisted of Surya, the sun; Indra, god of rain, the storm, and battle; and Agni, god of fire. More recently, recognition as a trinity is accorded to Brahma; Vishnu, the preserver; and Shiva, the destroyer and restorer. Within the Brahma-Vishnu-Shiva trinity, any one of the three may be regarded as *primus inter pares*. Thus, Kalidasa wrote (probably in the sixth century of the present era):

"Of Brahma, Vishnu, Siva, each may be
First, second, third amid the blessed Three."

(c) There are gods each of whom, although presiding over a special domain, is also sometimes thought of as the supreme god among the gods. In earlier times, such supremacy was accorded, by different worshipers, as well as by the same worshiper at different times, to Varuna, the sky god; Surya or Savitri, the sun; Indra; and Rudra, god of the storm, strength, and beauty.

(d) There are other gods, who command special attention for special purposes. Among these, worshiped particularly in earlier periods, are Ushas, goddess of the dawn; Kama, god of love; Soma, god of the fermented drink which is believed to bestow immortality; and Yama, king of the blessed in the afterworld. More recently, Kali, mother of all, has had some allegiance.

Western religion, by contrast, is mainly monotheistic.

THESIS 18. *Universal religion holds, first, that the spiritual in life is paramount; and, second, that the cosmos originated as the play or sport or whimsical willing ("lila") of a creator who molded available matter into an order which he himself designed.*

THAT THE SPIRITUAL in life is paramount is a concept on which Hindus and religious Westerners agree, at least in principle. It is, however, taken more seriously in practice by Hindus.

Of the belief that God made and rules the world through sport or whim, a strain runs through Western thought from Plato, who asserted that man is God's plaything, and other Greek thinkers, who held that τύχη (chance, contingency, caprice) is a component of the world, through Descartes, who said that God could have made the laws of nature entirely different from what they are, and Peirce, who said that the cosmos originated in sport. Other Western thinkers, however, from Aristotle to Einstein, disagree.

Thus many of the basic theses of Indian philosophy are reflected positively or negatively in Western thought. The reflection in some cases is conscious, that is, Western thinkers have known Indian thought and have agreed or disagreed with it; in other cases, it is not conscious, that is, Western thinkers, responding to universal

springs of wonder about the universe and man, have reached conclusions which parallel or oppose the conclusions reached by the
philosophers and seers of India. In any case, comprehension of
Indian philosophy deepens our grasp of Western philosophy, and
vice versa.

A CHRONOLOGY

LISTED BELOW ARE THE AUTHORS AND WRITINGS INCLUDED IN THE present volume—together with a few additional landmarks that are mentioned but not extensively covered.

The reader should bear in mind that authorities differ greatly on the period to which some of the earlier texts are to be assigned. While the dates shown here are based on good authority, in some instances equally good authority may be cited for quite different dates.

About 2000–500 B.C.	Vedic hymns.
About 1000–500 B.C.	Brahmanas, Aranyakas, and Upanishads (annexes to the collections of Vedic hymns).
About 600 B.C.	Brihaspati, leading hedonist.
Between 600 and 200 B.C.	Jaimini, author of the Mimamsa Sutras (basic text of one of the six traditional systems of Hindu philosophy).
About 580–500 B.C.	Mahavira, Jain leader.
563–483 B.C.	Buddha (Gautama Siddhartha).
About 550 B.C.	Gautama (not Buddha), author of the Nyaya Sutras (basic text of one of the six systems).
About 550 B.C.	Kapila, author of the Sankhya Sutras (basic text of one of the six systems).
Between 500 and 200 B.C.	Badarayana, author of the Brahma Sutras (basic text of one of the six systems).

Between 500 and 100 B.C.	*Bhagavad Gita.*
Between 450 and 250 B.C.	Dhammapada, Buddhist classic.
About 400 B.C.	Development of Theravada Buddhism (also called Hinayana Buddhism).
Between 300 and 50 B.C.	*Sutra Kritanga* (Discourse of Performed Precepts), Jain classic.
Between 300 and 50 B.C.	*Uttara Dhyayana* (Higher Meditation), Jain classic.
Between 300 B.C. and A.D. 200	*Mahabharata,* epic poem.
Between 300 B.C. and A.D. 500	*Ramayana,* epic poem.
About 250 B.C.	Kanada, author of the Vaishesika Sutras (basic text of one of the six systems).
Between 250 B.C. and A.D. 350	Patanjali, author of the Yoga Sutras (basic text of one of the six systems).
Between 200 B.C. and A.D. 200	Code of Manu.
Between 100 B.C. and A.D. 300	Tiruvalluvar, author of the *Kural,* a Tamil didactic poem.
About A.D. 50	Development of Mahayana Buddhism.
Between 50 and 200	*Lankavatara Sutra,* Mahayana Buddhist classic.
Between 100 and 300	Yajnavalkya, legal codifier.
Between 250 and 450	Kundakunda, Jain teacher.
Between 300 and 1500	Puranas, metrical compendiums of lore.
About 500	*Questions of King Milinda,* Theravada Buddhist classic.
About 500 to 1400	Tantras, esoteric religious rhapsodies.
About 800	Shankara, Vedantist teacher.
About 850	Guna-Bhadra, Jain teacher.
About 1050	Ramanuja, Vedantist teacher.
About 1200	Madhva, Vedantist teacher.
About 1350	Madhava, summarizer of systems.
About 1450 or 1500	Kabir, mystic poet.
1469–1538	Nanak, original Sikh teacher.

1563–1606	Arjun, Sikh teacher.
1828	Establishment of the Brahmo-Samaj, movement of reform Hinduism.
1836–1886	Ramakrishna, mystic leader.
1861–1941	Rabindranath Tagore, philosopher, poet, and novelist.
1863–1902	Vivekananda, mystic leader.
1869–1948	M. K. Gandhi, apostle of non-violence.
1871–1950	M. Hiriyanna, theoretician of value.
1872–1950	Aurobindo Ghose, mystic leader.
1876	Birth of S. C. Chatterjee, epistemologist and metaphysician.
1877–1947	A. K. Coomaraswamy, specialist in aesthetics.
1882	Establishment in India of the headquarters of the Theosophical Society.
1888	Birth of S. Radhakrishnan, philosopher, diplomat, and president of India.
1888	Birth of A. R. Wadia, social philosopher.
1892	Birth of D. M. Datta, analytic philosopher.
1895	Birth of Jiddu Krishnamurti, mystic leader.

The Mind of
I N D I A

I

"That Art Thou": Ancient
Vedantism

VEDANTISM IS THE PHILOSOPHY BASED ON (A) THE VEDIC HYMNS AND
(b) the interpretative essays annexed to the collections of Vedic
hymns.

"Veda," which is cognate with the Latin *video* ("I see"), means
"knowledge" or "lore." The hymns which came to be called
"Vedic" were composed probably in the thousand years preceding
1000 B.C. (some experts say 500 B.C.) and were collected about
1000 (or 500) B.C. into four anthologies:

> The Rig Veda (lore of praise), which contains the oldest hymns;
> The Sama Veda (lore of tunes), most of which is a duplication
> of hymns in the Rig Veda;
> The Yajur Veda (lore of prayer), consisting of two parts, the
> Black Yajur Veda and the White Yajur Veda; and
> The Atharva Veda (lore of the Atharva clan), which was the
> latest to be compiled and to be accorded canonical status, but
> which nevertheless contains some of the most primitive ideas.

The interpretative essays annexed to the collections of Vedic
hymns include some which are ritualistic and some which are
theoretical. The latter are called "Upanishads" ("sittings,"
"séances," or "dialogues"). There are over one hundred Upani-

shads, many of them in verse form. The ideas regarding the
cosmos which are set forth in the Upanishads are among the most
exalted in all philosophical and religious literature.

The basic tenets of Vedantism, as set forth in the Vedic hymns
and in the Upanishads, are as follows:

1. There are gods, or at least there are aspects of Godhood.

2. There is one supreme god. Sometimes one of the rank-and-
file gods is elevated to this position, but more commonly a god—
called "Brahma" or "Brahman"—is postulated whose prime function is to be the supreme god.

3. Although his rule of the universe is unexplainable, and
indeed is in the nature of play, nevertheless he is good.

4. If you can realize your essential identity with him and with
all other persons and things, i.e., if you can grasp the truth of
"That art thou," you have achieved the highest goal.

The Vedic corpus, broadly conceived, is made up of the following components:

A. Smirti (revealed scriptures)
  1. The Vedic hymns (mantras), grouped into four collections (samhitas) known as the Vedas, as listed above.
  2. The seven Brahmanas (treatises on ritual and folklore),
  one or more for each Veda. Annexed to the Brahmanas
  are (a) the Aranyakas (forest meditation documents) and
  (b) the Upanishads.
  3. The six Angas (further explanations, especially explanations of the Brahmanas). Included in the Angas are (a) the
  Kalpa Sutras (pronouncements on the ages of the world),
  which themselves include the Dharma Sutras (pronouncements on duty or justice), and (b) works on ceremonies,
  grammar, and astronomy.
B. Sruti (traditional scriptures)
  1. The four Upangas (additional explanations), which include (a) about twenty Dharma Shastras (poetic treatises
  on duty or justice, attributed to Manu, Yajnavalkya, and
  others; see Chapter IV of the present volume); (b) the
  Nyaya and Mimamsa Sutras and other epitomes (see Chapter IV of the present volume); and (c) the eighteen
  Puranas (cosmogonies, legends, etc.).

2. The four Upavedas (supplements to the Vedas), one for each Veda, on archery, music, sculpture, medicine, etc.

The present chapter includes selections from the Vedas and from the Upanishads. A few short excerpts from some of the other components of the corpus may illustrate their general character. Thus, the following appears in the Aitareya Brahmana, which is associated with the Rig Veda:

> "The pleasure
> A father has in his own son exceeds
> All other pleasures. Food is life, apparel
> Is a protection, gold an ornament,
> A loving wife the best of friends, a daughter
> An object of compassion, but a son
> Is like a light sent from the highest heaven."

Also in the Aitareya Brahmana is the following statement on the solar system: "The sun never sets nor rises. When people think to themselves the sun is setting, he . . . makes . . . day to what is on the other side. Then when people think he rises in the morning, he . . . makes . . . night to what is on the other side."

A conception of the nature of immortality appears in the following passage from the Satapatha Brahmana, which is associated with the Yajur Veda:

> "The gods lived constantly in dread of death—
> The mighty Ender—so with toilsome rites
> They worshipped and performed religious acts
> Till they became immortal. Then the Ender
> Said to the gods, 'As ye have made yourselves
> Imperishable, so will men endeavour
> To free themselves from me; what portion then
> Shall I possess in man?' The gods replied,
> 'Henceforth no being shall become immortal
> In his own body; this his mortal frame
> Shalt thou still seize; this shall remain thy own.
> He who through knowledge or religious works
> Henceforth attains to immortality
> Shall first present his body, Death, to thee.'"

Translations by Sir Monier Monier-Williams

The following selections are taken from the Taittiriya Aranyaka, which is an annex of the Yajur Veda:

"O Gods! in our desire for livelihood, whatever falsehood we might have uttered, from that sin, O All-gods having attachment to us, do you together free us."

"The Deities who are here, Prosperity, Shame at doing wrong, Fortitude, Penance, Intellect, Status, Faith, Truth, and Dharma (duty)—may all these rise along with me who am rising; may all these never leave me."

"That eye-like sun, beneficent to the gods, that rises up bright in the East, may we be seeing it for a hundred autumns; may we live a hundred autumns; may we delight and rejoice for a hundred autumns; may we be in our places for a hundred autumns; may we be hearing and speaking for a hundred autumns; may we be unvanquished for a hundred autumns; may we be able to see this sun for a long time."

"May the earth, water, fire, air and ether that make up my body become purified so that I may become the effulgent spirit free from sullying passion and sin. . . . May my thought, speech and action become purified so that I may become the effulgent spirit, free from sullying passion and sin. May my soul become purified so that I may become the effulgent spirit, free from sullying passion and sin."

Translations by V. Raghavan

In one of the Puranas, the Vishnu Purana, appears the following prayer:

>"Hail to thee, mighty Lord, all-potent Vishnu!
>Soul of the universe, unchangeable,
>Holy, eternal, always one in nature,
>Whether revealed as Brahma, Hari, Siva—
>Creator or Preserver or Destroyer—
>Thou art the cause of final liberation;
>Whose form is one, yet manifold; whose essence
>Is one, yet diverse; tenuous, yet vast;
>Discernible, yet undiscernible;

Root of the world, yet of the world composed;
Prop of the universe, yet more minute
Than earth's minutest particles; abiding
In every creature, yet without defilement,
Imperishable, one with perfect wisdom."

Translation by Sir Monier Monier-Williams

The Bhagavata Purana (Divine Purana) is the most celebrated of the eighteen Puranas. It is in the group sometimes called "Vaishnava Puranas" (those which extol Vishnu) and sometimes called "Sattvika Puranas" (those which exalt Vishnu as having the character of Sattva, goodness). Of it, the nineteenth-century mystic Ramakrishna wrote: "It is fried in the butter of Knowledge and steeped in the honey of Love." It includes in the eleventh book a sermon put into the mouth of Krishna, who is worshiped as an incarnation of the Divine Being. The following passages appear in the sermon:

"Worship me in the knowers of Truth through hospitality and service. Worship me in the devotee by welcoming him cordially. . . . Worship me in the air by seeing it as divine energy, and in water by accepting it as the symbol of divine purity. . . . worship me in the body by offering it food and drink . . .

"In all these abodes worship me . . . with a concentrated mind. He who thus worships me through work and meditation lives continuously in me . . .

"Even though apparently awake, one is still asleep if one sees multiplicity. Wake up from this dream of ignorance and see the one Self. . . . Meditate on the oneness of the Self with God . . . the one *I Am.* . . .

"The Yogi . . . should . . . practise holding his mind steady in meditation on the Atman, the divine Self. If the mind wanders restlessly while he is practising meditation, he should take still firmer hold on it and patiently try to control its vagaries. He must never lose sight of the course of the mind, but watch the thoughts that pass through it. . . .

"Though he may find it necessary to satisfy his desires, which he is unable for the time to give up, let him all the

while ponder on the emptiness of such gratification . . .
Desirelessness is said to be the highest good. Blessed therefore is he who has no desire. . . .

"Thy sense of happiness and misery is due to a false identification of thy Self with the body, which alone is subject to
changes. . . . Can it be that the progress of time causes happiness and misery? Even then the Atman remains unaffected,
for time exists only in the mind. . . .

"Wise is he who looks with an equal eye upon all beings,
seeing the one indwelling God in the hearts of all. He who
meditates on my divine nature as present in every man
becomes free from rivalry, from jealousy, from hatred . . .

"When a man, relinquishing all attachment, surrenders
himself to me, he realizes his oneness with me . . ."

Translation by Prabhavananda

VEDIC HYMNS

Atharva Veda, Book 4, Hymn 16

T HIS HYMN ASCRIBES OMNISCIENCE TO VARUNA (PRONOUNCED
"VURR-in-a"), god of the sky. The name "Varuna" corresponds
linguistically to "Uranos," the name of the oldest god in the Greek
pantheon, also god of the sky.

After presenting several illustrations of Varuna's omniscience, the
hymn introduces at the end two additional themes: Varuna's rule of
the cosmos as a game or sport; and a prayer that Varuna, in dispensing
good and evil, give preference to tellers of truth over tellers of lies.

> The mighty lord on high our deeds,
>   As if at hand, espies;
> The gods know all men do, though men
>   Would fain their acts disguise:
>
> Whoever stands, whoever moves,
>   Or steals from place to place,
> Or hides him in his secret cell,—
>   The gods his movements trace.
>
> Wherever two together plot,
>   And deem they are alone,
> King Varuna is there, a third,
>   And all their schemes are known.

This earth is his, to him belong
  Those vast and boundless skies;
Both seas within him rest, and yet
  In that small pool he lies.

Whoever far beyond the sky
  Should think his way to wing,
He could not there elude the grasp
  Of Varuna the king.

His spies, descending from the skies,
  Glide all this world around;
Their thousand eyes all-scanning sweep
  To earth's remotest bound.

Whate'er exists in heaven and earth,
  Whate'er beyond the skies,
Before the eyes of Varuna,
  The king, unfolded lies.

The ceaseless winkings all he counts
  Of every mortal's eyes,
He wields this universal frame
  As gamester throws his dice.

Those knotted nooses which thou fling'st,
  O god, the bad to snare,
All liars let them overtake,
  But all the truthful spare.

                    Translation by John Muir

Atharva Veda, Book 19, Hymn 59

TIME IS OF ALL CONCEPTS one of the most abstract. Any people whose mythology personifies time, as is done in this hymn, must be rated as philosophically sophisticated.

Time, like a brilliant steed with seven rays,
And with a thousand eyes, imperishable,
Full of fecundity, bears all things onward.
On him ascend the learned and the wise.

Time, like a seven-wheeled, seven-naved car, moves on.
His rolling wheels are all the worlds, his axle
Is immortality. He is the first of gods.
We see him like an overflowing jar;
We see him multiplied in various forms.

He draws forth and encompasses the worlds;
He is all future worlds; he is their father;
He is their son; there is no power like him.

The past and future issue out of Time,
All sacred knowledge and austerity.
From Time the earth and waters were produced;
From Time, the rising, setting, burning sun;
From Time, the wind;

                Through Time the earth is vast;
Through Time the eye perceives; mind, breath, and name
In him are comprehended.

                     All rejoice
When Time arrives—the monarch who has conquered
This world, the highest world, the holy worlds,
Yea, all the worlds—and ever marches on.

Translation by Sir Monier Monier-Williams

Rig Veda, Book 1, Hymn 50 (Excerpt)

To THE SUN are ascribed, in this hymn, omniscience, surpassing splendor, the benison of light, and the meting out of time.

By lustrous heralds led on high,
The omniscient Sun ascends the sky,
His glory drawing every eye.
All-seeing Sun, the stars so bright,
Which gleamed throughout the sombre night,
Now scared, like thieves, slink fast away,
Quenched by the splendour of thy ray.

Thy beams to men thy presence show;
Like blazing fires they seem to glow.
Conspicuous, rapid, source of light,
Thou makest all the welkin bright.
In sight of gods and mortal eyes,
In sight of heaven, thou scal'st the skies.
Bright god, thou scann'st with searching ken,
The doings all of busy men.
Thou stridest o'er the sky; thy rays
Create, and measure out, our days;
Thine eye all living things surveys.

Translation by John Muir

Rig Veda, Book 1, Hymn 121

THE ONE GOD above all others, who had a beginning but is now immortal, Creator and Ruler as well as Sustainer of the world and of life, praiseworthy and righteous, is implored not to harm us.

What god shall we adore with sacrifice?
Him let us praise, the golden child that rose
In the beginning, who was born the lord—
The one sole lord of all that is—who made
The earth, and formed the sky, who giveth life,
Who giveth strength, whose bidding gods revere,
Whose hiding-place is immortality,
Whose shadow, death; who by his might is king
Of all the breathing, sleeping, waking world—
Who governs men and beasts, whose majesty
These snowy hills, this ocean with its rivers
Declare; of whom these spreading regions form
The arms; by whom the firmament is strong,
Earth firmly planted, and the highest heavens
Supported, and the clouds that fill the air
Distributed and measured out; to whom
Both earth and heaven, established by his will,
Look up with trembling mind; in whom revealed
The rising sun shines forth above the world.

Where'er let loose in space, the mighty waters
Have gone, depositing a fruitful seed
And generating fire, there *he* arose,
Who is the breath and life of all the gods,
Whose mighty glance looks round the vast expanse
Of watery vapour—source of energy,
Cause of the sacrifice—the only God
Above the gods. May he not injure us!
He the Creator of the earth—the righteous
Creator of the sky, Creator too
Of oceans bright, and far-extending waters.

Translation by Sir Monier Monier-Williams

Rig Veda, Book 9, Hymn 112

THE THEME OF NON-ATTACHMENT, non-addiction to desire, which
flourished later, is not yet evident in this period, unless the writer of
the present hymn, in limning the varieties of desire, is also poking fun
at them.

Men's tastes and trades are multifarious;
And so their ends and aims are various.
The smith seeks something cracked to mend;
The leech would fain have sick to tend;
The priest desires a devotee
From whom he may extract a fee.
Each craftsman makes and mends his ware,
And hopes the rich man's gold to share.
My sire's a leech, and I a bard;
Corn grinds my mother, toiling hard.
All craving wealth, we each pursue
By different means, the end in view,
Like people running after cows,
Which too far off have strayed to brouse.
The draught-horse seeks an easy yoke,
The merry dearly love a joke,
Of pretty maidens men are fond,
And thirsty frogs desire a pond.

Translation by John Muir

Rig Veda, Book 10, Hymn 90

PURUSHA (pronounced "POOR-a-sha"), who in Hindu mythology was
the first male, is here said to be (a) immanent as a spirit in everything, (b) identical with the totality of things, (c) paradoxically both
parent and offspring of Viraj (the name is accented on the second
syllable), who is a secondary creative force comparable to Plato's
Demiurge, and (d) the source of the caste system.

> The embodied spirit has a thousand heads,
> A thousand eyes, a thousand feet, around
> On every side enveloping the earth,
> Yet filling space no larger than a span.
> He is himself this very universe,
> He is whatever is, has been, and shall be.
> He is the lord of immortality.
> All creatures are one-fourth of him, three-fourths
> Are that which is immortal in the sky.
> From him, called Purusha, was born Viraj,
> And from Viraj was Purusha produced
> Whom gods and holy men made their oblation.
> With Purusha as victim they performed
> A sacrifice. When they divided him,
> How did they cut him up? what was his mouth?
> What were his arms? and what his thighs and feet?
> The Brahman was his mouth, the kingly soldier
> Was made his arms, the husbandman his thighs,
> The servile Sudra issued from his feet.

Translation by Sir Monier Monier-Williams

Rig Veda, Book 10, Hymn 127

NIGHT, an intangible being, is personified here as the daughter of day
and the sister of morning.

> The goddess Night arrives in all her glory,
> Looking about her with her countless eyes.
> She, the immortal goddess, throws her veil
> Over low valley, rising ground, and hill,

But soon with bright effulgence dissipates
The darkness she produces; soon advancing
She calls her sister Morning to return,
And then each darksome shadow melts away.

Kind goddess, be propitious to thy servants
Who at thy coming straightway seek repose,
Like birds who nightly nestle in the trees.
Lo! men and cattle, flocks and winged creatures,
And e'en the ravenous hawks, have gone to rest.

Drive thou away from us, O Night, the wolf;
Drive thou away the thief, and bear us safely
Across thy borders. Then do thou, O Dawn,
Like one who clears away a debt, chase off
This black, yet palpable obscurity,
Which came to fold us in its close embrace.

Receive, O Night, dark daughter of the Day,
My hymn of praise, which I present to thee,
Like some rich offering to a conqueror.

Translation by Sir Monier Monier-Williams

Rig Veda, Book 10, Hymn 129

THE AUTHOR OF THIS HYMN, the most philosophical hymn in the Vedas, is not only sufficiently advanced to tackle the hardest problem of cosmology, how things got started, but is even more amazingly advanced in realizing that a prior question, how we can know such things anyhow, also demands an answer.

There then was neither Aught nor Nought,
  No air nor sky beyond.
What covered all? Where rested all?
  In watery gulf profound?

Nor death was there, nor deathlessness,
  Nor change of night and day.
That One breathed calmly, self-sustained:
  Nor else beyond It lay.

Gloom hid in gloom existed first—
  One sea eluding view.
That One, a void in chaos wrapt,
  By inward fervour grew.

Within It first arose desire,
  The primal germ of mind,
Which nothing with existence links,
  As sages searching find.

The kindling ray that shot across
  The dark and drear abyss,—
Was it beneath? Or high aloft?
  What bard can answer this?

There fecundating powers were found,
  And mighty forces strove,
A self-supporting mass beneath,
  And energy above.

Who knows, whoe'er hath told, from whence
  This vast creation rose?
No gods had then been born, who then
  Can e'er the truth disclose?

Whence sprang this world, and whether framed
  By hand divine or no,
Its lord in heaven alone can tell,—
  If even he can show.

Translation by John Muir

UPANISHADS

Isha Upanishad (Excerpts)

"ISHA" (PRONOUNCED "EE-SHA") MEANS "LORD." THIS UPANISHAD IS so named because "Isha" is the first word in it, following the invocation.

The best way to read this Upanishad is not to look for logical sequence from paragraph to paragraph, but to enjoy the rhapsodic, provocative force of each paragraph (or occasionally a pair of paragraphs) as a unit. The same is true of the Book of Psalms in the Old Testament.

The distinction between the seed of nature and the shapes of nature, near the end of this Upanishad, is presumably the distinction between fundamental reality and appearance, between (in twentieth-century terminology) the energy inside the atom on the one hand and visible everyday objects on the other.

The Isha Upanishad is a supplement to the Yajur Veda.

This is perfect. This is perfect. Perfect comes from perfect. Take perfect from perfect, the remainder is perfect.

May peace and peace and peace be everywhere.

Whatever lives is full of the Lord. . . . The Self is one. . . . Unmoving, it moves; is far away, yet near; within all, outside all.

Of a certainty the man who can see all creatures in himself, himself in all creatures, knows no sorrow.

How can a wise man, knowing the unity of life, seeing all creatures in himself, be deluded or sorrowful?

The Self is everywhere, without a body, without a shape, whole,

1 5

pure, wise, all knowing, far shining, self-depending, all transcending; in the eternal procession assigning to every period its proper
duty.

Pin your faith to natural knowledge, stumble through the darkness of the blind; pin your faith to supernatural knowledge,
stumble through a darkness deeper still.

Natural knowledge brings one result, supernatural knowledge
another. We have heard it from the wise who have clearly
explained it.

They that know and can distinguish between natural knowledge
and supernatural knowledge shall, by the first, cross the perishable
in safety; shall, passing beyond the second, attain immortal life.

Pin your faith to the seed of nature, stumble through the darkness of the blind; pin your faith to the shapes of nature, stumble
through a darkness deeper still.

The seed of nature brings one result; the shapes of nature
another. We have heard it from the wise who have clearly
explained it.

They that know and can distinguish between the shapes of
nature and the seed of nature shall, by the first, cross the perishable
in safety; shall, passing beyond the second, attain immortal life.

They have put a golden stopper into the neck of the bottle.
Pull it, Lord! Let out reality. I am full of longing.

Protector, Seer, controller of all, fountain of life, upholder, do
not waste light; gather light; let me see that blessed body—Lord
of all. I myself am He.

Life merge into the all prevalent, the eternal; body turn to
ashes. Mind! meditate on the eternal Spirit; remember past deeds.
Mind! remember past deeds; remember, Mind! remember.

Holy light! illuminate the way that we may gather the good we
planted. Are not our deeds known to you? Do not let us grow
crooked, we that kneel and pray again and again.

Translation by Purohit and W. B. Yeats

Kena Upanishad

"KENA" (which may suitably be Anglicized as "KEE-na," or alternatively pronounced "KAY-na," to conform more closely to the original)
is the first word of this Upanishad, following the invocation. It means
literally "By whom," and appears in the translation as "What."

The promise of immortality to those who see the one Spirit in all things, near the end of section 2, reflects the "feeling of eternity" which has characterized the mystic trance not only in India but also in the Western mystic tradition.

"Wedas," near the end of this Upanishad, is an alternate spelling of "Vedas."

The Kena Upanishad is a supplement to the Sama Veda.

1

Speech, eyes, ears, limbs, life, energy, come to my help. These books have Spirit for theme. I shall never deny Spirit, nor Spirit deny me. Let me be in union, communion with Spirit. When I am one with Spirit, may the laws these books proclaim live in me, may the laws live.

The enquirer asked: "What has called my mind to the hunt? What has made my life begin? What wags in my tongue? What God has opened eye and ear?"

The teacher answered: "It lives in all that lives, hearing through the ear, thinking through the mind, speaking through the tongue, seeing through the eye. The wise man clings neither to this nor that, rises out of sense, attains immortal life.

"Eye, tongue, cannot approach it nor mind know; not knowing, we cannot satisfy enquiry. It lies beyond the known, beyond the unknown. We know through those who have preached it, have learnt it from tradition.

"That which makes the tongue speak, but needs no tongue to explain, that alone is Spirit; not what sets the world by the ears.

"That which makes the mind think, but needs no mind to think, that alone is Spirit; not what sets the world by the ears.

"That which makes the eye see, but needs no eye to see, that alone is Spirit; not what sets the world by the ears.

"That which makes the ear hear, but needs no ear to hear, that alone is Spirit; not what sets the world by the ears.

"That which makes life live, but needs no life to live, that alone is Spirit; not what sets the world by the ears."

2

"If you think that you know much, you know little. If you think that you know It from study of your own mind or of nature, study again."

The enquirer said: "I do not think that I know much, I neither say that I know, nor say that I do not."

The teacher answered: "The man who claims that he knows, knows nothing; but he who claims nothing, knows.

"Who says that Spirit is not known, knows; who claims that he knows, knows nothing. The ignorant think that Spirit lies within knowledge, the wise man knows It beyond knowledge.

"Spirit is known through revelation. It leads to freedom. It leads to power. Revelation is the conquest of death.

"The living man who finds Spirit, finds Truth. But if he fail, he sinks among fouler shapes. The man who can see the same Spirit in every creature, clings neither to this nor that, attains immortal life."

3

Once upon a time, Spirit planned that the gods might win a great victory. The gods grew boastful; though Spirit had planned their victory, they thought they had done it all.

Spirit saw their vanity and appeared. They could not understand; they said: "Who is that mysterious Person?"

They said to Fire: "Fire! Find out who is that mysterious Person."

Fire ran to Spirit. Spirit asked what it was. Fire said: "I am Fire; known to all."

Spirit asked: "What can you do?" Fire said: "I can burn anything and everything in this world."

"Burn it," said Spirit, putting a straw on the ground. Fire threw itself upon the straw, but could not burn it. Then Fire ran to the gods in a hurry and confessed it could not find out who was that mysterious Person.

Then the gods asked Wind to find out who was that mysterious Person.

Wind ran to Spirit and Spirit asked what it was. Wind said: "I am Wind; I am the King of the Air."

Spirit asked: "What can you do?" and Wind said: "I can blow away anything and everything in this world."

"Blow it away," said Spirit, putting a straw on the ground. Wind threw itself upon the straw, but could not move it. Then Wind ran to the gods in a hurry and confessed it could not find out who was that mysterious Person.

Then the gods went to Light and asked it to find out who was that mysterious Person. Light ran towards Spirit, but Spirit disappeared upon the instant.

There appeared in the sky that pretty girl, the Goddess of Wisdom, snowy Himalaya's daughter. Light went to her and asked who was that mysterious Person.

4

The Goddess said: "Spirit, through Spirit you attained your greatness. Praise the greatness of Spirit." Then Light knew that the mysterious Person was none but Spirit.

That is how these gods—Fire, Wind and Light—attained supremacy; they came nearest to Spirit and were the first to call that Person Spirit.

Light stands above Fire and Wind; because closer than they, it was the first to call that Person Spirit.

This is the moral of the tale. In the lightning, in the light of an eye, the light belongs to Spirit.

The power of the mind when it remembers and desires, when it thinks again and again, belongs to Spirit. Therefore let Mind meditate on Spirit.

Spirit is the Good in all. It should be worshipped as the Good. He that knows it as the Good is esteemed by all.

You asked me about spiritual knowledge, I have explained it.

Austerity, self-control, meditation are the foundation of this knowledge; the Wedas are its house, truth its shrine.

He who knows this shall prevail against all evil, enjoy the Kingdom of Heaven, yes for ever enjoy the blessed Kingdom of Heaven.

Translation by Purohit and W. B. Yeats

Katha Upanishad

"KATHA" (which rhymes with "WHAT-a") is said by some authorities to mean "dialogue" here, and by others to be the family name associated with the portion of the Yajur Veda to which this Upanishad is a supplement.

In the first quoted paragraph of this Upanishad (third paragraph after the invocation), Nachiketas' statement that his father's cows were powerless is a way of saying that his father's cows were nonexistent.

The symbolic reference to fire, in Death's speeches (book 1, section 1), may perhaps best be taken as alluding to cosmic spiritual energy.

"Om" (rhymes with "foam"), in a later speech by Death, is a sound used by Hindus as an aid to meditative self-awareness, to shut out irrelevant sensations and ideas.

Death in one speech here expresses with utmost brevity the standard Hindu eschatological principle: anyone who fails to "find himself" before he dies (i.e., who is so involved in selfish living that he does not see his own self as part of the universal self) is doomed to take on another body and to live on earth again.

Poetic imagery of a high order and tense intellectual drama pervade this Upanishad. It is one of the most aesthetically appealing of the entire corpus and one of the most philosophical as well.

BOOK I

1

May He protect us both. May He take pleasure in us both. May we show courage together. May spiritual knowledge shine before us. May we never hate one another. May peace and peace and peace be everywhere.

Wajashrawas, wanting heaven, gave away all his property.

He had a son by name Nachiketas. While the gifts were passing, Nachiketas, though but a boy, thought to himself:

"He has not earned much of a heaven; his cows can neither eat, drink, calve nor give milk."

He went to his father and said: "Father, have you given me to somebody?" He repeated the question a second and a third time; at last his father said: "I give you to Death."

Nachiketas thought: "Whether I die now or later matters little; but what I would like to know is what happens if Death gets me now."

Wajashrawas would have taken back his words but Nachiketas said: "Think of those who went before, those that will come after: their word their bond. Man dies and is born again like a blade of grass."

Nachiketas went into the forest and sat in meditation within the house of Death. When Death appeared his servant said: "Lord! When a holy man enters a house as guest it is as if Fire entered. The wise man cools him down. So please give him water.

"If a holy man comes into a fool's house and is given nothing, the fool's family, public and private life, ambitions, reputation, property, hopes, alliances, all suffer."

Thereupon Death said to Nachiketas: "A guest should be respected; you have lived three days in my house without eating and drinking. I bow to you, holy man! Take from me three gifts and I shall be the better for it."

Nachiketas said: "I will take as my first gift that I may be reconciled to my father; that he may be happy; that he may keep no grudge against me but make me welcome."

Death said: "I shall so arrange things, that when your father gets you back he shall sleep well at night, his grudge forgotten and love you as before."

Nachiketas said: "There is no fear in the Kingdom of Heaven; because you are not there, nobody there is afraid of old age; man is beyond hunger, thirst and sorrow.

"Death! you know what Fire leads to heaven, show it, I am full of faith. I ask that Fire as my second gift."

Death said: "I will explain it, listen. Find the rock and conquer unmeasured worlds. Listen, for this came out of the cavern."

Death told him that out of Fire comes this world, what bricks and how many go to the altar, how best to build it. Nachiketas repeated all, Death encouraged ran on:

"I give you another gift. This Fire shall be called by your name.

"Count the links of the chain: worship the triple Fire: knowledge, meditation, practice; the triple process: evidence, inference, experience; the triple duty: study, concentration, renunciation; understand that everything comes from Spirit, that Spirit alone is sought and found; attain everlasting peace; mount beyond birth and death.

"When man understands himself, understands universal Self, the union of the two, kindles the triple Fire, offers the sacrifice; then shall he, though still on earth, break the bonds of death, beyond sorrow, mount into heaven.

"This Fire that leads to heaven is your second gift, Nachiketas! It shall be named after you. Now choose again, choose the third gift."

Nachiketas said: "Some say that when man dies he continues to exist, others that he does not. Explain, and that shall be my third gift."

Death said: "This question has been discussed by the gods, it is deep and difficult. Choose another gift, Nachiketas! Do not be hard. Do not compel me to explain."

Nachiketas said: "Death! you say that the gods have discussed it, that it is deep and difficult; what explanation can be as good as yours? What gift compares with that?"

Death said: "Take sons and grandsons, all long-lived, cattle and horses, elephants and gold, take a great kingdom.

"Anything but this; wealth, long life, Nachiketas! empire, anything whatever; satisfy the heart's desire.

"Pleasure beyond human reach, fine women with carriages, their musical instruments; mount beyond dreams; enjoy. But do not ask what lies beyond death."

Nachiketas said: "Destroyer of man! these things pass. Joy ends enjoyment, the longest life is short. Keep those horses, keep singing and dancing, keep it all for yourself.

"Wealth cannot satisfy a man. If he but please you, Master of All, he can live as long as he likes, get all that he likes; but I will not change my gift.

"What man, subject to death and decay, getting the chance of undecaying life, would still enjoy mere long life, thinking of copulation and beauty.

"Say where man goes after death; end all that discussion. This, which you have made so mysterious, is the only gift I will take."

2

Death said: "The good is one, the pleasant another; both command the soul. Who follows the good, attains sanctity; who follows the pleasant, drops out of the race.

"Every man faces both. The mind of the wise man draws him to the good, the flesh of the fool drives him to the pleasant.

"Nachiketas! Having examined the pleasures you have rejected them; turned from the vortex of life and death.

"Diverging roads: one called ignorance, the other wisdom. Rejecting images of pleasure, Nachiketas! you turn towards wisdom.

"Fools brag of their knowledge; proud, ignorant, dissolving, blind led by the blind, staggering to and fro.

"What can the money-maddened simpleton know of the future?

'This is the only world' cries he; because he thinks there is no other I kill him again and again.

"Some have never heard of the Self, some have heard but cannot find Him. Who finds Him is a world's wonder, who expounds Him is a world's wonder, who inherits Him from his Master is a world's wonder.

"No man of common mind can teach Him; such men dispute one against another. But when the uncommon man speaks, dispute is over. Because the Self is a fine substance, He slips from the mind and deludes imagination.

"Beloved! Logic brings no man to the Self. Yet when a wise man shows Him, He is found. Your longing eyes are turned towards reality. Would that I had always such a pupil.

"Because man cannot find the Eternal through passing pleasure, I have sought the Fire in these pleasures and, worshipping that alone, found the Eternal.

"Nachiketas! The fulfilment of all desire, the conquest of the world, freedom from fear, unlimited pleasure, magical power, all were yours, but you renounced them all, brave and wise man.

"The wise, meditating on God, concentrating their thought, discovering in the mouth of the cavern, deeper in the cavern, that Self, that ancient Self, difficult to imagine, more difficult to understand, pass beyond joy and sorrow.

"The man that, hearing from the Teacher and comprehending, distinguishes nature from the Self, goes to the source; that man attains joy, lives for ever in that joy. I think, Nachiketas! your gates of joy stand open."

Nachiketas asked: "What lies beyond right and wrong, beyond cause and effect, beyond past and future?"

Death said: "The word the Wedas extol, austerities proclaim, sanctities approach—that word is Om.

"That word is eternal Spirit, eternal distance; who knows it attains to his desire.

"That word is the ultimate foundation. Who finds it is adored among the saints.

"The Self knows all, is not born, does not die, is not the effect of any cause; is eternal, self-existent, imperishable, ancient. How can the killing of the body kill Him?

"He who thinks that He kills, he who thinks that He is killed, is ignorant. He does not kill nor is He killed.

"The Self is lesser than the least, greater than the greatest. He lives in all hearts. When senses are at rest, free from desire, man finds Him and mounts beyond sorrow.

"Though sitting, He travels; though sleeping is everywhere. Who but I Death can understand that God is beyond joy and sorrow.

"Who knows the Self, bodiless among the embodied, unchanging among the changing, prevalent everywhere, goes beyond sorrow.

"The Self is not known through discourse, splitting of hairs, learning however great; He comes to the man He loves; takes that man's body for His own.

"The wicked man is restless, without concentration, without peace; how can he find Him, whatever his learning?

"He has made mere preachers and soldiers His food, death its condiment; how can a common man find Him?"

3

"The individual self and the universal Self, living in the heart, like shade and light, though beyond enjoyment, enjoy the result of action. All say this, all who know Spirit, whether householder or ascetic.

"Man can kindle that Fire, that Spirit, a bridge for all who sacrifice, a guide for all who pass beyond fear.

"Self rides in the chariot of the body, intellect the firm-footed charioteer, discursive mind the reins.

"Senses are the horses, objects of desire the roads. When Self is joined to body, mind, sense, none but He enjoys.

"When a man lack steadiness, unable to control his mind, his senses are unmanageable horses.

"But if he control his mind, a steady man, they are manageable horses.

"The impure, self-willed, unsteady man misses the goal and is born again and again.

"The self-controlled, steady, pure man goes to that goal from which he never returns.

"He who calls intellect to manage the reins of his mind reaches the end of his journey, finds there all-pervading Spirit.

"Above the senses are the objects of desire, above the objects of desire mind, above the mind intellect, above the intellect manifest nature.

"Above manifest nature the unmanifest seed, above the unmanifest seed, God. God is the goal; beyond Him nothing.

"God does not proclaim Himself, He is everybody's secret, but the intellect of the sage has found Him.

"The wise man would lose his speech in mind, mind in the intellect, intellect in nature, nature in God and so find peace.

"Get up! Stir yourself! Learn wisdom at the Master's feet. A hard path the sages say, the sharp edge of a razor.

"He who knows the soundless, odourless, tasteless, intangible, formless, deathless, supernatural, undecaying, beginningless, endless, unchangeable Reality, springs out of the mouth of Death."

Those who hear and repeat correctly this ancient dialogue between Death and Nachiketas are approved by holy men.

He who sings this great mystery at the anniversary of his fathers to a rightly chosen company, finds good luck, good luck beyond measure.

BOOK II

1

Death said: "God made sense turn outward, man therefore looks outward, not into himself. Now and again a daring soul, desiring immortality, has looked back and found himself.

"The ignorant man runs after pleasure, sinks into the entanglements of death; but the wise man, seeking the undying, does not run among things that die.

"He through whom we see, taste, smell, feel, hear, enjoy, knows everything. He is that Self.

"The wise man, by meditating upon the self-dependent, all-pervading Self, understands waking and sleeping and goes beyond sorrow.

"Knowing that the individual self, eater of the fruit of action, is the universal Self, maker of past and future, he knows he has nothing to fear.

"He knows that He himself born in the beginning out of meditation, before water was created, enters every heart and lives there among the elements.

"That boundless Power, source of every power, manifesting itself as life, entering every heart, living there among the elements, that is Self.

"The Fire, hidden in the fire-stick like a child in the womb, worshipped with offerings, that Fire is Self.

"He who makes the sun rise and set, to Whom all powers do homage, He that has no master, that is Self.

"That which is here, is hereafter; hereafter is here. He who thinks otherwise wanders from death to death.

"Tell the mind that there is but One; he who divides the One, wanders from death to death.

"When that Person in the heart, no bigger than a thumb, is known as maker of past and future, what more is there to fear? That is Self.

"That Person, no bigger than a thumb, burning like flame without smoke, maker of past and future, the same today and tomorrow, that is Self.

"As rain upon a mountain ridge runs down the slope, the man that has seen the shapes of Self runs after them everywhere.

"The Self of the wise man remains pure; pure water, Nachiketas, poured into pure water."

2

"Who meditates on self-existent, pure intelligence, ruler of the body, the city of eleven gates, grieves no more, is free, for ever free.

"He is sun in the sky, fire upon the altar, guest in the house, air that runs everywhere, Lord of lords, living in reality. He abounds everywhere, is renewed in the sacrifice, born in water, springs out of the soil, breaks out of the mountain; power: reality.

"Living at the centre, adorable, adored by the senses, He breathes out, breathes in.

"When He, the bodiless, leaves the body, exhausts the body, what leaves? That is Self.

"Man lives by more than breath; he lives by the help of another who makes it come and go.

"Nachiketas! I will tell you the secret of undying Spirit and what happens after death.

"Some enter the womb, waiting for a moving body, some pass into unmoving things: according to deed and knowledge.

"Who is awake, who creates lovely dreams, when man is lost in sleep? That Person through whom all things live, beyond whom none can go; pure, powerful, immortal Spirit.

"As fire, though one, takes the shape of whatsoever it consumes, so the Self, though one, animating all things, takes the shape of whatsoever it animates; yet stands outside.

"As air, though one, takes the shape of whatsoever it enters, so the Self, though one, animating all things, takes the shape of whatsoever it animates; yet stands outside.

"As the sun, the eye of the world, is not touched by the impurity it looks upon, so the Self, though one, animating all things, is not moved by human misery but stands outside.

"He is One, Governor, Self of all, Creator of many out of one. He that dare discover Him within, rejoices; what other dare rejoice?

"He is imperishable among things that perish. Life of all life, He, though one, satisfies every man's desire. He that dare discover Him within, knows peace; what other dare know peace?"

Nachiketas asked: "Where shall I find that joy beyond all words? Does He reflect another's light or shine of Himself?"

Death replied: "Neither sun, moon, stars, fire nor lightning lights Him. When He shines, everything begins to shine. Everything in the world reflects His light."

3

"Eternal creation is a tree, with roots above, branches on the ground; pure eternal Spirit, living in all things and beyond whom none can go; that is Self.

"Everything owes life and movement to Spirit. Spirit strikes terror, hangs like a thunderbolt overhead; find it, find immortality.

"Through terror of God fire burns, sun shines, rain pours, wind blows, death speeds.

"Man, if he fail to find Him before the body falls, must take another body.

"Man, looking into the mirror of himself, may know Spirit there as he knows light from shade; but in the world of spirits It is known distorted as in a dream, in the choir of angels as though reflected on troubled water.

"He who knows that the senses belong not to Spirit but to the elements, that they are born and die, grieves no more.

"Mind is above sense, intellect above mind, nature above intellect, the unmanifest above nature.

"Above the unmanifest is God, unconditioned, filling all things. He who finds Him enters immortal life, becomes free.

"No eye can see Him, nor has He a face that can be seen, yet through meditation and through discipline He can be found in the heart. He that finds Him enters immortal life.

"When mind and sense are at rest, when the discrimination of intellect is finished, man comes to his final condition.

"Yoga brings the constant control of sense. When that condition is reached the Yogi can do no wrong. Before it is reached Yoga seems union and again disunion.

"He cannot be known through discourse, nor found by the mind or the eye. He that believes in His existence finds Him. How can a man who does not so believe find Him?

"Go backward from effect to cause until you are compelled to believe in Him. Once you are so compelled, truth dawns.

"When the desires of the heart are finished, man though still in the body is united to Spirit; mortal becomes immortal.

"When the knot of the heart is cut, mortal becomes immortal. This is the law.

"The heart has a hundred and one arteries; one of these—Sushumna—goes up into the head. He who climbs through it attains immortality; others drive him into the vortex.

"God, the inmost Self, no bigger than a thumb, lives in the heart. Man should strip him of the body, as the arrow-maker strips the reed, that he may know Him as perpetual and pure; what can He be but perpetual and pure?"

Then Nachiketas having learnt from Death this knowledge, learnt the method of meditation, rose above desire and death, found God: who does the like, finds Him.

Translation by Purohit and W. B. Yeats

Chandogya Upanishad (Excerpts)

IN THIS UPANISHAD, ascribed to the Chandogya family, appears the celebrated short formulation of the philosophy of interpersonal monism: "That art thou" (or, in the translation given here: "You are That"). Karma, mentioned near the end, is the burden that you carry with you of the consequences of your former moral conduct.

The Chandogya Upanishad is a supplement to the Sama Veda.

BOOK VI

1

Speech, eyes, ears, limbs, life, energy, come to my help. These books have Spirit for theme. I shall never deny Spirit, nor Spirit deny me. Let me be in union, communion with Spirit. When I am one with Spirit, may the laws these books proclaim live in me, may the laws live.

2

Om. Once upon a time there lived Shwetaketu, son of Uddalaka. Uddalaka said: "My son! Find a teacher, learn; none of our family has remained a Brahman in name only."

At twelve he found his teacher; at twenty-four, having completed the study of the Wedas, he returned home, stiff-necked, arrogant, self-willed.

Uddalaka said: "My son! You think such a lot of yourself, but did you ask your teacher about that initiation, which makes a man hear what is not heard, think what is not thought, know what is not known?"

"What is that initiation, Lord?" said Shwetaketu. Uddalaka said: "By knowing a lump of clay you know all things made of clay; they differ from one another as it were in language and in name, having no reality but their clay;

"By knowing one nugget of gold you know all things made of gold; they differ from one another as it were in language and in name, having no reality but their gold;

"By knowing one piece of base metal you know all things made of that metal; they differ from one another as it were in language and in name, having no reality but that metal.

"For the like reason, after that initiation, you know everything."

Shwetaketu said: "My revered teacher cannot have known that; had he known it he would have told me. Therefore, Lord! teach it."

3

"My son! In the beginning, there was mere being, one without a second. Some say there was mere nothing, nothing whatsoever; that everything has come out of nothing.

"But how can that be true, my son," said Uddalaka; "how could

that which is, come from that which is not? I put it otherwise; in
the beginning there was mere being, one without a second.

"That being thought: 'Would that I were many! I will create!'
He created light. Light thought: 'Would that I were many! I will
create!' Light created the waters. When anybody weeps or sweats,
the tears and the sweat are created by light.

"Those waters thought: 'Would that we were many! We will
create!' They created food. Whenever and wherever it rains, food
is abundant. Food is from water." . . .

9

Aruna's son, Uddalaka, said to Shwetaketu: "My son! know the
nature of sleep. When a man sleeps, he is united with that Being,
that is himself. We think it enough to say that he sleeps, yet he
sleeps with himself.

"A tethered bird, after flying in every direction, settles down on
its perch; the mind, after wandering in every direction, settles down
on its life; for, my son! mind is tethered to life.

"Know the nature of hunger and thirst. Man becomes hungry.
Water brings his food to his belly. Water brings his food, as
cowherd his cow, horseman his horse, general his army. Remember,
my son! that body sprouts from food; could it sprout without a
root?

"What is the root of all? What but food?

"Remember, my son! water is root, food its sprout; light is root,
water its sprout; in the same way, that Being is root, light its sprout.
All creatures have their root in that Being. He is their rock, their
home.

"Man becomes thirsty. Light brings the water to his gullet, as
cowherd his cow, horseman his horse, general his army. Remember,
my son! that food sprouts from water; could it sprout without a
root?

"What is the root of all? What but water?

"Light is root, water its sprout; that Being is root, light its sprout.
All creatures have their root in that Being; He is their rock, their
home. My son! I have already told you how the three first gods
became each of them threefold when in contact with body. When
a man is dying, his speech merges into mind, his mind into life, his
life into light, his light into the one Being.

"That Being is the seed; all else but His expression. He is truth, He is Self. Shwetaketu! You are That."

"Explain once more, Lord!" said Shwetaketu.

"I will explain!" said Uddalaka.

10

"My son! Bees create honey by gathering the sweet juices from different flowers, and mixing all into a common juice.

"And there is nothing in honey whereby the juice of a particular flower can be identified, so it is with the various creatures who merge in that Being, in deep sleep or in death.

"Whatever they may be, tiger, lion, wolf, boar, worm, moth, gnat, mosquito, they become aware of particular life when they are born into it or awake.

"That Being is the seed; all else but His expression. He is truth. He is Self, Shwetaketu! You are That."

"Explain once more, Lord!" said Shwetaketu.

"I will explain!" said Uddalaka.

11

"My son! Rivers, flowing east and west, rise from the sea, return to the sea, become the sea itself, forget their identities.

"These creatures do not know that they have risen from that Being, or returned to that Being.

"Whatever that may be, tiger, lion, wolf, boar, worm, moth, gnat, mosquito, they become aware of particular life when they are born into it or awake.

"That Being is the seed; all else but His expression. He is truth. He is Self. Shwetaketu! You are That."

"Explain once more, Lord!" said Shwetaketu.

"I will explain!" said Uddalaka.

12

"Strike at the bole of a tree, sap oozes but the tree lives; strike at the middle of the tree, sap oozes but the tree lives; strike at the top of the tree, sap oozes but the tree lives. The Self as life, fills the tree; it flourishes in happiness, gathering its food through its roots.

"If life leaves one branch, that branch withers. If life leaves a second branch, that branch withers. If life leaves a third branch, that branch withers. When life leaves the whole tree, the whole tree withers.

"Remember, my son! The body bereft of Self dies. Self does not die.

"That Being is the seed; all else but His expression. He is truth. He is Self, Shwetaketu! You are That."

"Explain once more, Lord!" said Shwetaketu.

"I will explain!" said Uddalaka.

13

Uddalaka asked his son to fetch a banyan fruit.

"Here it is, Lord!" said Shwetaketu.

"Break it," said Uddalaka.

"I have broken it, Lord!"

"What do you see there?"

"Little seeds, Lord!"

"Break one of them, my son!"

"It is broken, Lord!"

"What do you see there?"

"Nothing, Lord!" said Shwetaketu.

Uddalaka said: "My son! This great banyan tree has sprung up from a seed so small that you cannot see it. Believe in what I say, my son!

"That Being is the seed; all else but His expression. He is truth. He is Self, Shwetaketu! You are That."

"Explain once more, Lord!" said Shwetaketu.

"I will explain!" said Uddalaka.

14

"Put this salt into water, see me tomorrow morning," said Uddalaka. Shwetaketu did as he was told.

Uddalaka said: "Bring me the salt you put into water last night." Shwetaketu looked, but could not find it. The salt had dissolved.

Uddalaka asked his son how the top of the water tasted. Shwetaketu said: "It is salt."

Uddalaka asked how the middle of the water tasted.

Shwetaketu said: "It is salt."

Uddalaka asked how the bottom of the water tasted.

Shwetaketu said: "It is salt."

Uddalaka said: "Throw away the water; come to me."

Shwetaketu did as he was told and said: "The salt will always remain in the water."

Uddalaka said: "My son! Though you do not find that Being in the world, He is there.

"That Being is the seed; all else but His expression. He is truth. He is Self, Shwetaketu! You are That."

"Explain once more, Lord!" said Shwetaketu.

"I will explain!" said Uddalaka.

15

"My son! If a man were taken out of the province of Gandhara, abandoned in a forest blindfolded, he would turn here and there, he would shout: 'I have been brought here blindfolded and abandoned!'

"Thereupon some good man might take off the bandage and say: 'Go in that direction; Gandhara is there.' The bandage off, he would, if a sensible man, ask his way from village to village and come at last to Gandhara. In the same way the man initiated by his master, finds his way back into himself. Having remained in his body till all his Karma is spent, he is joined to Himself.

"That Being is the seed; all else but His expression. He is truth. He is Self. Shwetaketu! You are That."

"Explain once more, Lord!" said Shwetaketu.

"I will explain!" said Uddalaka.

16

"Relations gather round a sick man and say: 'Do you remember me? Do you remember me?' He remembers until his speech has merged in his mind, his mind in his life, his life in his light, his light in the one Being.

"When his speech is merged in his mind, his mind in his life, his life in his light, his light in that one Being, what can he remember?

"That Being is the seed; all else but His expression. He is truth. He is Self. Shwetaketu! You are That."

"Explain once more, Lord!" said Shwetaketu.

"I will explain!" said Uddalaka.

17

"My son! They bring a man in handcuffs to the magistrate,
charging him with theft. The magistrate orders the hatchet to be
heated. If the man has committed the theft and denies it, he is
false to himself, and having nothing but that lie to protect him
grasps the hatchet; and is burned.

"If he has not committed the theft, he is true to himself and,
with truth for his protector, grasps the hatchet; and is not burned.
He is acquitted.

"The man that was not burnt, lived in truth. Remember that all
visible things live in truth; remember that truth and Self are one.
Shwetaketu! You are That."

Shwetaketu understood what he said, yes, he understood what
his father said.

Translation by Purohit and W. B. Yeats

Brihadaranyaka Upanishad (Excerpts)

THE BRIHADARANYAKA (pronounced "BREE-ha-DAR-an-YA-ka")
Upanishad is, from its name, a "forest Upanishad"; it is a supplement
to the Yajur Veda.

This Upanishad is an early document of negative theology. God is
said in it to be *neti, neti* ("not this, not that").

BOOK III

Spirit has two aspects: measurable, immeasurable; mortal, immortal; stable, unstable; graspable, ungraspable.

Everything on this earth except wind and sky is measurable,
mortal, stable, graspable; it comes from the graspable, from the
sun that shines in the heavens, the substance of the graspable.

Wind and sky are immeasurable, immortal, unstable, ungraspable; they come from the ungraspable, from God that shines
through the sun, the substance of the ungraspable.

This is the material aspect of Spirit.

Now the divine aspect of Spirit.

Everything in the body except life and heart is measurable,
mortal, stable, graspable; it comes from the graspable, from the
eye, the substance of the graspable.

Life and heart are immeasurable, immortal, unstable, ungraspable; they come from the ungraspable, from God that shines in
the right eye, the substance of the ungraspable.

And what is the shape of that God? It is like a saffron-coloured
garment, like a white woolen garment, like red cochineal, like the
flame of fire, like the white lotus, like a sudden flash of lightning.
Who knows Him thus, his glory flashes like lightning.

They describe Spirit as "Not this; not that." The first means:
"There is nothing except Spirit"; the second means: "There is
nothing beyond Spirit." They call Spirit the "Truth of all truths."
The senses are true, but He is the truth of them all. . . .

BOOK V

This earth is the honey of all beings; all beings the honey of this
earth. The bright eternal Self that is in earth, the bright eternal
Self that lives in this body, are one and the same; that is immortality, that is Spirit, that is all.

Water is the honey of all beings; all beings the honey of water.
The bright eternal Self that is in water, the bright eternal Self that
lives in human seed, are one and the same; that is immortality, that
is Spirit, that is all.

Fire is the honey of all beings; all beings the honey of fire. The
bright eternal Self that is in fire, the bright eternal Self that lives
in speech, are one and the same; that is immortality, that is Spirit,
that is all.

Wind is the honey of all beings; all beings the honey of wind.
The bright eternal Self that is in wind, the bright eternal Self that
lives in breath, are one and the same; that is immortality, that is
Spirit, that is all.

The sun is the honey of all beings; all beings the honey of the
sun. The bright eternal Self that is in the sun, the bright eternal
Self that lives in the eye, are one and the same; that is immortality,
that is Spirit, that is all.

The quarters are the honey of all beings; all beings the honey of
the quarters. The bright eternal Self that is in the quarters, the
bright eternal Self that lives in the ear, are one and the same; that
is immortality, that is Spirit, that is all.

The moon is the honey of all beings; all beings the honey of
the moon. The bright eternal Self that is in the moon, the bright

eternal Self that lives in the mind, are one and the same; that is immortality, that is Spirit, that is all.

Lightning is the honey of all beings, all beings the honey of lightning. The bright eternal Self that is in lightning, the bright eternal Self that lives in the light of the body, are one and the same; that is immortality, that is Spirit, that is all.

Thunder is the honey of all beings; all beings the honey of thunder. The bright eternal Self that is in thunder, the bright eternal Self that lives in the voice, are one and the same; that is immortality, that is Spirit, that is all.

Air is the honey of all beings; all beings the honey of air. The bright eternal Self that is in air, the bright eternal Self that lives in the hollow of the heart, are one and the same; that is immortality, that is Spirit, that is all.

Law is the honey of all beings; all beings are the honey of law. The bright eternal Self that is in law, the bright eternal Self that lives as the law in the body, are one and the same; that is immortality, that is Spirit, that is all.

Truth is the honey of all beings; all beings the honey of truth. The bright eternal Self that is truth, the bright eternal Self that lives as the truth in man, are one and the same; that is immortality, that is Spirit, that is all.

Mankind is the honey of all beings; all beings the honey of mankind. The bright eternal Self that is mankind, the bright eternal Self that lives in a man, are one and the same; that is immortality, that is Spirit, that is all.

Self is the honey of all beings; all beings the honey of Self. The bright eternal Self that is everywhere, the bright eternal Self that lives in a man, are one and the same; that is immortality, that is Spirit, that is all.

This Self is the Lord of all beings; as all spokes are knit together in the hub, all things, all gods, all men, all lives, all bodies, are knit together in that Self.

Translation by Purohit and W. B. Yeats

II

The Road to Nirvana: Ancient Buddhism

THE BASIC TENETS OF BUDDHISM ARE: (A) MAN IS IN BONDAGE TO his desires, and suffering is therefore his lot; (b) man can find release from desires and consequently from suffering by attaining a deep trance of self-awareness; (c) an exceptionally deep trance, called "nirvana" (the annihilation of attachment) or "enlightenment," is achieved from time to time by a "buddha" (an enlightened one); and (d) one such buddha, Siddhartha (given name) Gautama (family name) Sakyamuni (honored member of the Sakya clan), who was born in 563 B.C. and died eighty years later, is *par excellence* the Buddha of the present cycle of the ages, or more simply Buddha.

Classical Buddhist literature consists of the canonical works of an older sect (founded within a century after Buddha's death), the canonical works of a newer sect (first century of the Christian era), and a set of neutral works.

Those who belong to the older of the two sects are often called "Hinayana" (or little vehicle) Buddhists, but this name was applied to them by the rival, self-styled "Mahayana" (great vehicle) Buddhists. The members of the older sect call themselves not "Hinayana" but "Theravada" (older teaching) Buddhists.

The scriptures of the older—Theravada—creed, written in the Pali language, are called the *Tipitaka* (Three Baskets) and consist of the *Vinaya Pitaka* (Basket of Discipline), the *Sutta Pitaka* (Basket of Discourses), and the *Abhidhamma Pitaka* (Basket of Doctrinal Elaborations). The scriptures of the later-organized sect, written in Sanskrit, consist of *sutras* (discourses), *shastras* (philosophical treatises), and other works.

The neutral works, written (like the Mahayana scriptures) in Sanskrit but sacred to both sects, include notably an epic poem of surpassing literary excellence entitled *Buddha Carita* (Life of Buddha), by Ashvaghosa, a writer of the second century in the Christian era. (The "C" in *Carita* is pronounced like "ch" in "church.")

BASIC TEXTS

Sermons, by Buddha (Excerpts)

GAUTAMA, CALLED "BUDDHA" (563–483 B.C.), WAS BORN IN Kapilavastu, in northeastern India, at the foot of the Himalayas, the son of a local monarch belonging to the warrior caste. When the prince was twenty-nine years old, and had just become the father of a son, he became unbearably aware of the intensity of suffering in the world, and left his home and family for a life of meditation in the forest and of instruction under religious teachers.

One day, after six years of such efforts to find an understanding of the world's suffering, while deep in concentration under a tree, he achieved "enlightenment." Thereafter, for forty-five years, he taught that the way to release from suffering is open to all, through the annihilation of attachment.

All of the six excerpts from Buddha's sermons which are included here are taken from the *Sutta Pitaka* (Basket of Discourses): the first and second, from the *Samyutta Nikaya* (division of connected discourses); the third, fourth, and fifth, from the *Digha Nikaya* (division of long discourses); and the sixth, from the *Majjhima Nikaya* (division of medium-length discourses).

"Nibbana," as used in the sermons, is the Pali-language equivalent of the Sanskrit *nirvana*. "Ariyan" means "noble." The groups of dots (. . .) appear for the most part in the full translation; they take the place of what the translator considered to be needless repetitions, except in a few places in the fifth and sixth excerpts, where the dots indicate omissions necessary for condensation of the text for the present collection.

Although, in some passages, Buddha is referred to in the third person, the sermons are nevertheless believed to represent his actual teachings, if not (in such passages) his exact words.

1

These two extremes, brethren, should not be followed by one who has gone forth as a wanderer:

Devotion to the pleasures of sense—a low and pagan practice, unworthy, unprofitable, the way of the world (on the one hand), and on the other hand devotion to self-mortification, which is painful, unworthy, unprofitable.

By avoiding these two extremes He who hath won the Truth (the Buddha) hath gained knowledge of that Middle Path which giveth Vision, which giveth Knowledge, which causeth Calm, Insight, Enlightenment, and Nibbana.

And what, brethren, is that Middle Path which giveth Vision, which giveth Knowledge, which causeth Calm, Insight, Enlightenment, and Nibbana?

Verily it is this Ariyan Eightfold Path, that is to say:

Right view, right aim, right speech, right action, right living, right effort, right mindfulness, right contemplation.

This, brethren, is that Middle Path, which giveth Vision, which giveth Knowledge, which causeth Calm, Insight, Enlightenment, and Nibbana.

Now this, brethren, is the Ariyan Truth about Suffering:

Birth is Suffering, Decay is Suffering, Sickness is Suffering, Death is Suffering, likewise Sorrow and Grief, Woe, Lamentation and Despair. To be conjured with things which we dislike, to be separated from things which we like—that also is Suffering. Not to get what one wants—that also is Suffering. In a word, this Body, this fivefold Mass which is based on Grasping, that is Suffering.

Now this, brethren, is the Ariyan Truth about The Origin of Suffering:

It is that Craving that leads downwards to birth, along with the Lure and the Lust that lingers longingly now here, now there: namely, the Craving for Sensation, the Craving to be born again, the Craving to have done with rebirth. Such, brethren, is the Ariyan Truth about The Origin of Suffering.

And this, brethren, is the Ariyan Truth about The Ceasing of Suffering:

Verily it is the utter passionless cessation of, the giving up, the forsaking, the release from, the absence of longing for, this Craving.

Now this, brethren, is the Ariyan Truth about The Way leading to the Ceasing of Suffering. Verily it is this Ariyan Eightfold Path, that is:

Right view, right aim, right speech, right action, right living, right effort, right mindfulness, right contemplation.

At the thought, brethren, of this Ariyan Truth of Suffering, concerning things unlearnt before, there arose in me Vision, Insight, Understanding: there arose in me Wisdom, there arose in me Light.

At the thought, brethren, "this Ariyan Truth about the Origin of Suffering is to be understood," concerning things unlearnt before, there arose in me Vision, Insight, Understanding: there arose in me Wisdom, there arose in me Light.

At the thought, brethren, "this Ariyan Truth of Suffering has been understood," concerning things unlearnt before, there arose in me Vision, Insight, Understanding: there arose in me Wisdom, there arose in me Light.

Again, at the thought, brethren, of this Ariyan Truth of the Origin of Suffering, concerning things unlearnt before, there arose in me Vision, Insight, Understanding: there arose in me Wisdom, there arose in me Light.

At the thought, brethren, "the Origin of Suffering must be put away," concerning things unlearnt before, there arose in me Vision, Insight, Understanding: there arose in me Wisdom, there arose in me Light.

So also at the thought "The Origin of Suffering has been put away" . . . there arose in me Light.

Again, at the thought, brethren, of this Ariyan Truth of the Ceasing of Suffering . . . there arose in me Light.

At the thought, brethren, "the Ceasing of Suffering must be realized" . . . there arose in me Light.

At the thought, brethren, "the Ceasing of Suffering has been realized" . . . there arose in me Light.

Finally, brethren, at the thought of This Ariyan Way leading to the Ceasing of Suffering . . . there arose in me Light.

At the thought, brethren, "the Way leading to the Ceasing of Suffering is to be developed" . . . there arose in me Light.

At the thought, brethren, "the Way leading to the Ceasing of

Suffering has been developed" . . . concerning things unlearnt before, there arose in me Vision, Insight, Understanding: there arose in me Wisdom, there arose in me Light.

2

Body, brethren, is without the Self. If body, brethren, were the Self, body would not be involved in sickness, and one would be able to say of body: "Thus let my body be: thus let my body not be."

But, brethren, inasmuch as body is not the Self, that is why body is involved in sickness, and one cannot say of body: "Thus let my body be: thus let my body not be."

So also with regard to feelings, perception, the activities and consciousness . . . they are not the Self.

For if consciousness, brethren, were the Self, then consciousness would not be involved in sickness, and one could say of consciousness: "Thus let my consciousness be: thus let my consciousness not be." But inasmuch as consciousness is not the Self, that is why consciousness is involved in sickness. That is why one cannot say of this consciousness: "Thus let my consciousness be: thus let my consciousness not be."

Now what think ye, brethren? Is body permanent or impermanent?

Impermanent, Lord.

And what is impermanent, is that weal or woe?

Woe, Lord.

Then what is impermanent, woeful, unstable by nature, is it fitting to regard it thus: "This is mine: I am this: this is the Self of me"?

Surely not, Lord.

So also is it with feeling, perception, the activities and consciousness. Therefore, brethren, every body whatever, be it past, future, or present: be it inward or outward, gross or subtle, low or high, far or near—every body should be thus regarded, as it really is, by right insight,—"This is not mine: this am not I: this is not the Self of me."

Every feeling whatever, every perception whatever, all activities whatsoever (must be so regarded).

Every consciousness whatever, be it past, future or present, gross or subtle, low or high, far or near,—every consciousness, I say, must be thus regarded, as it really is, by right insight: "This is not mine: this am not I: this is not the Self of me."

So seeing, brethren, the well-taught Ariyan disciple feels disgust for body, feels disgust for feeling, feels disgust for perception, for the activities, feels disgust for consciousness. So feeling disgust, he is repelled: being repelled, he is freed: knowledge arises that "in the freed is the freed thing": so that he knows: "Destroyed is rebirth: lived is the righteous life: done is my task: for life in terms like these there is no hereafter."

3

Now what, brethren, is right view?

The knowledge about Ill, the Arising of Ill, the Ceasing of Ill, and the Way leading to the Ceasing of Ill,—that, brethren, is called Right View.

And what, brethren, is right aim?

The being set on Renunciation, on Non-resentment, on Harmlessness,—that, brethren, is called Right Aim.

And what, brethren, is right speech?

Abstinence from lying speech, from backbiting and abusive speech, and from idle babble,—that, brethren, is called Right Speech.

And what, brethren, is right action?

Abstinence from taking life, from taking what is not given, from wrong-doing in sexual passions,—that, brethren, is called Right Action.

And what, brethren, is right living?

Herein, brethren, the Ariyan disciple, by giving up wrong living, gets his livelihood by right living,—that, brethren, is called Right Living.

And what, brethren, is right effort?

Herein, brethren, a brother generates the will to inhibit the arising of evil immoral conditions that have not yet arisen: he makes an effort, he sets energy afoot, he applies his mind and struggles. Likewise (he does the same) to reject evil immoral conditions that have already arisen. Likewise (he does the same) to cause the arising of good conditions that have not yet arisen. Likewise he does the same to establish, to prevent the corruption, to cause the increase, the practice, the fulfillment of good conditions that have already arisen. This, brethren, is called Right Effort.

And what, brethren, is right mindfulness?

Herein, brethren, a brother dwells regarding body as a compound, he dwells ardent, self-possessed, recollected, by controlling the covetousness and dejection that are in the world. So also with regard to Feelings, with regard to Perception, with regard to the Activities . . . with regard to Thought. This, brethren, is called Right Mindfulness.

And what, brethren, is right contemplation?

Herein, brethren, a brother, remote from sensual appetites, remote from evil conditions, enters upon and abides in the First Musing, which is accompanied by directed thought and sustained thought (on an object). It is born of solitude, full of zest and happiness.

Then, by the sinking down of thought directed and sustained, he enters on and abides in the Second Musing, which is an inner calming, a raising up of the will. In it there is no directed thought, no sustained thought. It is born of contemplation, full of zest and happiness.

Then again, brethren, by the fading away of the zest, he becomes balanced (indifferent) and remains mindful and self-possessed, and while still in the body he experiences the happiness of which the Ariyans aver "the balanced thoughtful man dwells happily." Thus he enters on the Third Musing and abides therein.

Then again, brethren, rejecting pleasure and pain, by the coming to an end of the joy and sorrow which he had before, he enters on and remains in the Fourth Musing, which is free from pain and free from pleasure, but is a state of perfect purity of balance and equanimity. This is called Right Contemplation.

This, brethren, is called the Ariyan Truth of the Way leading to the Ceasing of Woe.

4

Through not understanding, through not penetrating the Four Ariyan Truths, brethren, we have run on and wandered round this long, long journey (of rebirth), both you and I. What are those four?

The Ariyan Truth of Ill: the Ariyan Truth of the Arising of Ill: the Ariyan Truth of the Ceasing of Ill: the Ariyan Truth of the Way leading to the Ceasing of Ill.

But, brethren, when these Four Ariyan Truths are understood and penetrated, then is uprooted the craving for existence, cut off is the thread that leadeth to rebirth, then is there no more coming to be.

5

This is the Only Way, brethren, that leads to the purification of beings, to passing beyond sorrow and lamentation, to the destruction of grief and despair, to the attainment of the Method, to the realizing of Nibbana, thus: The Four Ways of Establishing Mindfulness. What are the four?

(*Contemplation of Body.*) Herein, brethren, a brother abides regarding Body (as a compound); he is ardent, self-possessed, and concentrated by controlling the covetousness and dejection that are in the world. So also with regard to Feelings, and Thought, and Mental States (Ideas).

And how, brethren, does a brother abide regarding body (as a compound)?

In this method, brethren, a brother goes to the forest or to the foot of a tree or to a lonely place, and there sits down cross-legged, and holds his body straight, establishing concentration in front of him. Then he breathes in mindfully, and mindfully breathes out. As he draws a long breath he knows, "A long breath I draw in." As he breathes out a long breath he knows, "A long breath I breathe out." As he draws in a short breath he knows, "A short breath I draw in." As he breathes out a short breath he knows, "A short breath I breathe out." . . .

Just as, brethren, a clever turner or turner's 'prentice when he gives a long pull (to his lathe-string) is aware "I am giving a long pull," or when he gives a short pull is aware "I am giving a short pull,"—even so does a brother train himself (by conscious in-breathing and out-breathing). . . .

Thus, brethren, does a brother abide in the Contemplation of Body.

Then again, brethren, a brother when he walks is conscious "I am walking," or when he stands still he is conscious "I am standing still." When he sits, or lies, he is conscious of so doing: and whatever the posture of the body he is aware of it. . . .

Then again, brethren, both in advancing and retreating he acts mindfully. In looking forward or backward, in bending or straightening, in wearing his robes or carrying bowl and robe, he acts mindfully. In eating, drinking, chewing, or tasting, in his bodily functions, he acts mindfully. In going, standing, sitting, sleeping, waking, speaking, or keeping silence he acts mindfully. . . .

(*Contemplation of Feelings.*) In this method, brethren, a brother when feeling a pleasant feeling is aware "I feel a pleasant feeling": or when feeling a painful feeling is aware "I am feeling a painful feeling": or when the feeling is neither pleasant nor painful is aware "I am feeling a neutral feeling." . . .

Thus, inwardly or outwardly or both, he abides contemplating his feelings. He abides contemplating the rise of things in feelings or the fall of things in feelings or the rise-and-fall of things in feelings. He says to himself, "It is feeling," and thus his mindfulness of feelings is established, just sufficiently for him to know their existence and to become concentrated. Thus he abides detached and he grasps at nothing at all in the world.

That, brethren, is how a brother abides in the Contemplation of Feelings.

(*Contemplation of Thought.*) And how, brethren, does a brother abide in the Contemplation of Thought as such? In this method, a brother is aware of a passionate thought that it is passionate: of a dispassionate thought that it is dispassionate. Of a hateful thought he is aware that it is hateful; of a thought free from hate he is aware that it is so. Of a confused thought he is aware that it is confused, and of a clear thought he is aware that it is clear. Of a concentrated thought he is aware that it is concentrated, and of a diffuse thought he is aware that it is diffuse. Of a lofty thought he is aware that it is lofty, of a low thought he is aware that it is low. Of a thought concerned with the higher he is aware that it is so: of a thought concerned with the lower he is also aware. Of a thought composed or discomposed, of one that is liberated or bound, in each case he is aware that it is so.

Thus, either inwardly or outwardly or both inwardly and outwardly, he abides contemplating thought. He contemplates the rise of things in thought or the fall of things in thought, or the rise-and-fall of things in thought. Thinking "It is thought," his mindfulness about thought is established, just sufficiently for him to know its existence and to become concentrated. Thus does he abide detached and he grasps at nothing at all in the world.

That is how, brethren, a brother abides, as regards thought, in the Contemplation of Thought.

(*Contemplation of Ideas.*) And how, brethren, does a brother, as regards ideas, abide in the Contemplation of Ideas? . . .

In this method, brethren, a brother is aware of an inner sensual desire that it is sensual, and when he has no inner sensual desire he is aware of it. When there arises in him a sensual desire not felt before, he is aware of it. When there is a rejection of a sensual desire that has arisen, he is aware of it. Also he is aware that when he has rejected such a desire it will not rise up again.

So also with regard to Ill-will, Sloth and Torpor, Excitement and Worry, and Wavering. Of each of these he is aware in the same way, that it is present or absent, of the arising of such when not felt before, of its rejection when felt, and of its never rising again when once rejected.

6

Brethren, there are these five ways of speech which other men may use to you:—speech seasonable or unseasonable: speech true or false: speech gentle or bitter: speech conducive to profit or to loss: speech kindly or resentful.

When men speak evil of ye, thus must ye train yourselves: "Our heart shall be unwavering, no evil word will we send forth, but compassionate of others' welfare will we abide, of kindly heart without resentment: and that man who thus speaks will we suffuse with thoughts accompanied by love, and so abide: and, making that our standpoint, we will suffuse the whole world with loving thoughts, far-reaching, wide-spreading, boundless, free from hate, free from ill-will, and so abide." Thus, brethren, must ye train yourselves.

Moreover, brethren, though robbers, who are highwaymen, should with a two-handed saw carve you in pieces limb by limb, yet if the mind of any one of you should be offended thereat, such a one is no follower of my gospel. . . .

Translation by F. L. Woodward

Dhammapada (Excerpts)

THE MOST FAMOUS of all the Theravada Buddhist scriptures is the *Dhammapada* (Way of Duty), which is included in the *Khuddaka*

Nikaya (division of minor discourses) of the *Sutta Pitaka* (Basket of Discourses). It was written between the fifth and third centuries before the Christian era.

CHAPTER I

The Twin Verses

All that we are is the result of what we have thought: it is founded on our thoughts, it is made up of our thoughts. If a man speaks or acts with an evil thought, pain follows him, as the wheel follows the foot of the ox that draws the wagon.

All that we are is the result of what we have thought: it is founded on our thoughts, it is made up of our thoughts. If a man speaks or acts with a pure thought, happiness follows him, like a shadow that never leaves him.

"He abused me, he beat me, he defeated me, he robbed me,"— in those who harbour such thoughts hatred will never cease.

"He abused me, he beat me, he defeated me, he robbed me,"— in those who do not harbour such thoughts hatred will cease.

For never does hatred cease by hatred here below: hatred ceases by love; this is an eternal law.

The world does not know that we must all come to an end here; but those who know, their quarrels cease at once.

He who lives looking for pleasures only, his senses uncontrolled, immoderate in his food, idle and weak, him Mara (the tempter) will surely overthrow, as the wind throws down a weak tree.

He who lives without looking for pleasures, his senses well controlled, moderate in his food, faithful and strong, him Mara will certainly not overthrow, any more than the wind throws down a rock mountain.

He who wishes to put on the yellow robe though still impure and disregardful of temperance and truth is unworthy of the yellow robe.

But whoever has cleansed himself from impurity, is well-grounded in all virtues, and regards also temperance and truth, is indeed worthy of the yellow robe.

They who imagine truth in untruth, and see untruth in truth, never arrive at truth, but follow vain desires.

They who know truth in truth and untruth in untruth, arrive at truth and follow true desires.

As rain breaks through an ill-thatched house, lust breaks through an ill-trained mind.

As rain does not break through a well-thatched house, lust will not break through a well-trained mind.

The evil-doer mourns in this world and he mourns in the next; he mourns in both. He mourns and suffers when he sees the evil of his own work.

The virtuous man delights in this world, and he delights in the next; he delights in both. He delights and rejoices when he sees the purity of his own work.

The evil-doer suffers in this world and he suffers in the next; he suffers in both. He suffers when he thinks of the evil he has done: he suffers even more when he has gone in the evil path (to hell).

The virtuous man is happy in this world and he is happy in the next; he is happy in both. He is happy when he thinks of the good he has done. He is even happier when he has gone on the good path (to heaven).

The slothful man even if he can recite many sacred verses, but does not act accordingly, has no share in the priesthood, but is like a cowherd counting another's kine.

If a man can recite but few sacred verses but is a follower of the Law, and, having forsaken lust and ill-will and delusion, possesses true knowledge and serenity of mind, he, clinging to nothing in this world or that to come, has indeed a share in the priesthood.

CHAPTER II

On Earnestness

Earnestness is the path of immortality, thoughtlessness the path of death. Those who are earnest do not die, those who are thoughtless are as if dead already.

Those who, having understood this clearly, are advanced in earnestness, delight therein, rejoicing in the knowledge of the Ariyas (the elect).

These wise people, meditative, persevering, always possessed of strong powers, attain to Nirvana, the highest happiness.

If a man is earnest and exerts himself, if he is ever-mindful, if his deeds are pure, if he acts with consideration and restraint and lives according to the Law,—then his glory will increase.

By rousing himself, by earnestness, by temperance and self-control, the wise man may make for himself an island which no flood can overwhelm.

Senseless and foolish folk fall into sloth. The wise man guards earnestness as his best treasure.

Follow not after vanity, nor after the enjoyment of love and lust. He who is earnest and meditative obtains ample joy.

When the learned man drives away vanity by earnestness, he, the wise, climbing the terraced heights of wisdom, looks down upon the fools, free from sorrow he looks upon the sorrowing crowd, as one that stands on a mountain looks down upon them that stand upon the plain.

Earnest among the slothful, awake among the sleepers, the wise man advances like a racer, leaving behind the hack.

By earnestness did Maghavan (Indra) rise to the lordship of the gods. People praise earnestness; thoughtlessness is always blamed.

A mendicant who delights in earnestness, who looks with fear on thoughtlessness, advances like a fire, burning all his fetters both great and small.

A mendicant who delights in earnestness, who looks with fear on thoughtlessness, cannot fall away (from his perfect state)—he is close upon Nirvana.

CHAPTER III

Thought

As a fletcher makes straight his arrow, a wise man makes straight his trembling and unsteady thought, which is difficult to guard, difficult to hold back.

As a fish taken from his watery home and thrown on the dry ground, our thought quivers all over in its effort to escape the dominion of Mara (the tempter).

It is good to tame the mind, which is difficult to hold in and flighty, rushing wherever it listeth; a tamed mind brings happiness.

Let the wise man guard his thoughts which are difficult to perceive, very artful and rushing wherever they list: thoughts well guarded bring happiness.

Those who bridle their mind which travels far, moves about alone, is without a body, and hides in the chamber (of the heart), are freed from the bonds of Mara (the tempter).

If a man's thoughts are unsteady, if he does not know the true Law, his knowledge will never be perfect.

If a man's thoughts are free from lust, if his mind is not perplexed, if he has renounced merit and demerit, then there is no fear for him while he is watchful.

Knowing that this body is (fragile) like a jar, and making this thought firm like a fortress, one should attack Mara (the tempter) with the weapon of knowledge, one should watch him when conquered and should never falter.

Before long, alas! this body will lie on the ground, despised, bereft of consciousness, like a useless log.

Whatever a hater may do to a hater, or an enemy to an enemy, a wrongly-directed mind will do us greater mischief.

Not a mother, not a father will do so much, nor any other relative; a well-directed mind will do us greater service.

CHAPTER IV

Flowers

Who shall overcome this Earth, and the world of Yama (the lord of the departed), and the world of the gods? Who shall find out the well-taught path of virtue, even as a clever (garland weaver) picks out the (right) flower?

The disciple will overcome the Earth, and the world of Yama, and the world of the gods. The disciple will find out the well-taught path of virtue, even as a clever (garland-weaver) picks out the right flower.

He who knows that this body is like froth and has learned that it is as unsubstantial as a mirage, will break the flower-tipped arrow of Mara, and never see the King of death.

Death carries off a man who is gathering flowers and whose mind is distracted, as a flood carries off a sleeping village.

Death overpowers a man who is gathering flowers, and whose mind is distracted, before he is satiated in his pleasures.

As the bee collects nectar and departs without injuring the flower of its colour or scent, so let a sage go about a village.

Not the perversities of others, not what they have done or left undone should a sage take notice of.

Like a beautiful flower, full of colour, but without scent, are the fair but fruitless words of him who does not act accordingly.

Like a beautiful flower, full of colour and full of scent, are the pure and fruitful words of him who acts accordingly.

Even as one may make many kinds of wreaths from a heap of flowers, so should one born to the mortal lot perform good deeds manifold.

The scent of flowers does not travel against the wind, nor that of sandal-wood, or of Tagara and Mallika flowers; but the fragrance of good people travels even against the wind; a good man pervades every place.

Sandal-wood or Tagara, a lotus-flower or a Vassiki, among these sorts of perfumes the perfume of virtue is preeminent.

Mean is the scent that comes from Tagara and sandal-wood;— the perfume of those who possess virtue rises up to the gods as the highest.

Of the people thus excellently virtuous, abiding in earnestness and emancipated through true knowledge, Mara (the tempter) never finds the way.

As on a heap of rubbish cast upon the highway the lotus will grow full of sweet perfume and delight, thus the disciple of the truly enlightened Buddha shines forth by his knowledge among those who are like rubbish, among the people who walk in darkness.

CHAPTER V

The Fool

Long is the night to him who is awake; long is a league to him who is tired; long is the round of rebirth to the foolish who do not know the true law.

If a traveller does not meet with one who is his better or his equal, let him keep firmly to his solitary journey; there is no companionship with a fool.

"These sons belong to me, and this wealth belongs to me," with such thoughts a fool is tormented. He himself does not belong to himself; how much less sons and wealth!

The fool who knows his foolishness is wise at least so far. But a fool who thinks himself wise, he is called a fool indeed.

If a fool be associated with a wise man even all his life, he will perceive the truth as little as a spoon perceives the taste of soup.

If an intelligent man be associated for one minute only with a wise man, he will soon perceive the truth, as the tongue perceives the taste of soup.

Fools of little understanding are their own greatest enemies, for they do evil deeds which must bear bitter fruits.

That deed is not well done of which a man must repent, and the reward of which he receives crying and with a tearful face.

No, that deed is well done of which a man does not repent and the reward of which he receives gladly and cheerfully.

As long as the evil deed done does not bear fruit, the fool thinks it is like honey; but when it ripens, then the fool suffers grief.

Let a fool month after month eat his food (like an ascetic) with the tip of a blade of Kusha grass, yet is he not worth the sixteenth part of those who have well-weighed the Law.

An evil deed like newly-drawn milk does not turn at once; smouldering like fire covered with ashes, it follows the fool.

The knowledge that a fool acquires, so far from profiting him, destroys his good fortune, nay, it cleaves his head.

Let the fool wish for a false reputation, for precedence among the monks, for lordship in the monasteries, for honour among other people.

"May both laymen and those who have left the world think that this is done by me; may they be subject to me in everything which is to be done or is not to be done": thus is the mind of the fool, and his desire and pride increase.

One is the road that leads to wealth, another the road that leads to Nirvana; if the monk, the disciple of Buddha, has learnt this he will not delight in the praise of men, he will strive after separation from the world.

CHAPTER VI

The Wise Man

If you see an intelligent man who detects faults and blames what is blame-worthy, follow that wise man as though he were a revealer of (hidden) treasures.

Let him admonish, let him teach, let him forbid what is improper!—he will be beloved of the good, by the bad he will be hated.

Do not have evil-doers for friends, do not have low people for friends: have virtuous people for friends, have for friends the best of men.

He who drinks in the Law lives happily with a serene mind; the wise man ever rejoices in the Law as taught by the elect (Ariyas).

Irrigators guide the water (wherever they like); fletchers bend the arrow; carpenters bend a log of wood; wise people fashion themselves.

As a solid rock is not shaken by the wind, wise people falter not amidst blame and praise.

Wise people, after they have listened to the laws, become serene like a deep, clear and still lake.

Good people walk on, whatever befall; the good do not prattle, longing for pleasure; whether touched by happiness or sorrow, wise people never appear elated or depressed.

If, whether for his own sake or for the sake of others, a man wishes neither for a son nor for wealth, nor for lordship, and if he does not wish for his own success by unfair means, then he is good, wise and upright.

Few are there among men who arrive at the other shore (become Arhats); the other people here merely run up and down the shore.

But those who, when the Law has been well preached to them, follow the Law, will reach the further shore of the dominion of death, hard to traverse though it be.

A wise man should leave the way of darkness and follow the way of light. After going from his home to the houseless state, he should in his retirement look for enjoyment where enjoyment is hard to find. Leaving all pleasure behind, and calling nothing his own, the wise man should purge himself from all the impurities of the heart.

Those whose minds are well-grounded in the (seven) elements of knowledge, who rejoice in the renunciation of affections and in freedom from attachment, whose evil proclivities have been overcome and who are full of light, are completely liberated even in this world.

Translation by Irving Babbitt

LATER DISCOURSES

THE LATER DISCOURSES OF BUDDHISM WERE PRODUCED BY THE various sects. The distinctions between the two major sects, namely, Theravada (or Hinayana) Buddhism and Mahayana Buddhism, may be summarized as follows:

Chronological status—Theravada Buddhism is the older view (founded about 400 B.C.); Mahayana Buddhism (founded in the first century of the Christian era), the younger.

Attitude toward the other—Theravadists regard Mahayana Buddhism as wrong-headed and heretical; Mahayanists, by contrast, regard the Theravadists' view as right but incomplete. This contrast is paralleled roughly by the Old Testament-based Jewish view of Christianity as wrong, and the New Testament-emphasizing Christian view of the Old Testament as right but incomplete.

Numerical preponderance—Mahayana Buddhism has more adherents than Theravada Buddhism.

Geographical strongholds—Theravada Buddhism (sometimes called "Southern Buddhism") is strong in Ceylon, Burma, and Thailand. Mahayana Buddhism (sometimes called "Northern Buddhism") is strong in Nepal, Tibet, China, Korea, and Japan. The Communist regime in China and Tibet has not suppressed Buddhism, but controls it to the same extent to which the Soviet regimes in Eastern Europe control the Christian churches.

View of Buddha—Theravadists regard Buddha as a man. Mahayana Buddhists regard him as an embodiment of the transcendental Buddha, with whose essence one can be united by achieving nirvana and thus becoming, oneself, a Buddha.

View on eligibility for nirvana—Theravadists emphasize the eligibility of monks; Mahayana Buddhists, that of the laity.

View on the nature of those who achieve nirvana—According to Theravadists, nirvana is achieved by Arhats, or Arhants (saints), who are liberated in the present life, once for all, from the cycle of life and death. According to Mahayana Buddhists, nirvana is achieved after the endurance of several lives by Bodhisattvas (those who possess the essence, *sat-*, of enlightenment, *bodh-*), who, though desiring to become Buddhas, postpone their entrance into nirvana in order to help many suffering creatures.

The foregoing distinctions between the views of the two sects are not fully reflected in the Theravada and Mahayana scriptures, but are evidenced mainly in practice. Nevertheless, the scriptures are revealing. The classical scriptures, the *Three Baskets*, are revered by both groups and are regarded by the Theravadists as containing the whole of the basic doctrine. Therefore, the later discourses of the Theravadists are essentially explanatory, while those of the Mahayana Buddhists contain additional, or supplementary, doctrines.

Although Theravadism is the older view, its important later discourses are not necessarily older than the important later discourses of Mahayana Buddhism. Indeed, the Theravada discourse included here, the *Questions of King Milinda*, happens to have been written after the Mahayana selection included here. But the Theravada selection is given first, as representative of the older view. Readers who wish to take the actual readings (as distinguished from the development of the sects) in a more strictly chronological order are invited to read the Mahayana selection first.

Theravada View of Nirvana: Questions of King Milinda (*Excerpts*)

THE POST-CANONICAL Theravada literature includes most notably the *Path of Purity*, by Buddhaghosha (called "the Great," to distinguish him from others of the same name), who lived about 450 in the Christian era, and the *Questions of King Milinda,* by an unknown writer who lived about fifty years later.

The *Questions of King Milinda* presents a series of doctrinal questions supposedly asked by one of the Greco-Persian kings of southern India, Menander ("Milinda" in the Indian tongues), who reigned about 150 B.C., together with the answers supposedly given to Milinda by a monk named Nagasena. The excerpts printed here emphasize (a) that only some, not all, can win nirvana, and (b) that those who win nirvana only "realize," or acquire awareness of, that state, but do not "produce" it, for it exists independently of its being won.

The special terms used in the excerpt have the following meanings:

Arhats—Saints.
Dharma—Duty, law, or justice.
Jina—Conqueror or hero, i.e., Buddha.
Karma—Burden of the consequences of one's past moral conduct.
Sariputra—An important first-generation disciple of Buddha.
Triple Jewel—According to T. W. Rhys Davids, who translated the *Questions of King Milinda* for Max Müller's monumental *Sacred Books of the East,* this expression refers to Buddha, his religion, and his order. But it seems equally or more likely that the expression refers to the threefold way of life epitomized in Buddhist writings as dharma (the moral side), artha (wealth or utility, the practical side), and kama (desire or love, the aesthetic side).

CHAPTER 4

Emancipation and Nirvana

(*Problems of Nirvana.*) The king asked: "Is cessation Nirvana?"
"Yes, your majesty!"
"How is that, Nagasena?"
"All the foolish common people take delight in the senses and their objects, are impressed by them, are attached to them. In that way they are carried away by the flood, and are not set free from birth, old age, and death, from grief, lamentation, pain, sadness, and despair—they are, I say, not set free from suffering. But the well-informed holy disciples do not take delight in the senses and their objects, are not impressed by them, are not attached to them, and in consequence their craving ceases; the cessation of craving

leads successively to that of grasping, of becoming, of birth, of old age and death, of grief, lamentation, pain, sadness, and despair— that is to say to the cessation of all this mass of ill. It is thus that cessation is Nirvana."

"Very good, Nagasena!"

The king asked: "Do all win Nirvana?"

"No, they do not. Only those win Nirvana who, progressing correctly, know by their superknowledge those dharmas which should be known by superknowledge, comprehend those dharmas which should be comprehended, forsake those dharmas which should be forsaken, develop those dharmas which should be developed, and realize those dharmas which should be realized."

"Very good, Nagasena!"

The king asked: "Do those who have not won Nirvana know how happy a state it is?"

"Yes, they do."

"But how can one know this about Nirvana without having attained it?"

"Now what do you think, your majesty? Do those who have not had their hands and feet cut off know how bad it is to have them cut off?"

"Yes, they do."

"And how do they know it?"

"From hearing the sound of the lamentations of those whose hands and feet have been cut off."

"So it is by hearing the words of those who have seen Nirvana that one knows it to be a happy state."

"Very good, Nagasena!"

(*The Nature of Nirvana.*) King Milinda said: "I will grant you, Nagasena, that Nirvana is absolute Ease, and that nevertheless one cannot point to its form or shape, its duration or size, either by simile or explanation, by reason or by argument. But is there perhaps some quality of Nirvana which it shares with other things, and which lends itself to a metaphorical explanation?"

"Its form, O king, cannot be elucidated by similes, but its qualities can."

"How good to hear that, Nagasena! Speak then, quickly, so that I may have an explanation of even one of the aspects of Nirvana! Appease the fever of my heart! Allay it with the cool sweet breezes of your words!"

"Nirvana shares one quality with the lotus, two with water, three with medicine, ten with space, three with the wishing jewel, and five with a mountain peak. As the lotus is unstained by water, so is Nirvana unstained by all the defilements. As cool water allays feverish heat, so also Nirvana is cool and allays the fever of all the passions. Moreover, as water removes the thirst of men and beasts who are exhausted, parched, thirsty, and overpowered by heat, so also Nirvana removes the craving for sensuous enjoyments, the craving for further becoming, the craving for the cessation of becoming. As medicine protects from the torments of poison, so Nirvana from the torments of the poisonous passions. Moreover, as medicine puts an end to sickness, so Nirvana to all sufferings. Finally, Nirvana and medicine both give security. And these are the ten qualities which Nirvana shares with space. Neither is born, grows old, dies, passes away, or is reborn; both are unconquerable, cannot be stolen, are unsupported, are roads respectively for birds and Arhats to journey on, are unobstructed and infinite. Like the wishing jewel, Nirvana grants all one can desire, brings joy, and sheds light. As a mountain peak is lofty and exalted, so is Nirvana. As a mountain peak is unshakeable, so is Nirvana. As a mountain peak is inaccessible, so is Nirvana inaccessible to all the passions. As no seeds can grow on a mountain peak, so the seeds of all the passions cannot grow in Nirvana. And finally, as a mountain peak is free from all desire to please or displease, so is Nirvana."

"Well said, Nagasena! So it is, and as such I accept it."

(*The Realization of Nirvana.*) King Milinda said: "In the world one can see things produced of karma, things produced from a cause, things produced by nature. Tell me, what in the world is not born of karma, or a cause, or of nature?"

"There are two such things, space and Nirvana."

"Do not, Nagasena, corrupt the Jina's words, do not answer the question ignorantly!"

"What did I say, your majesty, that you speak thus to me?"

"What you said about space not being born of karma, or from a cause, or from nature, that was correct. But with many hundreds of arguments has the Lord proclaimed to his disciples the way to the realization of Nirvana—and then you say that Nirvana is not born of a cause!"

"It is true that the Lord has with many hundreds of arguments proclaimed to his disciples the way to the realization of Nirvana;

but that does not mean that he has spoken of a cause for the production of Nirvana."

"Here, Nagasena, we do indeed enter from darkness into greater darkness, from a jungle into a deeper jungle, from a thicket into a denser thicket, inasmuch as we are given a cause for the realization of Nirvana, but no cause for the production of that same dharma (i.e., Nirvana). If there is a cause for the realization of Nirvana, we would also expect one for its production. If there is a son's father, one would for that reason also expect the father to have had a father; if there is a pupil's teacher, one would for that reason also expect the teacher to have had a teacher; if there is a seed for a sprout, one would for that reason also expect the seed to have had a seed. Just so, if there is cause for the realization of Nirvana, one would for that reason also expect a cause for its production."

"Nirvana, O king, is not something that should be produced. That is why no cause for its production has been proclaimed."

"Please, Nagasena, give me a reason, convince me by an argument, so that I can understand this point!"

"Well then, O king, attend carefully, listen closely, and I will tell you the reason for this. Could a man with his natural strength go up from here to the Himalaya mountains?"

"Yes, he could."

"But could that man with his natural strength bring the Himalaya mountains here?"

"No, he could not."

"Just so it is possible to point out the way to the realization of Nirvana, but impossible to show a cause for its production. Could a man, who with his natural strength has crossed in a boat over the great ocean, get to the farther shore?"

"Yes, he could."

"But could that man with his natural strength bring the farther shore of the great ocean here?"

"No, he could not."

"Just so one can point out the way to the realization of Nirvana, but one cannot show a cause for its production. And what is the reason for that? Because that dharma, Nirvana, is unconditioned."

"Is then, Nagasena, Nirvana unconditioned?"

"So it is, O king, unconditioned is Nirvana, not made by anything. Of Nirvana one cannot say that it is produced, or unproduced, or that it should be produced; that it is past, or future, or present; or that one can become aware of it by the eye, or the ear, or the nose, or the tongue, or the body."

"In that case, Nagasena, you indicate Nirvana as a dharma which is not, and Nirvana does not exist."

"Nirvana is something which is. It is cognizable by the mind. A holy disciple, who has followed the right road, sees Nirvana with a mind which is pure, sublime, straight, unimpeded and disinterested."

"But what then is that Nirvana like? Give me a simile, and convince me by arguments. For a dharma which exists can surely be illustrated by a simile!"

"Is there, great king, something called 'wind'?"

"Yes, there is such a thing."

"Please, will your majesty show me the wind, its colour and shape, and whether it is thin or thick, long or short."

"One cannot point to the wind like that. For the wind does not lend itself to being grasped with the hands, or to being touched. But nevertheless there is such a thing as 'wind.'"

"If one cannot point to the wind, one might conclude that there is no wind at all."

"But I know, Nagasena, that there is wind, I am quite convinced of it, in spite of the fact that I cannot point it out."

"Just so, your majesty, there is Nirvana, but one cannot point to Nirvana, either by its colour or its shape."

"Very good, Nagasena. Clear is the simile, convincing is the argument. So it is, and so I accept it: there is a Nirvana."

(*The Saints and Their Bodies.*) The king asked: "Does someone who is no more reborn feel any unpleasant feelings?"

The Elder replied: "Some he feels, and others not."

"Which ones does he feel, and which ones not?"

"He feels physical, but not mental, pain."

"How is that?"

"The causes and conditions which produce feelings of physical pain have not ceased to operate, whereas those which produce feelings of mental pain have. And so it has been said by the Lord: 'Only one kind of feelings he feels, physical, and not mental.'"

"And when he feels a physical pain, why does he not escape into final Nirvana, by dying quickly?"

"An Arhat has no more likes or dislikes. Arhats do not shake

down the unripe fruit, the wise wait for it to mature. And so it has
been said by the Elder Sariputra, the Dharma's general:
> 'It is not death, it is not life I cherish.
> I bide my time, a servant waiting for his wage.
> It is not death, it is not life I cherish.
> I bide my time, in mindfulness and wisdom.' "

"Well put, Nagasena!" . . .

(*Conclusion.*) The king, as a result of his discussions with the
Venerable Nagasena, was overjoyed and humbled; he saw the value
in the Buddha's religion, gained confidence in the Triple Jewel,
lost his spikiness and obstinacy, gained faith in the qualities of the
Elder—in his observation of the monastic rules, his spiritual
progress and his general demeanour—because trusting and resigned,
free from conceit and arrogance. Like a cobra whose fangs have
been drawn, he said: "Well said, well said, Nagasena! You have
answered my questions, which would have given scope to a
Buddha, you have answered them well! Apart from the Elder
Sariputra, the supreme general of the Dharma, there is no one in
this religion of the Buddha who can deal with questions as well as
you do. Forgive my transgressions, Nagasena! May the Venerable
Nagasena accept me as a lay-follower, as one who takes his refuge
with the Triple Jewel, from to-day onwards, as long as I shall live!"

Translation by Edward Conze

Mahayana View of Nirvana: Lankavatara Sutra (Excerpts)

MAHAYANA BUDDHISM, in addition to a more or less standard form
(with variations) in Nepal, Tibet, China, and Korea, includes also
the Tantric wing in Bengal, the Shin wing (which is a merger of
Buddhism and Shinto) in Japan, and Zen wherever it is practiced.

Mahayana discourses, produced after the classical period, include
(a) *sutras*, which are discourses ascribed to Buddha; (b) *shastras*,
which are commentaries or textbooks, partly limited in authority to
individual subsects or wings within the Mahayana persuasion; and
(c) *tantras*, which are secret texts, for members of a given subsect only,
intentionally shocking and obscure in phrasing, to throw outsiders off
the track. In some listings, the third group includes, instead of the
tantras, or in addition to them, a Sanskrit version of the Pali Theravada scripture, *Vinaya Pitaka* (Basket of Discipline). Regarding a

non-Buddhist category of *tantras*, see the last part of Chapter IV of this volume.

Of the *sutras*, which have more philosophical appeal than the *shastras* or the *tantras*, the best known are the *Diamond Sutra* (which is part of a collection of sutras known as the *Perfection of Wisdom*), the *Sutra Concerning the Lotus of the True Doctrine*, and the *Lankavatara Sutra* (Discourse on the Entry into Lanka, i.e., discourse on a legendary visit by Buddha to Ceylon).

The *Lankavatara Sutra* was probably composed in the first two centuries of the Christian era. The special terms used in the excerpts from it which are printed here have the following meanings:

Arhat—A saint.
Bodhisattva-Mahasattva—A greatly superior possessor of the essence of enlightenment.
Dharmakaya—The attribute of justice or duty or cosmic law.
Samadhi—A deep trance of self-awareness, leading to enlightenment; or (in this passage) one who experiences such a trance.
Sugata—He who has well gone (i.e., to nirvana), namely, Buddha.
Tathagata—He who, or one who, has thus gone (i.e., to nirvana), namely, Buddha or any other fully enlightened being.

CHAPTER I

Discrimination

Thus have I heard. The Blessed One once appeared in the Castle of Lanka which is on the summit of Mount Malaya in the midst of the great Ocean. . . . The Blessed One, knowing of the mental agitations going on in the minds of those assembled (like the surface of the ocean stirred into waves by the passing winds), and his great heart moved by compassion, smiled and said:

In the days of old the Tathagatas of the past who were Arhats and fully-enlightened Ones came to the castle of Lanka on Mount Malaya and discoursed on the Truth of Noble Wisdom that is beyond the reasoning knowledge of the philosophers as well as being beyond the understanding of ordinary disciples and masters; and which is realisable only within the inmost consciousness; for your sakes, I too would discourse on the same Truth. All that is seen in the world is devoid of effort and action because all things in the world are like a dream, or like an image miraculously projected. This is not comprehended by the philosophers and the ignorant, but those who thus see things see them truthfully. Those who see things otherwise walk in discrimination and, as they depend upon discrimination, they cling to dualism.

The world as seen by discrimination is like seeing one's own image reflected in a mirror, or one's shadow, or the moon reflected in water, or an echo heard in the valley. People grasping their own shadows of discrimination become attached to this thing and that thing and failing to abandon dualism they go on forever discriminating and thus never attain tranquility. By tranquility is meant Oneness, and Oneness gives birth to the highest Samadhi which is gained by entering into the realm of Noble Wisdom that is realisable only within one's inmost consciousness.

Then all the Bodhisattva-Mahasattvas rose from their seats and respectfully paid him homage and Mahamati the Bodhisattva-Mahasattva sustained by the power of the Buddhas drew his upper garment over one shoulder, knelt and pressing his hands together, praised him in the following verses:

As thou reviewest the world with thy perfect intelligence and compassion, it must seem to thee like an ethereal flower of which one cannot say: it is born, it is destroyed, for the terms being and non-being do not apply to it.

As thou reviewest the world with thy perfect intelligence and compassion, it must seem to thee like a dream of which it cannot be said: it is permanent or it is destructible, for being and non-being do not apply to it.

As thou reviewest all things by thy perfect intelligence and compassion, they must seem to thee like visions beyond the reach of the human mind, as being and non-being do not apply to them.

With thy perfect intelligence and compassion which are beyond all limit, thou comprehendest the egolessness of things and persons, and art free and clear from the hindrances of passion and learning and egoism.

Thou dost not vanish into Nirvana, nor does Nirvana abide in thee, for Nirvana transcends all duality of knowing and known, of being and non-being.

Those who see thee thus, serene and beyond conception, will

be emancipated from attachment, will be cleansed of all
defilement, both in this world and in the spiritual world
beyond.

In this world whose nature is like a dream, there is place for
praise and blame, but in the ultimate Reality of Dharmakaya which is far beyond the senses and the discriminating
mind, what is there to praise? O thou most Wise!

Then said Mahamati the Bodhisattva-Mahasattva: O blessed
One, Sugata, Arhat and Fully-enlightened One, pray tell us about
the realisation of Noble Wisdom which is beyond the path and
usage of the philosophers; which is devoid of all predicates such
as being and non-being, oneness and otherness, bothness and
not-bothness, existence and non-existence, eternity and non-
eternity; which has nothing to do with individuality and generality,
nor false-imagination, nor any illusions arising from the mind
itself; but which manifests itself as the Truth of Highest Reality.
By which, going up continuously by the stages of purification, one
enters at last upon the stage of Tathagatahood, whereby, by the
power of his original vows unattended by any striving, one will
radiate its influence to infinite worlds, like a gem reflecting its
variegated colors, whereby I and other Bodhisattva-Mahasattvas
will be enabled to bring all beings to the same perfection of virtue.

Said the Blessed One: Well done, well done, Mahamati! And
again, well done, indeed! It is because of your compassion for the
worlds, because of the benefit it will bring to many people both
human kind and celestial, that you have presented yourself before
us to make this request. Therefore, Mahamati, listen well and truly
reflect upon what I shall say, for I will instruct you.

Then Mahamati and the other Bodhisattva-Mahasattvas gave
devout attention to the teaching of the Blessed One.

Mahamati, the ignorant and simple-minded, not knowing that
the world is only something seen of the mind itself, cling to the
multitudinousness of external objects, cling to the notions of being
and non-being, oneness and otherness, bothness and not-bothness,
existence and non-existence, eternity and non-eternity, and think
that they have a self-nature of their own, all of which rises from
the discriminations of the mind and is perpetuated by habit-energy,
and from which they are given over to false imagination. It is all

like a mirage in which springs of water are seen as if they were real. They are thus imagined by animals who, made thirsty by the heat of the season, run after them.

Animals, not knowing that the springs are an hallucination of their own minds, do not realise that there are no such springs. In the same way, Mahamati, the ignorant and simple-minded, their minds burning with the fires of greed, anger and folly, finding delight in a world of multitudinous forms, their thoughts obsessed with ideas of birth, growth and destruction, not well understanding what is meant by existent and non-existent, and being impressed by the erroneous discriminations and speculations since beginningless time, fall into the habit of grasping this and that and thereby becoming attached to them. . . .

CHAPTER XIII

Nirvana

Then said Mahamati to the Blessed One: Pray tell us about Nirvana.

The Blessed One replied: The term, Nirvana, is used with many different meanings, by different people, but these people may be divided into four groups: There are people who are suffering, or who are afraid of suffering, and who think of Nirvana; there are the philosophers who try to discriminate Nirvana; there are the class of disciples who think of Nirvana in relation to themselves; and, finally, there is the Nirvana of the Buddhas.

Those who are suffering, or who fear suffering, think of Nirvana as an escape and a recompense. They imagine that Nirvana consists in the future annihilation of the senses and the sense-minds; they are not aware that Universal Mind and Nirvana are One, and that this life-and-death world and Nirvana are not to be separated. These ignorant ones, instead of meditating on the imagelessness of Nirvana, talk of different ways of emancipation. Being ignorant of, or not understanding, the teachings of the Tathagatas, they cling to the notion of Nirvana that is outside what is seen of the mind and, thus, go on rolling themselves along with the wheel of life and death.

As to the Nirvanas discriminated by the philosophers: there really are none. Some philosophers conceive Nirvana to be found where the mind-system no more operates owing to the cessation of the elements that make up personality and its world; or is found where there is utter indifference to the objective world and its impermanency. Some conceive Nirvana to be a state where there is no recollection of the past or present, just as when a lamp is extinguished, or when a seed is burnt, or when a fire goes out; because then there is the cessation of all the substrata, which is explained by the philosophers as the non-rising of discrimination. But this is not Nirvana, because Nirvana does not consist in simply annihilation and vacuity. . . .

These views severally advanced by the philosophers with their various reasonings are not in accord with logic nor are they acceptable to the wise. They all conceive Nirvana dualistically and in some causal connection; by these discriminations philosophers imagine Nirvana, but where there is no rising and no disappearing, how can there be discrimination? Each philosopher relying on his own textbook, from which he draws his understanding, sins against the truth, because truth is not where he imagines it to be. The only result is that it sets his mind to wandering about and becoming more confused as Nirvana is not to be found by mental searching, and the more his mind becomes confused the more he confuses other people.

As to the notion of Nirvana as held by disciples and masters who still cling to the notion of an ego-self, and who try to find it by going off by themselves into solitude: their notion of Nirvana is an eternity of bliss like the bliss of the Samadhis—for themselves. They recognise that the world is only a manifestation of mind and that all discriminations are of the mind, and so they forsake social relations and practise various spiritual disciplines and in solitude seek self-realisation of Noble Wisdom by self-effort. They follow the stages to the sixth and attain the bliss of the Samadhis, but as they are still clinging to egoism they do not attain the "turning-about" at the deepest seat of consciousness and, therefore, they are not free from the thinking-mind and the accumulation of its habit-energy. Clinging to the bliss of the Samadhis, they pass to their nirvana, but it is not the Nirvana of the Tathagatas. They are of those who have "entered the stream"; they must return to this world of life and death. . . .

The Tathagata's Nirvana is where it is recognized that there is nothing but what is seen of the mind itself; is where, recognizing the nature of the self-mind, one no longer cherishes the dualisms of discrimination; is where there is no more thirst nor grasping; is where there is no more attachment to external things. Nirvana is where the thinking-mind with all its discriminations, attachments, aversions and egoism is forever put away; is where logical measures, as they are seen to be inert, are no longer seized upon; is where even the notion of truth is treated with indifference because of its causing bewilderment; is where, getting rid of the four propositions, there is insight into the abode of Reality. Nirvana is where the twofold passions have subsided and the twofold hindrances are cleared away and the twofold egolessness is patiently accepted; is where, by the attainment of the "turning-about" in the deepest seat of consciousness, self-realisation of Noble Wisdom is fully entered into,—that is the Nirvana of the Tathagatas.

Translation by D. T. Suzuki and Dwight Goddard

III

Reverence for Life: Ancient Jainism

THE WORD "JAIN" COMES FROM THE ROOT "JI" ("TO CONQUER").
It signifies the viewpoint or status of those who have conquered
desire, including the desire to hurt.

Jainism is as old as Buddhism, or older. Indeed, its greatest
leader, Vardhamana (about 580–500 B.C.), called by the title
"Mahavira" (Great Hero), was probably an older contemporary
of Buddha. Its canonical literature, however, is of later vintage
than that of Buddhism.

Jainism shares with Vedantism and Buddhism the hypothesis
that man undergoes a cycle of lives of suffering but can end the
cycle and enter nirvana by concentrated meditation on the self.
Jainism adds to this the doctrine that life—even the life of insects—
is sacred and should under no circumstances be crushed.

Besides cherishing the addition of the commandment not to kill
or hurt, Jainism also differs from Vedantism and Buddhism in
that, whereas they speculate on ultimate being, Jainism philos-
ophizes about everyday reality. Jain theories about reality include
the following:

a. Basic substance, material or nonmaterial, endures forever, while the everyday things that are composed of basic

69

substance endure only for a time. Everyday things traverse the stages of production, continuance, and destruction, as their basic substance acquires and loses qualities.

b. Everyday things exhibit "indefiniteness of being," and many "syat" (maybe) propositions can be asserted about them. For example, of a gray clay jar one can assert that "maybe it will change its color," "maybe it will change its form," etc. Some Jain writers call this "the theory of the relativity of things."

c. The elements of things—earth, water, fire, and wind— have rudimentary souls.

Jainism has two sects, the Svetambaras (white-clad), whose monks wear white, and the Digambaras (sky-clad), who traditionally have gone naked but now wear loincloths. Digambaras deny that women can reach liberation from the cycle of lives.

BASIC TEXTS

T HE COLLECTION OF JAIN CANONICAL WORKS IS KNOWN AS THE *Siddhanta* (Complete Teaching). It consists of eleven Angas (Books of Precepts), four Mulasutras (Basic Discussions), and other works. Its consolidation occurred about the year 500 in the Christian era.

Discourse of Performed Precepts (Excerpts)

THE *Sutra Kritanga* (Discourse of Performed Precepts) is the second of the eleven Angas. Its paragraphs were probably composed a few centuries before the Christian era, but they do not seem to have been consolidated and written down in an organized arrangement until some centuries later.

The special terms used in the excerpts printed here have the following meanings:

Arhat—A saint.
Brahman, or Brahma—The world soul.
Brahmana—A member of the highest caste.
Isvara, or Ishvara—The creator god.
Karman, or karma—The burden of the consequences of one's moral conduct.
Sramana, or samana—An ascetic.

LECTURE I (*"The Doctrine"*), CHAPTER I

One should know what causes the bondage of Soul, and knowing it one should remove it.

Gambusvamin asked Sudharman:

What causes the bondage of Soul according to Mahavira? and what must one know in order to remove it?

Sudharman answered:

He who owns even a small property in living or lifeless things, or consents to others holding it, will not be delivered from misery.

If a man kills living beings, or causes other men to kill them, or consents to their killing them, his iniquity will go on increasing.

A sinner who makes the interests of his kinsmen and companions his own, will suffer much; for the number of those whose interest he takes to heart constantly increases. . . .

"Everybody, fool or sage, has an individual soul. These souls exist as long as the body, but after death they are no more; there are no souls which are born again.

"There is neither virtue nor vice, there is no world beyond; on the dissolution of the body the individual ceases to be. . . ."

How can those who hold such opinions explain the variety of existence in the world? They go from darkness to utter darkness, being fools and engaged in works. . . .

CHAPTER II

Again some say: "It is proved that there are individual souls; they experience pleasure and pain; and on dying they lose their state of life.

". . . Pleasure and misery, final beatitude and temporal pleasure and pain are not caused by the souls themselves, nor by others; but the individual souls experience them; it is the lot assigned them by destiny." This is what they say.

Those who proclaim these opinions are fools who fancy themselves learned; they have no knowledge, and do not understand that things depend partly on fate, and partly on human exertion. . . .

Shaking off greed, pride, deceit, and wrath, one becomes free from Karman. This is a subject which an ignorant man, like a brute animal, does not attend to.

The unworthy heretics who do not acknowledge this, will incur death an endless number of times, like deer caught in a snare. . . .

The mind of those who sin in thoughts is not pure; they are wrong, they do not conduct themselves carefully. . . .

CHAPTER III

We hear also of another error of some philosophers: some say that the world has been created or is governed by the gods, others, by Brahman.

Some say that it has been created by the Isvara, others that it was produced from chaos, this world with living beings and lifeless things, with its variety of pleasure and pain.

Some Brahmanas and Sramanas say that the universe was produced from the primeval egg, and He Brahman created the things. These ignorant men speak untruth.

Those who on arguments of their own maintain that the world has been created, do not know the truth. Nor will the world ever perish. . . .

CHAPTER IV

This is the quintessence of wisdom: not to kill anything. Know this to be the legitimate conclusion from the principle of the reciprocity with regard to non-killing.

Living according to the rules of conduct, and without greed, one should take care of the highest good.

In walking, in sitting and lying down, and in food and drink: with regard to these three points a monk should always control himself.

And he should leave off pride, wrath, deceit, and greed. . . .

LECTURE II (*"The Destruction of Karman"*), CHAPTER I

Rishabha said to his sons:

Acquire perfect knowledge of the Law! why do you not study it? It is difficult to obtain instruction in it after this life. The days that are gone by will never return, nor is it easy a second time to obtain human birth.

See, young and old men, even children in the mother's womb die. As a hawk catches a quail, so life will end when its time is spent. . . .

Notwithstanding their pleasures and relations, all men must suffer in due time the fruit of their works; as a cocoa-nut detaching itself from its stalk falls down, so life will end when its time is spent.

Even a very learned or virtuous man, or a Brahmana or an ascetic, will be severely punished for his deed when he is given to actions of deceit. . . .

Exert and control yourself! For it is not easy to walk on ways where there are minutely small animals. Follow the commandments which the Arhats have well proclaimed.

Heroes of faith who desist from sins and exert themselves aright, who subdue wrath, fear, will never kill living beings; they desist from sins and are entirely happy.

It is not myself alone who suffers, all creatures in the world suffer; this a wise man should consider, and he should patiently bear such calamities as befall him, without giving way to his passions. . . .

As a bird covered with dust removes the grey powder by shaking itself, so a worthy and austere Brahmana, who does penance, annihilates his Karman.

His father and mother, his children and wife who claim him, will admonish him: "See, you are our supporter; care not for the next world in order to support us."

Some people are foolishly attached to others, and are thereby deluded; the unrighteous make them adopt unrighteousness, and they exult in their wickedness.

Therefore a worthy and wise man should be careful, ceasing from sin and being entirely happy. The virtuous heroes of faith have chosen the great road, the right and certain path to perfection.

He who has entered the road leading to the destruction of Karman, who controls his mind, speech, and body, who has given up his possessions and relations and all undertakings, should walk about subduing his senses.

CHAPTER II

A man who insults another will long whirl in the Circle of Births; to blame others is not good. Considering this a sage is not conceited.

He who is independent, and he who is the servant of a servant, if they but observe the Vow of Silence, they have no reason to be ashamed . . .

Indifferent and pure with regard to every kind of control, a Sramana should walk about; he who entertains pure thoughts during his whole life, dies as a worthy and wise man.

The sage who sees the far-off goal (liberation), past and future things, will practise indifference, though he suffer corporal punishment and be beaten.

Possessing perfect wisdom, a sage always vanquishes his passions; he correctly expounds the Law; he never neglects even the smallest duty; he is neither angry nor proud. . . .

Seeing that numerous living beings lead an individual life, and that every one feels pleasure and pain just as the others, a wise man, who observes the Vow of Silence, leaves off injuring them.

A sage has completely mastered the Law, and has ceased to do actions; but the selfish grieve . . .

Who will lead a domestic life when he knows that everything must perish?

One should know and renounce the great attachment to the world, and respect and honours on earth; for conceit is a very thin thorn difficult to pull out. A wise man, therefore, should abandon worldliness. . . .

When a monk quarrels and uses very bad language, he will suffer great spiritual loss; therefore a wise man should not quarrel. . . .

A monk should not tell stories, nor ask idle questions, nor gossip. But, knowing the highest Law, he should perform his religious duties, and regard nothing his own.

A monk should not indulge deceit, greed, pride, and wrath. Those are virtuous who have arrived at the right understanding of these passions, and who have well practised control.

A monk should be free from attachment, wise, controlling himself, seeking the Law, earnest in the performance of austerities, and subduing his senses. . . .

Many men who thought this Law to be the highest good and conducive to their spiritual welfare, obeyed their preceptors, ceased from works, and have crossed the great flood of worldly existence. . . .

CHAPTER III

If a monk who abstains from actions, suffers pain for acts done through ignorance, that Karman will be annihilated through control. The wise reach perfection getting rid of death. . . .

Pleasure-seeking men who are greedy and are absorbed by amusements, are reckless and like the wretched; they do not know that meditation has been enjoined as a duty. . . .

Lest the lot of the wicked should fall to you, escape the influence of the senses, and discipline yourself! The wicked will much and strongly grieve, groan, and wail.

See, life in this world is transient; though your life lasts a hundred years, you die as a short-lived man; mind that your years swiftly pass. . . .

Those who engage in undertakings, who work the perdition of their souls, and who kill living beings, will go to the world of the wicked . . .

Though life cannot be prolonged, as the saying is, still foolish people sin recklessly thinking: "We are only concerned with the present time; who has seen the next world and returned thence?" . . .

The man also who still lives in the house, should, in accordance with his creed, be merciful to living beings; we are bidden to be fair and equal with all; thereby even a householder goes to the world of the gods. . . .

Knowing the truth, one should live up to it, seeking the Law, earnest in the performance of austerities . . .

The fool thinks that his wealth, cattle, and relations will save him; they him, or he them. But they are no help, no protection.

When calamity befalls him, or the end of his life draws near, he must go and come alone; the wise believe that there is nothing to protect him.

All living beings owe their present form of existence to their own Karman; timid, wicked, suffering latent misery, they err about in the Circle of Births, subject to birth, old age, and death. . . .

Do not kill living beings in the threefold way (by acts, order, or assent), being intent on your spiritual welfare and abstaining from sins. In this way numberless men have reached perfection, and others, who live now, and who are to come, will reach it. . . .

Translation by Hermann Jacobi (adapted)

Higher Meditation (Excerpts)

THE *Uttara Dhyayana* (Higher Meditation) is the first of the four Jain Mulasutras (Basic Discussions). Its paragraphs, like those of the Discourse of Performed Precepts, were probably written in the first centuries before the Christian era, and were consolidated and written down a number of centuries afterward.

The special terms used in the excerpts printed here have the following meanings:

Karman, or karma—The burden of the consequences of one's moral conduct.

Kasyapa—Mahavira.

Kasyapa Gotra—A church, group, or order of which Mahavira was a member.

Sramana, or samana—An ascetic.

LECTURE I (*"On Discipline"*)

I shall explain in due order the discipline of a houseless monk, who has got rid of all worldly ties. Listen to me.

A monk who, on receiving an order from his superior, walks up to him, watching his nods and motions, is called well-behaved.

But a monk who, on receiving an order from his superior, does not walk up to him, being insubordinate and inattentive, is called ill-behaved.

As a bitch with sore ears is driven away everywhere, thus a bad, insubordinate, and talkative pupil is turned out.

As a pig leaves a trough filled with grain to feed on faeces, so a brute of a man turns away from virtue, and takes to evil ways.

Hearing a man thus compared to a dog and a pig, he who desires his own welfare should adhere to good conduct.

Therefore be eager for discipline, that you may acquire righteousness; a son of the wise, who desires liberation, will not be turned away from anywhere.

One should always be meek, and not be talkative in the presence of the wise; one should acquire valuable knowledge, and avoid what is worthless.

When reprimanded, a wise man should not be angry, but he should be of a forbearing mood; he should not associate, laugh, and play with mean men.

He should do nothing mean, nor talk much; but after having learned his lesson, he should meditate by himself.

If he by chance does anything mean, he should never deny it, but if he has done it, he should say: "I have done it"; if he has not done it, "I have not done it."

He should not, in every case, wait for the express command of the teacher like an unbroken horse for the whip of the rider, but like a broken horse which sees the whip of the rider he should commit no evil act.

Disobedient, rough speaking, ill-behaved pupils will exasperate even a gentle teacher; but those will soon win even a hot-tempered teacher who humour him and are polite.

He should not speak unasked, and asked he should not tell a lie; he should not give way to his anger, and bear with indifference pleasant and unpleasant occurrences.

Subdue your Self, for the Self is difficult to subdue; if your Self is subdued, you will be happy in this world and in the next.

Better it is that I should subdue my Self by self-control and penance, than be subdued by others with fetters and corporal punishment.

He should never do anything disagreeable to the wise, neither in words nor deeds, neither openly nor secretly. . . .

If spoken to by the superior, he should never remain silent, but should consider it as a favour; asking for his command, he should always politely approach his teacher.

If the teacher speaks little or much, he should never grow impatient; but an intelligent pupil should rise from his seat and answer the teacher's call modestly and attentively. . . .

He should not tell anything sinful or meaningless (such as "There goes a barren woman, bearing a chaplet of sky-flowers, having bathed in the water of a mirage, and carrying a bow made of a hare's horn"; explanation inserted by the commentator Devendra) or hurtful, neither for his own sake nor for anybody else's, nor without such a motive.

In barbers' shops or houses, on the ground separating two houses, or on the highway a single monk should not stand with a single woman, nor should he converse with her.

Any instruction the wise ones may give me in a kind or a rough way, I shall devotedly accept, thinking that it is for my benefit.

The teacher's instruction, his manner of giving it, and his blaming evil acts are considered blissful by the intelligent, but hateful by the bad monk.

Wise, fearless monks consider even a rough instruction as a benefit, but the fools hate it, though it produces patience and purity of mind.

He should occupy a low, firm seat, which does not rock; seldom rising and never without a cause, he should sit motionless.

At the right time a monk should sally forth, and he should return at the right time; avoiding to do anything out of time, he should do what is appropriate for each period of the day. . . .

LECTURE II (*"On Troubles"*)

The Venerable Ascetic Mahavira of the Kasyapa Gotra has declared twenty-two troubles which a monk must learn and know, bear and conquer, in order not to be vanquished by them when he lives the life of a wandering mendicant. These, then, are the twenty-two troubles declared by the Venerable Ascetic Mahavira, which a monk must learn and know, bear and conquer, in order not to be vanquished by them when he lives the life of a wandering mendicant:

(1) Hunger, (2) thirst, (3) cold, (4) heat, (5) gad-flies and gnats.

(6) Nakedness, (7) to be discontented with the objects of control, (8) women, (9) erratic life, (10) place for study.

(11) Lodging, (12) abuse, (13) corporal punishment, (14) to ask for something, (15) to be refused.

(16) Illness, (17) pricking of grass, (18) dirt, (19) kind and respectful treatment, (20) understanding.

(21) Ignorance, (22) righteousness.

The enumeration of the troubles has been delivered by the Kasyapa, I shall explain them to you in due order. Listen to me.

1. Though his body be weakened by hunger . . . though emaciated like the joint of a crow's leg and covered with a network of veins, he should know the permitted measure of food and drink, and wander about with a cheerful mind.

2. Though overcome by thirst, he should drink no cold water,

restrained by shame and aversion from forbidden things; he should try to get distilled (boiled and lifeless) water.

Wandering about on deserted ways, in pain, thirsty, with dry throat, and distressed, he should bear this trouble of thirst.

3. If a restrained, austere ascetic occasionally suffers from cold on his wanderings, he should not walk beyond the prescribed time . . .

4. If he suffers from the heat of hot things, or from the heat of his body, or from the heat of summer, he should not lament the loss of comfort.

A wise man, suffering from heat, should not long for a bath, or pour water over his body, or fan himself.

5. Suffering from insects, a great sage remains undisturbed. As an elephant at the head of the battle kills the enemy, so does a hero in self-control conquer the internal foe.

He should not scare away insects, nor keep them off, nor be in the least provoked to passion by them. Tolerate living beings, do not kill them, though they eat your flesh and blood.

6. "My clothes being torn, I shall soon go naked," or "I shall get a new suit"; such thoughts should not be entertained by a monk.

At one time he will have no clothes, at another he will have some; knowing this to be a salutary rule, a wise monk should not complain about it.

7. A houseless and poor monk who wanders from village to village may become tired of ascetic life: he should bear this trouble.

A sage should turn away from this discontent; he should wander about free from sins, guarded in himself, a tabernacle as it were of the Law, doing no actions, and perfectly passionless.

8. In this world men have a natural liking for women; he who knows and renounces them, will easily perform his duties as a Sramana.

A wise man who knows that women are a slough, as it were, will get no harm from them, but will wander about searching for the Self.

9. Alone, living on allowed food, he should wander about, bearing all troubles, in a village or a town or a market-place or a capital.

Different from other men a monk should wander about, he should acquire no property; but not being attached to house-holders, he should live without a fixed residence.

10. In a burial-place, or a deserted house, or below a tree he should sit down, alone, without moving, and he should not drive away any one.

Sitting there he should brave all dangers; when seized with fear, he should not rise and go to some other place.

11. A monk who does penance and is strong in self-control, will not be affected beyond measure by good or bad lodgings, but an evil-minded monk will.

Having obtained a good or bad lodging in an empty house, he should stay there thinking: "What does it matter for one night?"

12. If a layman abuses a monk, he should not grow angry against him; because he would be like a child, a monk should not grow angry.

If a monk hears bad words, cruel and rankling ones, he should silently overlook them, and not take them to heart.

13. A monk should not be angry if beaten, nor should he there-fore entertain sinful thoughts; knowing patience to be the highest good, a monk should meditate on the Law.

If somebody strikes a restrained, resigned Sramana somewhere, he should think: "I have not lost my life."

14. It will always cause difficulties to a houseless monk to get everything by begging, and nothing without begging.

The hand of the giver is not always kindly stretched out to a monk when he is on his begging tour; but he should not think that it would be better to live as a householder.

15. He should beg food from the householder when his dinner is ready; a wise man should not care whether he gets alms or not.

"I get nothing to-day, perhaps I shall get something to-morrow"; a monk who thinks thus will not be grieved by his want of success.

16. If any misfortune happens and he suffers pain, he should cheerfully steady his mind, and bear the ills that attack him.

He should not long for medical treatment, but he should continue to search for the welfare of his soul; thus he will be a true Sramana by neither acting himself nor causing others to act.

17. When a naked, rough, restrained ascetic lies on the grass, his body will be hurt.

In the sun his pain will grow insupportable; still a monk, though hurt by the grass, will not use clothes.

18. When by the heat of summer his body sweats and is covered with dirt and dust, a wise monk should not lament his loss of comfort.

He should bear all this, waiting for the destruction of his Karman, and practising the noble, excellent Law; he should carry the filth on his body till he expires.

19. It may be that a gentleman salutes a monk, or rises from his seat on his approach, or invites him to accept alms in his house: a monk should evince no predilection for men of this sort, who show him such marks of respect.

Not resentful, having few wants, begging from strangers, and not being dainty, a wise man should not long for pleasant things, nor be sorry afterwards for not having got them.

20. "Forsooth, in bygone times I have done actions productive of ignorance, for I do not remember them when asked by anybody anywhere." . . . (Understanding this as the reason for your not remembering bad actions,) comfort yourself, knowing the consequences of actions.

21. (Do not despair over your ignorance, saying,) "It was of no use to turn away from the lust of the senses and to live restrainedly, for I do not properly recognise good and bad things," and "Though in practising austerities and religious observances I live according to strict rules, still the hindrances to knowledge will not go off."

22. A monk should not think (debating the merits of righteousness): "There is, indeed, no life to come, nor an exalted state to be acquired by penances; in short, I have been deceived."

Translation by Hermann Jacobi (adapted)

LATER DISCOURSES

Essence of the Scripture, by Kundakunda (Excerpts)

K UNDAKUNDA, WHO PROBABLY LIVED IN THE THIRD, FOURTH, OR fifth century of the Christian era, wrote an essay entitled *Pravacana-Sara* (Essence of the Doctrine, or Essence of the Scripture). Part 1 deals with knowledge; Part 2 (of which some excerpts are given here), with reality; and Part 3, with conduct.

The special terms used in the excerpts printed here have the following meanings:

Dharma—Duty, or law, or justice.
Jina—Conqueror, or hero; i.e., Mahavira.
Para-samayikas—Attached to "the other."
Svaka-samayikas—Attached to the self.

The object, indeed, consists of substance; the substances are said to have their essence in qualities. And through these (the qualities), occur the modifications. . . .

The souls which find satisfaction in the modifications are called *para-samayikas*; but those who rely on the innate nature of the self must be esteemed *svaka-samayikas*.

That which, whilst it does not forsake its innate nature, is connected with origination, annihilation and stability and which possesses qualities and modifications, they call a substance. . . .

Existence is the innate nature of a substance . . .

The Jina, the Excellent Hero, when he preached the dharma, declared that one, omnipresent characteristic, "to be an existent," belongs here to all things with their manifold characterizations. . . .

There is no coming-into-existence without destruction; there is no destruction devoid of origination; neither origination nor destruction can truly be without stability.

Origination, continuance and dissolution are in the modifications . . .

One modification of a substance arises and another vanishes; the substance has not vanished and has not arisen. . . .

There is without substance no quality whatever, no modification . . .

Substance, which in innate nature is suchlike, always attains a manifestation . . .

A man is not a god, nor is a god a man or a liberated soul; being thus "not," how does the soul admit of identity?

Every substance is, according as one chooses the point-of-view-of-modification or the point-of-view-of-substance, other and not other . . .

Substance is, is not . . . and with regard to some modification or other is taught to be both or something else.

Translation by Barend Faddegon (adapted)

Discourse to the Soul, by Guna-Bhadra (Excerpts)

GUNA-BHADRA lived about the year 850 in the Christian era.

The meanings of the special terms used in the excerpts printed here from his *Atmanushasana* (Discourse to the Soul) are as follows:

Dharma—Duty (or the performance of one's duty), law (or conformity to law), or justice (or the doing of justice).

Jinavani—Victorious one, i.e., Mahavira.

Karma, or karman—The burden of the consequences of one's moral conduct.

Oh soul! thou art always afraid of pain, and desirous of pleasure. Therefore I also offer thee the object of thy desire, which tends to give pleasure and remove pain.

If perchance in this advice there be something which, though sweet at fruition, is yet unpalatable, be thou not afraid of that, just as a sick person is not afraid of bitter medicine.

Persons who are vain and full of talk, and clouds which thunder but give no rain, are easy to find. But it is difficult to find those kind-hearted persons who desire to uplift the world, just as it is difficult to find clouds full of rain and beneficial to the world.

He who is wise, well-versed in the essence of the Jaina scriptures, aware of the ways of the world, with no sense-desires, brilliant, calm-minded, ever ready with answers, patient of a volley of questions, powerful, attracting other minds, leader of saints, a repository of good qualities, and with speech clear and sweet, should deliver religious discourses without speaking ill of others.

Perfect knowledge of the scripture; pure conduct; inclination to persuade others to the right path; keen interest in the propagation of the right path of liberation; obeisance to the learned; pridelessness; knowledge of the world; gentleness; desirelessness; whoever possesses these and other qualities of the leader of ascetics, be he the teacher of worthy people.

The promising one, who ponders over the *summum bonum* for the self, who is very anxious to avoid worldly sufferings, who seeks happiness, whose intellectual greatness lies in listening, retaining, etc., who having heard the truth (which brings eternal happiness) properly meditates upon it, who is full of the quality of compassion, who is established by reason and by scriptural authority, and who accepts the sacred doctrine . . . such a person is worthy of being taught.

Demerit produces pain, happiness follows Dharma. This is well known to all. Therefore the man who desires happiness should always refrain from demerit, and follow Dharma.

All men desire the early attainment of true happiness; it arises from the destruction of all Karmas, which results from right conduct; right conduct depends upon knowledge. And that is acquired from the Scriptures. These are based on Jinavani, and this emanates from the discoursing Omniscient, and that is free from all defects. Defects are attachment and others. Therefore after duly reasoned-out contemplation of Him, the source of all happiness, let the worthy resort to Him for their benefit. . . .

The tranquillity, knowledge, vows, and austerities of a person are of the value of a stone. But they become adorable, like a great jewel, if accompanied by right belief.

A gentle remedy is prescribed, as for a child, for thee, who art a sufferer from the disease of wrong belief, and do not know what good is to be pursued, and what evil is to be avoided.

Having taken the poison of sense-enjoyments, thou hast got the fever of delusion; from this has arisen thy keen thirst for sense-gratification, and thou hast become feeble. . . .

Whether happy or miserable in this world, thou must exercise piety; if happy, to increase thy happiness; and if miserable, to remove thy misery.

The pleasures derived from all sense-objects are fruits of the trees of the garden of piety. Therefore preserve thou the trees, and pluck the fruits by all means. . . .

The person who in consequence of piety has acquired prosperity may have enjoyments while preserving piety, like the peasant who gets corn from the seed, but preserves the seed of that corn. . . .

So long as piety abides well in the heart, the man does not slay even his slayer. When that religion goes away, the father and the son are found killing each other. Therefore the protection of this world depends verily upon Dharma only.

There is no demerit in enjoying pleasures; but there is demerit in doing what tends to destroy their source. Indigestion is not caused by sweet food, but by eating it beyond its limit. . . .

Know this body of thine to be a prison house, built of a number of thick bones as stone pillars, fastened by nerves and muscles, covered over with skin, plastered with wet flesh, well-protected by its wicked enemies, the Karmas . . . O bereft of wisdom! Have no foolish love for it. . . .

Having renounced the world without regret, having mastered thyself, having washed away the dust of Karmas by rule of right conduct, having freed thyself from mundane existence, and having become supremely happy, enjoy this bliss of self-realization.

The poor are discontented for not obtaining wealth, and the rich too are so for want of contentment. Alas! all are in trouble. Only an ascetic is happy.

Happiness dependent upon others leads to pain. Only independent happiness is commendable. Else how could the ascetics be called happy? . . .

Living beings are like fruits, falling down from the palm-tree of birth. How long can they be in the intervening space before they reach the ground of death? . . .

May all living beings be free from anxiety on seeing that Death is sudden and has no fixed place, time, mode, and cause.

Translation by B. J. L. Jaini (adapted)

IV

Ancient and Medieval Epitomes and Commentaries

FOLLOWING THE PERIOD OF CLASSICAL CREATIVITY—THE PERIOD mainly of Vedic writers, the Upanishads, Buddha, Mahavira, and the early successors of Buddha and Mahavira—came a period of consolidation and interpretation. The early portions of this period overlapped with the later portions of the classical period, as follows:

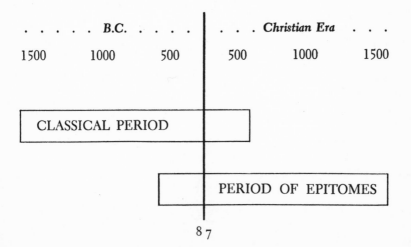

The period of epitomes (and commentaries) brought into being (a) documents exemplifying fatalism and hedonism, (b) the standard epitomes of the "six philosophical systems," and (c) law codes, books of proverbs, and spiritual rhapsodies.

FATALISM AND
HEDONISM

TWO SIGNIFICANT DOCUMENTS OF THIS PERIOD WHICH ARE OUTSIDE the scope of the six orthodox systems are, first, the *Bhagavad Gita* (Celestial Song, or Song of God), which is outside the systems in that its basic doctrine, acceptance of fate, is not peculiar to any one of them but rather is common to all of them, and, second, an epitome of hedonism, a doctrine which is outside the six systems in that it is rejected by all of them.

Bhagavad Gita, by Veda Vyasa (Excerpts)

THE *Bhagavad Gita*, which is often called "the Bible of the Hindus," dates from about 500 to 100 B.C. Its author, according to Western scholars, is unknown. Indian writers ascribe it to a sage named Veda Vyasa.

In the legendary, and perhaps historic, war between the Pandava princes and their cousins the Kurus, the blind king, Dhritarashtra, the ancestor of both groups, sent a messenger, Sanjaya, to the battlefield to learn the state of affairs. Sanjaya returned and reported to Dhritarashtra that Arjuna, the second of the Pandavas, and their greatest champion, had been struck with remorse at the prospect of slaughtering his relatives in the opposite camp, and had appealed for advice to his charioteer, Krishna, who, according to the tale, was an incarnation of the Supreme Being.

Krishna, as Sanjaya reported to Dhritarashtra, told the hesitant

Arjuna that all life is one, that if a warrior is fated to kill, he may as well kill with the realization of the ultimate unity of all life anyway, and that in the last analysis all things, including the non-living, are one.

The dialogue between the charioteer, Lord Krishna, and the warrior, Prince Arjuna, as reported by Sanjaya to King Dhritarashtra, is the content of the *Bhagavad Gita*. The dialogue is basically an episode in the sixth book of the epic account of the war between the Pandavas and the Kurus, the *Mahabharata* (Saga of the Great Bharata Clan). It is commonly believed to have been composed independently of the *Mahabharata* and inserted in the *Mahabharata* in the final stages of the consolidation of that epic.

Of the special terms used in the excerpts printed here, many are explained by the context. For example, Govinda, Janardana, Keshav, Madhava, and Madhusudan can be readily identified as designations of Krishna. The following are less self-explanatory:

Kalpa—A cycle of years; an era.
Mahatma—A great-souled one.
Mantra—A scriptural verse.
Om—Syllable used in meditation; symbolic of the world soul, or
  of the one life that pervades all living things.
Prakriti—Nature.
Sat and asat—Being and nonbeing.
Three worlds—Heaven, earth, and the underworld.
Veds—The four collections of Vedic hymns.
Yog—Yoga, union with the world soul.

BOOK 1

Arjuna:
Krishna! as I behold, come here to shed
Their common blood, yon concourse of our kin,
My members fail, my tongue dries in my mouth,
A shudder thrills my body, and my hair
Bristles with horror; from my weak hand slips
Gandiv, the goodly bow; a fever burns
My skin to parching; hardly may I stand;
The life within me seems to swim and faint;
Nothing do I foresee save woe and wail!
It is not good, O Keshav! nought of good
Can spring from mutual slaughter! Lo, I hate
Triumph and domination, wealth and ease,
Thus sadly won! Aho! what victory

Can bring delight, Govinda! what rich spoils
Could profit; what rule recompense; what span
Of life itself seem sweet, bought with such blood?
Seeing that these stand here, ready to die,
For whose sake life was fair, and pleasure pleased,
And power grew precious:—grandsires, sires, and sons,
Brothers, and fathers-in-law, and sons-in-law,
Elders and friends! Shall I deal death on these
Even though they seek to slay us? Not one blow,
O Madhusudan! will I strike to gain
The rule of all Three Worlds; then, how much less
To seize an earthly kingdom! Killing these
Must breed but anguish, Krishna! If they be
Guilty, we shall grow guilty by their deaths;
Their sins will light on us, if we shall slay
Those sons of Dhritarashtra, and our kin;
What peace could come of that, O Madhava?
For if indeed, blinded by lust and wrath,
These cannot see, or will not see, the sin
Of kingly lines o'erthrown and kinsmen slain,
How should not we, who see, shun such a crime—
We who perceive the guilt and feel the shame—
Oh, thou Delight of Men, Janardana? . . .

BOOK 2

Better to live on beggar's bread
    With those we love alive,
Than taste their blood in rich feasts spread,
    And guiltily survive!

Ah! were it worse—who knows?—to be
    Victor or vanquished here,
When those confront us angrily
    Whose death leaves living drear?

In pity lost, by doubtings tossed,
    My thoughts—distracted—turn
To Thee, the Guide I reverence most,
    That I may counsel learn:

I know not what would heal the grief
    Burned into soul and sense,
If I were earth's unchallenged chief—
    A god—and these gone thence! . . .

Krishna:
Thou grievest where no grief should be! thou speak'st
Words lacking wisdom! for the wise in heart
Mourn not for those that live, nor those that die.
Nor I, nor thou, nor any one of these,
Ever was not, nor ever will not be,
For ever and for ever afterwards.
All, that doth live, lives always! To man's frame
As there come infancy and youth and age,
So come there raisings-up and layings-down
Of other and of other life-abodes,
Which the wise know, and fear not. This that irks—
Thy sense-life, thrilling to the elements—
Bringing thee heat and cold, sorrows and joys,
'Tis brief and mutable! Bear with it, Prince!
As the wise bear. The soul which is not moved,
The soul that with a strong and constant calm
Takes sorrow and takes joy indifferently,
Lives in the life undying! That which is
Can never cease to be; that which is not
Will not exist. To see this truth of both
Is theirs who part essence from accident,
Substance from shadow. Indestructible,
Learn thou! the Life is, spreading life through all;
It cannot anywhere, by any means,
Be anywise diminished, stayed, or changed.
But for these fleeting frames which it informs
With spirit deathless, endless, infinite,
They perish. Let them perish, Prince! and fight!
He who shall say, "Lo! I have slain a man!"
He who shall think "Lo! I am slain!" those both
Know naught! Life cannot slay. Life is not slain!

Never the spirit was born; the spirit shall cease to be
    never;

Never was time it was not; End and Beginning are
　　dreams!
Birthless and deathless and changeless remaineth the
　　spirit for ever;
Death hath not touched it at all, dead though the
　　house of it seems! . . .

　　　　Nay, but as when one layeth
　　　　　His worn-out robes away,
　　　　And, taking new ones, sayeth,
　　　　　"These will I wear to-day!"

　　　　So putteth by the spirit
　　　　　Lightly its garb of flesh,
　　　　And passeth to inherit
　　　　　A residence afresh.

I say to thee weapons reach not the Life,
Flame burns it not, waters cannot o'erwhelm,
Nor dry winds wither it. Impenetrable,
Unentered, unassailed, unharmed, untouched,
Immortal, all-arriving, stable, sure,
Invisible, ineffable, by word
And thought uncompassed, ever all itself,
Thus is the Soul declared! How wilt thou, then,
Knowing it so,—grieve when thou shouldst not grieve?
How, if thou hearest that the man new-dead
Is, like the man new-born, still living man—
One same, existent Spirit—wilt thou weep?
The end of birth is death; the end of death
Is birth: this is ordained! and mournest thou,
Chief of the stalwart arm! for what befalls
Which could not otherwise befall? The birth
Of living things comes unperceived; the death
Comes unperceived; between them, beings perceive:
What is there sorrowful herein, dear Prince? . . .

　　　　　　　When one, O Pritha's Son!—
Abandoning desires which shake the mind—
Finds in his soul full comfort for his soul,

He hath attained the Yog—that man is such!
In sorrows not dejected, and in joys
Not overjoyed; dwelling outside the stress
Of passion, fear, and anger; fixed in calms
Of lofty contemplation;—such an one
Is Muni, is the Sage, the true Recluse!
He, who to none and nowhere overbound
By ties of flesh, takes evil things and good
Neither desponding nor exulting, such
Bears wisdom's plainest mark! He who shall draw,
As the wise tortoise draws its four feet safe
Under its shield, his five frail senses back
Under the spirit's buckler from the world
Which else assails them, such an one, my Prince!
Hath wisdom's mark! . . .

BOOK 4

Manifold the renewals of my birth
Have been, Arjuna! and of thy births, too!
But mine I know, and thine thou knowest not,
O Slayer of thy Foes! Albeit I be
Unborn, undying, indestructible,
The Lord of all things living; not the less—
By Maya, by my magic which I stamp
On floating Nature-forms, the primal vast—
I come, and go, and come. When Righteousness
Declines, O Bharata! when Wickedness
Is strong, I rise, from age to age, and take
Visible shape, and move a man with men,
Succoring the good, thrusting the evil back,
And setting Virtue on her seat again.
Who knows the truth touching my births on earth
And my divine work, when he quits the flesh
Puts on its load no more, falls no more down
To earthly birth: to Me he comes, dear Prince!

Many there be who come! from fear set free,
From anger, from desire; keeping their hearts

Fixed upon me—my Faithful—purified
By sacred flame of Knowledge. Such as these
Mix with my being. . . .

BOOK 7

I will declare to thee that utmost lore,
Whole and particular, which, when thou knowest,
Leaveth no more to know here in this world.
Of many thousand mortals, one, perchance,
Striveth for Truth; and of those few that strive—
Nay, and rise high—one only—here and there—
Knoweth Me, as I am, the very Truth.
Earth, water, flame, air, ether, life, and mind,
And individuality—those eight
Make up the showing of Me, Manifest. . . .

I am the fresh taste of the water; I
The silver of the moon, the gold o' the sun,
The word of worship in the Veds, the thrill
That passeth in the ether, and the strength
Of man's shed seed. I am the good sweet smell
Of the moistened earth, I am the fire's red light,
The vital air moving in all which moves,
The holiness of hallowed souls, the root
Undying, whence hath sprung whatever is;
The wisdom of the wise, the intellect
Of the informed, the greatness of the great,
The splendor of the splendid. . . .
                              Hard it is
To pierce that veil divine of various shows
Which hideth Me; yet they who worship Me
Pierce it and pass beyond. I am not known
To evil-doers, nor to foolish ones,
Nor to the base and churlish; . . .
Four sorts of mortals know me: he who weeps,
Arjuna! and the man who yearns to know;
And he who toils to help; and he who sits
Certain of me, enlightened. . . .

But I, Arjuna; know all things which were,
And all which are, and all which are to be,
Albeit not one among them knoweth Me! . . .

BOOK 9

Now will I open unto thee—whose heart
Rejects not—that last lore, deepest-concealed,
That farthest secret of My Heavens and Earths,
Which but to know shall set thee free from ills,—
A Royal lore! a Kingly mystery!
Yea! for the soul such light as purgeth it
From every sin; a light of holiness
With inmost splendor shining; plain to see;
Easy to walk by, inexhaustible!
They that receive not this, failing in faith
To grasp the greater wisdom, reach not Me,
Destroyer of thy foes! They sink anew
Into the realm of Flesh, where all things change!
By Me the whole vast Universe of things
Is spread abroad;—by Me, the Unmanifest!
In Me are all existences contained;
Not I in them! Yet they are not contained,
Those visible things! Receive and strive to embrace
The mystery majestical! My Being—
Creating all, sustaining all—still dwells
Outside of all! See! as the shoreless airs
Move in the measureless space, but are not space,
And space were space without the moving airs;
So all things are in Me, but are not I.
At closing of each Kalpa, Indian Prince!
All things which be back to My Being come:
At the beginning of each Kalpa, all
Issue new-born from Me. By Energy
And help of Prakriti, my outer Self,
Again, and yet again, I make go forth
The realms of visible things—without their will—
All of them—by the power of Prakriti.
Yet these great makings, Prince! involve Me not,

Enchain Me not! I sit apart from them,
Other, and Higher, and Free; nowise attached!
Thus doth the stuff of worlds, moulded by Me,
Bring forth all that which is, moving or still,
Living or lifeless! Thus the worlds go on!
The minds untaught mistake Me, veiled in form;—
Naught see they of My secret Presence, nought
Of My hid Nature, ruling all which lives.
Vain hopes pursuing, vain deeds doing; fed
On vainest knowledge, senselessly they seek
An evil way, the way of brutes and fiends.
But My Mahatmas, those of noble soul
Who tread the path celestial, worship Me
With hearts unwandering,—knowing Me the Source,
Th' Eternal Source, of Life. Unendingly
They glorify Me; seek Me; keep their vows
Of reverence and love, with changeless faith
Adoring Me. Yea, and those too adore,
Who, offering sacrifice of wakened hearts,
Have sense of one pervading Spirit's stress,
One Force in every place, though manifold!
I am the Sacrifice! I am the Prayer!
I am the Funeral-Cake set for the dead!
I am the healing herb! I am the ghee,
The Mantra, and the flame, and that which burns!
I am—of all this boundless Universe—
The Father, Mother, Ancestor, and Guard!
The end of Learning! That which purifies
In lustral water! I am Om! I am
Rig-Veda, Sama-Veda, Yajur-Ved;
The Way, the Fosterer, the Lord, the Judge,
The Witness; the Abode, the Refuge-House,
The Friend, the Fountain and the Sea of Life
Which sends, and swallows up; Treasure of Worlds
And Treasure-Chamber! Seed and Seed-Sower,
Whence endless harvests spring! Sun's heat is mine;
Heaven's rain is mine to grant or to withhold;
Death am I, and Immortal Life I am,
Arjuna! Sat and Asat, Visible Life,

And Life Invisible! . . .
Whoso shall offer Me in faith and love
A leaf, a flower, a fruit, water poured forth,
That offering I accept . . .

BOOK 10

I am the Spirit seated deep
   In every creature's heart;
From Me they come; by Me they live;
   At My word they depart! . . .

By day I gleam, the golden Sun
   Of burning cloudless Noon;
By Night, amid the asterisms
   I glide, the dappled Moon! . . .

And of the viewless virtues,
   Fame, Fortune, Song am I,
And Memory, and Patience;
   And Craft, and Constancy: . . .

The policy of conquerors,
   The potency of kings,
The great unbroken silence
   In learning's secret things;
The lore of all the learned,
   The seed of all which springs.

Living or lifeless, still or stirred,
   Whatever beings be,
None of them is in all the worlds,
   But it exists by Me!

BOOK 14

He who with equanimity surveys
Lustre of goodness, strife of passion, sloth
Of ignorance, not angry if they are,
Not angry when they are not: he who sits

A sojourner and stranger in their midst
Unruffled, standing off, saying—serene—
When troubles break, "These are the Qualities!"
He unto whom—self-centred—grief and joy
Sound as one word; to whose deep-seeing eyes
The clod, the marble, and the gold are one;
Whose equal heart holds the same gentleness
For lovely and unlovely things, firm-set,
Well-pleased in praise and dispraise; satisfied
With honor or dishonor; unto friends
And unto foes alike in tolerance,
Detached from undertakings,—he is named
Surmounter of the Qualities!

Translation by Sir Edwin Arnold

Epitome of Hedonism, by Madhava (Excerpts)

BRIHASPATI, India's chief hedonist, lived about 600 B.C. His system is called "Charvaka" or "Lokayata." The first of these names comes from the root *charv-*, "to eat," and reflects the principle "eat, drink, and be merry." The second name (accented on the second syllable) comes from the root *loka-*, "world," and reflects the belief that only this world exists. Writers in English designate the system as "hedonism" or "materialism."

Brihaspati's sutras are extant only in brief quotations which appear in the writings of those who disagree with him. The longest known quotation appears near the end of the chapter on the Charvaka system in the *Sarva-Darsana-Samgraha* (Collection of Summaries of Systems) written by Madhava Acharya (Master Madhava) about the year 1350 in the Christian era.

Apart from terms which are explained by the context (such as the names of sacrifices), the special terms appearing in the excerpts have the following meanings:

Major and minor—In Western terminology, the minor premise and the conclusion of a syllogism, respectively (see "Sign," below).

Manu—Legendary, or perhaps historical, author of a legal code, the Code of Manu.

Sastra, or shastra—Philosophical teaching.

Sign or middle term—In Western terminology, the major premise of a syllogism; or that aspect of an inference which shows
a universal connection between two terms; thus, in the argument "Where there is smoke, there is fire; here is smoke;
therefore here is fire," the "sign or middle term" is the universal proposition "Where there is smoke, there is fire," since it
includes both smoke and fire and shows their connection.

Sruti—Revealed teaching (in this case, a reference to the
Brihadaranyaka Upanishad, from which Madhava took his
quotation).

The poet—The author of a passage in the Atharva Veda, which
Madhava paraphrased.

Vaidic—Vedic.

We have said in our preliminary invocation "salutation to
Siva, the abode of eternal knowledge, the storehouse of supreme
felicity," but how can we attribute to the Divine Being the giving
of supreme felicity, when such a notion has been utterly abolished
by Charvaka, the crest-gem of the atheistical school, the follower
of the doctrine of Brihaspati? The efforts of Charvaka are indeed
hard to be eradicated, for the majority of living beings hold by
the current rerfain—

> While life is yours, live joyously;
> None can escape Death's searching eye:
> When once this frame of ours they burn,
> How shall it e'er again return?

The mass of men, in accordance with the Sastras of policy and
enjoyment, considering wealth and desire the only ends of man,
and denying the existence of any object belonging to a future
world, are found to follow only the doctrine of Charvaka. Hence
another name for that school is Lokayata—a name well accordant
with the thing signified.

In this school the four elements, earth, &c., are the original
principles; from these alone, when transformed into the body,
intelligence is produced, just as the inebriating power is developed
from the mixing of certain ingredients; and when these are
destroyed, intelligence at once perishes also. They quote the Sruti
for this, "Springing forth from these elements, itself solid knowledge, it is destroyed when they are destroyed,—after death no
intelligence remains." . . .

The only end of man is enjoyment produced by sensual pleasures. Nor may you say that such cannot be called the end of man as they are always mixed with some kind of pain, because it is our wisdom to enjoy the pure pleasure as far as we can, and to avoid the pain which inevitably accompanies it; just as the man who desires fish takes the fish with their scales and bones, and having taken as many as he wants, desists; or just as the man who desires rice, takes the rice, straw and all, and having taken as much as he wants, desists.

It is not therefore for us, through a fear of pain, to reject the pleasure which our nature instinctively recognizes as congenial. Men do not refrain from sowing rice, because forsooth there are wild animals to devour it; nor do they refuse to set the cooking-pots on the fire, because forsooth there are beggars to pester us for a share of the contents. If any one were so timid as to forsake a visible pleasure, he would indeed be foolish like a beast, as has been said by the poet—

> The pleasure which arises to men
> From contact with sensible objects
> Is to be relinquished as accompanied by pain,—
> Such is the reasoning of fools.

> The berries of paddy,
> Rich with the finest white grains,
> What man, seeking his true interest,
> Would fling away because covered with husk and dust?

If you object that, if there be no such thing as happiness in a future world, then how should men of experienced wisdom engage in the agnihotra and other sacrifices, which can only be performed with great expenditure of money and bodily fatigue, your objection cannot be accepted as any proof to the contrary, since the agnihotra, &c., are only useful as means of livelihood, for the Veda is tainted by the three faults of untruth, self-contradiction, and tautology; then again the imposters who call themselves Vaidic pundits are mutually destructive . . .

Hence it follows that there is no other hell than mundane pain produced by purely mundane causes, as thorns, &c.; the only Supreme is the earthly monarch whose existence is proved by all the world's eyesight; and the only Liberation is the dissolution of the body. By holding the doctrine that the soul is identical with the body, such phrases as "I am thin," "I am black," &c., are at once intelligible . . . and the use of the phrase "my body" is metaphorical. . . .

Those who maintain the authority of inference (as showing the existence of God and a future world) accept the sign or middle term as the causer of knowledge, which middle term must be found in the minor and be itself invariably connected with the major. . . . What then is a means of this connection's being known?

We will first show that it is not perception. Now perception is held to be of two kinds, external and internal. The former is not the required means; for although it is possible that the actual contact of the senses and the object will produce the knowledge of the particular object thus brought in contact, yet as there can never be such contact in the case of the past or the future, the universal proposition which was to embrace the invariable connection of the middle and major terms in every case becomes impossible to be known. . . .

Nor is internal perception the means, since you cannot establish that the mind has any power to act independently towards an external object, since all allow that it is dependent on the external senses . . .

Nor can inference be the means of the knowledge of the universal proposition, since in the case of this inference we should also require another inference to establish it, and so on, and hence would arise the fallacy of an *ad infinitum* retrogression.

Nor can testimony be the means thereof, since . . . there is no more reason for our believing on another's word that smoke and fire are invariably connected, than for our receiving the *ipse dixit* of Manu, &c., which, of course, we Charvakas reject. . . .

From this it follows that fate, &c., do not exist, since these can only be proved by inference. . . . And all this has been also said by Brihaspati—

> There is no heaven, no final liberation,
> Nor any soul in another world,
> Nor do the actions of the four castes, orders, &c.,
> Produce any real effect.

The Agnihotra, the three Vedas, the ascetic's three staves,
And smearing one's self with ashes,
Were made by Nature as the livelihood
Of those destitute of knowledge and manliness.
If a beast slain in the Jyotishtoma rite
Will itself go to heaven,
Why then does not the sacrificer
Forthwith offer his own father?
If the Sraddha produces gratification
To beings who are dead,
Then here, too, in the case of travellers when they start,
It is needless to give provisions for the journey. . . .
While life remains let man live happily,
Let him feed on ghee even though he runs in debt;
When once the body becomes ashes,
How can it ever return again?
If he who departs from the body
Goes to another world,
How is it that he comes not back again,
Restless for love of his kindred?
Hence it is only as a means of livelihood
That Brahmans have established here
All these ceremonies for the dead,—
There is no other fruit anywhere. . . .

Translation by E. B. Cowell and A. E. Gough

THE SIX SYSTEMS

THE SO-CALLED "ORTHODOX" SYSTEMS OF HINDU PHILOSOPHY are often grouped in three couples as follows (a rough English equivalent of the main emphasis of each system is given in parentheses):

First couple
1. Nyaya (rationalism)
2. Vaishesika (pluralism)

Second couple
3. Sankhya (evolutionism)
4. Yoga (perfectionism)

Third couple
5. Mimamsa or Purva Mimamsa (moralism)
6. Vedanta or Uttara Mimamsa or Brahmanism (pantheism)

The six systems evolved in the 600 years just preceding the Christian era. They were summarized in sets of sutras (precepts) during that period or in the early centuries of the Christian era.

(1) *Nyaya Sutras, by Gautama (Excerpts)*

THE GAUTAMA who composed the Nyaya (Nee-AH-ya) Sutras is not the same as the Gautama who came to be called Buddha, but he lived at about the same time as Buddha. He is apparently responsible for the first version of this summary of the Nyaya philosophy, but the summary underwent changes at the hands of editors and compilers. The form in which we now have the sutras presumably resembles Gautama's version in essence if not in exact phraseology.

"Nyaya" means "going into a subject," i.e., analysis, or the rational approach, or rationalism.

BOOK 1

1. Proof; that which is the object of right notion; doubt; motive; familiar fact; scholastic tenet; confutation; ascertainment; disquisition; controversy; cavil; semblance of a reason; perversion; futility; and unfitness to be argued with;—from knowing the truth in regard to these, there is the attainment of the *summum bonum*.

2. Pain, birth, activity, fault, false notions—since, on successive annihilation of each of these in turn, there is the annihilation of the one next it, there is Beatitude.

3. Proofs are the deliverance of sense; the recognition of signs; the recognition of likeness; and words.

4. By a deliverance of sense is meant knowledge which has arisen from the contact of a sense with its object,—indeterminate but not erroneous, or determinate.

10. Desire, Aversion, Volition, Pleasure, Pain, and Knowledge are the sign of the Soul.

11. The body is the site of action, of the organs of sensation, and of the sentiments.

12. The organs of sensation from the Elements are Smell, Taste, Sight, Touch, and Hearing.

13. Earth, Water, Light, Air, Ether,—these are the Elements.

32. The members of a demonstration are the Proposition, the Reason, the Example, the Application, and the Conclusion.

33. The Proposition is the declaration of what is to be established.

34. The Reason is the means for the establishing of what is to be established; through the Example's having the nature, or in like manner through its having the reverse of the nature.

35. The Example is some familiar case of the fact—which, through the invariable attendedness by what is to be established, causes that nature to be which is to be established.

36. Or inversely the Example, on the contrary, may be one where we have a case of invariable abandonedness.

37. The Application is the collecting with respect to the Example, what is to be established as being so, or not so.

38. The Conclusion is the re-stating of the Proposition because of the mention of the Reason.

39. Confutation—for the ascertaining of the truth in regard to a question, the truth in regard to which is not accurately apprehended—is reasoning from the supposition of the cessation of the cause to the cessation of the effect.

40. Ascertainment is the determination of a question by hearing what is to be said for and against it, after having been in doubt.

44. The Semblances of a reason are the Erratic, the Contradictory, the Equally available on both sides, that which is In the same case with what is to be proved, and the Mistimed.

45. That is Erratic which arrives at more ends than the one required.

46. That is the Contradictory which is repugnant to what is proposed as that which is to be established.

47. That from which a question may arise as to whether the case stands this way or the other way, if employed with the view of determining the state of the case, is equally available for both sides.

48. And it is in the same case with what is to be proved, if, in standing itself in need of proof, it does not differ from that which is to be proved.

49. That is Mistimed which is adduced when the time is not that when it might have availed.

50. Unfairness is the opposing of what is propounded by means of assuming a different sense.

51. It is of three kinds, Fraud in respect of a term, Fraud in respect of a genus, and Fraud in respect of a trope.

52. Fraud in respect of a term is the assuming a meaning other than was intended by the speaker when he named the thing by a term that happened to be ambiguous.

53. Fraud in respect of a genus is the assuming that something is spoken of in respect whereof the thing asserted is impossible, because this happens to be the same in kind with that of which the thing asserted is possible.

54. Fraud in respect of a trope is the denial of the truth of the matter, when the assertion was made in one or other of the modes, literal or metaphorical.

Translation by J. R. B.

(2) *Vaishesika Sutras, by Kanada (Excerpts)*

"KANADA" (accented on the second syllable) is the nickname rather than the actual name of the author of the Vaishesika (rhymes with "my BAsic!—ah") Sutras, just as "Plato" is the nickname rather than the actual name of the great Greek philosopher. The actual name of the author of the Vaishesika Sutras was apparently "Kasyapa" (accented on the first syllable), but he was called "Kanada" ("atom-eater") because of his emphasis on the multiplicity of real things, i.e., his division of reality into numerous small particles. He probably lived about 250 B.C.

"Vaishesika" means "what distinguishes one thing from another," i.e., the particular, or particularism, or pluralism.

BOOK 1, *Lesson* 1

1. Now, then, we will explain what merit is.

2. Merit is that from which results attainment of elevation and of the highest good.

5. Earth, water, light, air, ether, time, space, soul, and the internal organ are the substances.

6. Colour, taste, smell and touch, numbers, extensions, individuality, conjunction and disjunction, priority and posteriority, intellections, pleasure and pain, desire and aversion, and volitions are the qualities.

7. Throwing upwards, throwing downwards, contracting, expanding, and going are the actions.

8. Existence, transitoriness, inhesion in substance, effect, cause, and possession of generality and particularity are the common elements of substances, qualities, and actions.

9. The common property of substance and quality is that they originate things of the same class.

10. Substances originate another substance, and qualities another quality.

15. The definition of substance is that it is possessed of actions and qualities, and is a coinherent cause.

16. That it has substance as a substratum, that it is without qualities, and that it is not a cause of conjunctions and disjunctions, being unconcerned with them, is the definition of quality.

17. That it abides in one substance, is without qualities, and is the absolute cause of conjunctions and disjunctions, is the definition of action.

25. Numbers from duality upward, individuality, conjunction, and disjunction are originated by more than one substance.

BOOK 1, *Lesson* 2

1. From non-existence of cause is non-existence of effect.

2. But there is not from non-existence of effect non-existence of cause.

3. Generality and particularity both depend upon intellection.

5. The essences of substance, quality, and action are general and particular.

6. With the exception of the ultimate particulars.

9. Existence is neither an action nor a quality, because it exists in qualities and actions.

11. The essence of substance is explained by means of its inherence in many substances.

13. In like manner the universal in quality is explained from its existence in qualities.

15. The essence of action is explained from its existence in actions.

BOOK 2, *Lesson* 1

1. Earth is possessed of colour, taste, smell, and touch.

2. Water is possessed of colour, taste, and touch and is fluid and viscid.

3. Light has colour and touch.

4. Air is possessed of touch.

5. Those qualities do not exist in ether.

20. Egress and ingress,—such is the mark of the existence of ether.

26. Since it inheres in something else and is known by per-

ception, sound is neither a quality of the soul nor a quality of the internal organ.

27. It remains that sound is a mark of ether.

B O O K 2, *Lesson 2*

4. Heat is the characteristic of light.
5. Cold is the characteristic of water.
6. The notions of posteriority . . . of simultaneity, of slowness, and quickness are marks of the existence of time.
10. The mark pertaining to space is that whence the knowledge arises that one thing is remote or not remote from another.

B O O K 3, *Lesson 1*

19. Activity and inactivity observed in one's own soul are the mark of the existence of other souls.

B O O K 3, *Lesson 2*

1. Existence and non-existence of knowledge on contact of the soul with the objects of sense are the mark of the existence of an internal organ.
3. Because of non-simultaneity of volitions, and non-simultaneity of cognitions, it is one in each body.
4. The ascending and descending vital airs, the opening and closing of the eyes, life, motions of the internal organ, affections of the other organs of sense, pleasure and pain, desire and aversion, and volition are marks of the existence of soul.
9. Existence of the soul, being the *conditio sine qua non* of the use of the word I, is not evidenced only by revelation.
14. The cognition of the Ego is a perception of a distinctive entity, since it applies to self-reflective soul, and not to ought else.
19. Because of the indifference of the origin of pleasure, pain, and knowledge, soul is one.
20. Because of its circumstances, soul is manifold.

B O O K 5, *Lesson 1*

1. Action in the hand is by means of conjunction with, and volition of, soul.

BOOK 5, *Lesson* 2

25. By qualities, space is explained.
26. By cause, time is explained.

Translation by A. E. Gough

(3) *Sankhya Sutras, by Kapila (Excerpts)*

KAPILA (accented on the first syllable) may have lived at about the same time as Buddha.

"Sankhya" (rhymes with "KONK-ya") means number. The system is called "Sankhya" because of its emphasis on numerical speculations about cosmic evolution. It corresponds roughly to evolutionism in Western thought.

According to some authorities, the genuine Sankhya Sutras, by Kapila, are lost, and what we have under that designation is a substitute composed by Vijnanabhikshu about 1450.

1. From the injurious effects of the threefold kinds of pain (natural and intrinsic, natural and extrinsic, and supernatural) arises a desire to know the means of removing it. . . .

4. Perception, inference, and fit testimony are the threefold kinds of accepted proof . . .

5. Perception is the application of the senses to special objects of sense. . . .

6. The knowledge of formal or generic existence is by perception; of things beyond the senses by inference; that which cannot be determined by this and cannot be perceived must be determined by fitting means.

10. That which is visible or developed has a cause; it is not eternal or universal; it is mobile (modifiable), multiform, dependent, attributive, conjunct, and subordinate. The undeveloped principle is the reverse.

15, 16. From the finite nature of specific objects, from the homogeneous nature of genera and species, from the active energy of evolution, from the separateness of cause and effect, and from the undividedness of the whole universe, there is a primary cause, the Unmanifested . . .

17. Because . . . there must be a superintending power, because

there must be a nature that enjoys, and because of active exertion . . . therefore soul exists.

51. The eight perfections are reasoning, word or oral instruction, study or reading, the suppression of the three kinds of pain, acquisition of friends and liberality. . . .

62. . . . not any Soul is bound, or is liberated, or migrates. It is Nature, which has many receptacles, which is bound, or is liberated, or migrates.

67. By the attainment of complete knowledge, virtue and the rest have become no longer a real cause; yet a body continues to be held, as a potter's wheel continues to revolve from the force of the previous impulse.

68. This separation from body being obtained, when Nature ceases to act because her purpose has been accomplished, then the soul obtains an abstraction from matter which is both complete and eternal.

Translation by John Davies

(4) Yoga Sutras, by Patanjali (Excerpts)

DIFFERENT SCHOLARS assign Patanjali (accented on the second syllable) to different periods, ranging from 250 B.C. to about 350 in the Christian era.

"Yoga" means "union," i.e., union with God. Since the method of achieving such unity is the perfecting of the self, yoga is sometimes equated with perfectionism. Yoga practitioners admit all castes and outcasts to their group.

There are five kinds of yoga, of which the first is usually listed separately and is disposed of summarily, so that one often reads that there are four kinds of yoga. This first kind is *hatha yoga*, union through bodily exercises. The other four, i.e., "the four kinds of yoga," are: *jnana yoga*, union through rational meditation (*jna-* is cognate with *know*); *bhakti yoga*, union through religious devotions; *karma yoga*, union through righteous conduct; and *raja* (kingly) *yoga*, union through spiritual exercises.

Apart from terms which are explained by the context, the special terms appearing in the excerpts have the following meanings:

Karma—The burden of the consequences of one's moral conduct.
Om—Syllable used in exercises in concentration.

The three qualities—Darkness or obscurity, goodness, and essence or passion.

Yogi—Practitioner of yoga.

CHAPTER I

We now begin the exposition of yoga. Yoga is controlling the activities of mind.

When mind is controlled, Self stays in His native condition. Otherwise He conforms to the nature of mind's activities.

The activities are five-fold; some painful, other pleasurable. They are: experience, perversion, delusion, sleep, recollection.

Experience comes from perception, inference, evidence.

Perversion is an idea of an object, not conforming to its nature.

Delusion is an idea conveyed by words, without any reality.

Sleep is a condition, which depends on the cessation of perception.

Recollection is the calling up of past experience.

Control the activities by practice and detachment.

Practice is effort towards concentration.

Long unremitting sincere practice develops into habit.

Detachment is the deliberate renunciation of desire for objects seen or heard. The highest form of detachment is the automatic renunciation of the three qualities, the result of Self-experience.

Sampradnyata Samadhi is that condition of conscious illumination, where mind is mixed up with consciousness of sentiment or consciousness of discrimination or consciousness of joy or consciousness of personality.

Asampradnyata Samadhi is that unmixed condition of conscious illumination, where by constant renunciation of all knowledge, mind retains past impressions only.

They who have lost attachment to body or have merged in nature, attain this condition when they are born again.

But others have to attain it through faith, effort, recollection, concentration, discrimination.

Success is immediate where effort is intense.

Success varies according to whether the effort is mild, moderate or intense.

Illumination is also attained by devotion to God.

God is the One unique Personality, untouched by desire, affliction, action or its result.

In Him lies the seed of omniscience.

He is the master of even the ancient masters, being beyond the limits of time.

His name is Om.

Repeat it constantly; meditate on its meaning.

Devotion to God enlightens the soul, removes every obstacle.

Disease, lack of enthusiasm, doubt, irregularity, lethargy, yearning for sensual pleasure, hallucination, failure to attain a step, failure to maintain that step, are obstacles that distract the mind.

Pain, nervousness, sulkiness, irregular breathing, follow. To destroy these, meditate on one object.

Mind attains peace by associating with the happy, pitying the miserable, appreciating the virtuous, and avoiding the vicious. Also by expulsion and retention of breath.

Mind attains peace, when meditation produces extra-ordinary sense-perceptions. Or by meditation on the inner light that leads beyond sorrow. Or by meditation on saints who have attained desirelessness. Or by meditation on the knowledge gained through dream or sleep. Or by meditation on anything you will.

Thus mind masters everything from the smallest to the greatest.

When mind's activity is controlled, illumination results, mind reflects the nature of either the seer, the seen, or the seeing, as pure crystal reflects the colour of whatever is placed on it. . . .

CHAPTER II

Austerity, study, devotion to God, constitute practical yoga. The aim is to attain illumination and to destroy afflictions.

Ignorance, egoism, desire, aversion, fear, are afflictions. Ignorance is the cause, the others are the effects, whether they are dormant, weak, suppressed or aggravated.

Ignorance thinks of the perishable as imperishable, of the pure as impure, of the painful as pleasurable, of the non-Self as Self.

Egoism is the identification of the Seer with the limitations of the eye. Desire is longing for pleasure. Aversion is recoiling from pain. Fear is that constant natural terror of death, that is rooted even in the minds of the learned.

The finer afflictions disappear as mind disappears in illumination. The grosser afflictions disappear through meditation.

Karma, whether fulfilled in present or future life, has its root in afflictions.

So long as the root is present, karma remains, creates re-birth, governs its fulfilment and duration of fulfilment.

It creates pleasure or pain as it springs from virtue or vice. . . .

Future misery is to be avoided.

The link between the Seer and the seen creates misery, is to be broken.

Purity, passion, ignorance, constitute the seen; element and sense its modifications; enjoyment and liberation its aim. . . .

The Seer is sight itself, but though untainted, appears as if tainted through the vagaries of the intellect.

The seen exists for the Seer alone.

The seen is dead to him who has attained liberation, but is alive to others, being common to all.

The Seer and the seen are linked together that the real nature of each may be known.

The cause of this link is ignorance.

No ignorance, no link. The breaking of the link reveals the independence of the Seer.

Unwavering discrimination between Self and non-Self destroys ignorance. . . .

Impurities having been washed away by the practice of meditation, the light of knowledge shines till discrimination is complete. . . .

Refusal of violence, refusal of stealing, refusal of covetousness, with telling truth and continence, constitute the Rules.

These are sacred vows, to be observed, independent of time, place, class or occasion.

Purity, austerity, contentment, repetition of sacred words, devotion to God, constitute the Regulations.

If wrong sentiments disturb, cultivate right thoughts.

Think that wrong actions, violence and the like, whether committed, caused or abetted, whether provoked by anger, avarice or infatuation, whether they seem important or unimportant, obstruct meditation, bring endless ignorance and misery.

When non-violence is firmly rooted, enmity ceases in the yogi's presence.

When truth is firmly rooted, the yogi attains the result of action without acting.

When non-stealing is firmly rooted, riches are attained.

When continence is firmly rooted, the yogi becomes potent.

When non-covetousness is firmly rooted, the yogi knows his past, present, future.

When purity is attained, the yogi shrinks from his body, avoids the touch of others.

He attains as well clarification of intellect, cheerfulness of mind, subjugation of sense, power of concentration, that fit him for Self-experience.

Contentment brings supreme happiness.

Austerity destroys impurity, awakens physical and mental powers.

Repetition of sacred words brings you in direct contact with the God you worship.

Illumination is attained by devotion to God. . . .

CHAPTER III

Samadhi is that condition of illumination where union as union disappears, only the meaning of the object on which the attention is fixed being present. . . .

Concentration is necessary to mount the various steps. . . .

At every moment distractions and impressions of distractions lessen, control and impressions of control increase, until mind clings to the condition of control.

When the impressions of control prevail, mind flows peacefully.

When mind rejects all objects but one, illumination results. . . .

Concentrate separately on the word, the meaning and the object, which are mixed up in common usage . . .

Concentrate on friendship, mercy, joy; excel in them.

Concentrate on strength like that of the elephant; get that strength.

Concentrate on inner Light; know the fine, the obscure, the remote. . . .

Concentrate on the navel; know the organism of the body.

Concentrate on the hollow of the throat; go beyond hunger and thirst. . . .

Concentrate on the Light in the head; meet the Masters. . . .

Concentrate on the real Self; know that Self. . . .

Concentration on the present moment, the moment gone, and

the moment to come, brings enlightenment, the result of discrimination. . . .

When intellect becomes as pure as Self, liberation follows.

CHAPTER IV

In reality, past and future exist as much as present; they are not seen because they exist on different planes. . . .

No object depends on one mind only; otherwise what becomes of it when that mind sees it no longer? . . .

The activities of mind are known to the Self; for Self is the Lord, who remains unaffected. . . .

Mind cannot at the same time know itself and any other object. . . .

He who sees clearly, refuses to identify mind with Self.

Intent on discrimination, his mind longs for liberation.

Sometimes in Illumination, impressions of the waking mind intervene. . . .

When the yogi attains final discrimination, renounces even that, he attains the condition called "Rain-cloud of Divinity."

Then action and affliction come to an end.

Translation by Purohit

(5) *Mimamsa Sutras, by Jaimini (Excerpts)*

OF THE TWO Mimamsa (pronounced "Mee-MAHM-sa") systems, one—sometimes called "Purva Mimamsa" (Early Mimamsa)—is more often called simply "Mimamsa," while the other—sometimes called "Uttara Mimamsa" (Later Mimamsa)—is more often called "Vedanta" or "Brahmanism."

"Mimamsa" means "thinking," or "investigation," but the investigation conducted by the system covers mainly obligatory beliefs and actions, and the system may therefore be thought of as a form of moralism. Jaimini (rhymes with "HI-minny") apparently lived between 600 and 200 B.C.

The references which may require explanation have the following meanings:

Badarayana—Author of the Brahma Sutras.
Dharma—Duty.

Let us understand what is Dharma. It may be defined as the highest good; and so let us inquire into its cause.

The idea of Dharma does not arise from sense-perception, because the latter is limited to what is present, while the idea of Dharma goes beyond the present. As it is conceived to be the highest good, its idea can best be imparted by a competent teacher, which is a valid means of acquiring knowledge, and does not require the authority of a Badarayana to prove it.

Some people say that Dharma arises from action, and prove their point by referring to the actual facts of life; and so they believe that the idea of Dharma is not permanent.

Dharma is indeed linked up with action, for we often say that a person does his Dharma, and that implies action. Action is part of our nature, for we see that all of us are engaged in some kind of action at the same time; and we see it in . . . Nature in all its modifications. We also see that success in action is often the result of a number of persons acting together.

At the same time we find that there are some who believe that we should be indifferent to all that is in the world. But even he who is said to be indifferent, acts. He might appear to be inactive, but is not really so . . . for the sun may appear to be inactive, but it is acting all the time; and so are creatures too.

There is an immutable law of action at work within all forms of life, according to which all must act. For instance, we see things growing in size, but without apparent action; yet there is sound, motion, or vibration within them unperceived. . . .

The object of action is the achievement of more and more perfection . . . It is this that makes the mode of our life continuous or whole . . .

If there is a doubt about what has happened, we can find it out from its description. We cannot say that there are things that cannot be described in words, because it is all within the power of the mind to describe them; and it is the mind that enables us to make a correct use of words. . . .

There can be no extinction of action, because some part of it will always remain . . .

Even in the most excellent hymns of the Vedas there is no mention of the powers of the mind which can know the origin of things. . . .

Those who are intelligent know the existence of the soul because of memory . . .

Translation by N. V. Thadani

(6a) *Brahma Sutras, by Badarayana (Excerpts)*

BRAHMANISM (which is close to pantheism) is also called "Vedantism" (Adherence to the Vedas) or "Uttara Mimamsa" (Later Investigation).

Badarayana (accented on the third syllable) probably lived some time between 500 B.C. and the year 200 in the Christian era.

Then therefore the enquiry into Brahman.

Brahman is that from which the origin etc. (the origin, subsistence, and dissolution) of this world proceed.

The omniscience of Brahman follows from its being the source of Scripture. . . .

The one within is the highest Lord . . .

The akasa, i.e. ether, is Brahman . . .

Breath is Brahman.

The light is Brahman . . .

That which consists of mind is Brahman . . .

The person within the eye is Brahman . . .

The abode of heaven, earth, and so on is Brahman . . .

The Imperishable is Brahman . . .

The small is Brahman . . .

The (scriptural) passages speaking of Non-being do not intimate absolute Non-existence. . . .

Brahman is the material cause also (besides being the spiritual cause) . . . both the origin and the dissolution of the world being directly declared to have Brahman for their material cause. . . .

"Brahman is not the creator of the world . . . since beings engaged in any action have a motive (and Brahman has none)." But Brahman's creative activity has no motive (needs no motive); it is mere sport . . .

The beginninglessness of the world recommends itself to reason and is seen from Scripture.

And because all the qualities required in the cause of the world are present in Brahman. . . .

The nonexistence of external things cannot be maintained, on account of our consciousness of them.

And on account of their difference in nature, the ideas of the waking state are not like those of a dream. . . .

Translation by George Thibaut (adapted)

(6b) *Monistic Brahma Meditations, by Shankara*

SHANKARA ACHARYA (pronounced "SHAHN-kara A-CHAR-ya"), or Shankaracharya (Master Shankara), lived about the year 800 in the Christian era. He wrote a celebrated commentary on the Brahma Sutras. His emphasis on non-dualism, or the unity of being, is appealingly reflected in his Meditations on the South-Facing Form, or Brahma Meditations.

The special terms or references in these meditations have the following meanings:

Auspicious hand-sign—Tip of the thumb touching the tip of the first finger, thus forming a circle which means "I know" or "wisdom" or "knowing, I am."

Eight ways of unfolding the divine power—Through unlimited smallness, unlimited largeness, unlimited lightness, unlimited heaviness, unlimited vision, unlimited movement, unlimited creativeness, and unlimited control.

Maya—Illusion.

Yogi—Practitioner of yoga.

I

Devotion to that Glorious Presence,
Infinite Instructor,
Who,
Seeing the universe as if outside,
Though it arose in himself,
Through maya,
Just as in a dream,
Or like a city being seen in the inner depths
        of a looking-glass,
In the awakening,
Discloses his own nature,
Than which there is no other.

II

Devotion to that Glorious Presence,
Infinite Instructor,
Who,
By donning space and time, produced by maya
Like a conjuror, or rather a great yogi,
Opens up and spreads out this world,
At first formless,
Like a sprout within a seed,
And afterwards wonderful in its diversity.

III

Devotion to that Glorious Presence,
Infinite Instructor,
Whose coming forth reveals the nature of true being,
Amidst the objects produced in false being.
To those who turn to him,
He gives direct knowledge,
By means of the wise saying "That, thou art."
As result of that experience there is no return
To the ocean of things.

IV

Devotion to that Glorious Presence,
Infinite Instructor,
Whose consciousness,
Brilliant as the radiance of a big lamp,
Stationed inside a pot pierced with many holes,
Spreads externally
Through the agency of the eye
And other organs of sense.
Only after that shining as "I know"
Shines this aggregate, the world.

V

Devotion to that Glorious Presence,
Infinite Instructor,
Destroyer of the great bewilderment
Sportively produced by the power of maya,

Whereby extremely misguided thinkers assert:
"I am the body"
Or—"the vital functions,"
Or—"the senses,"
Or—"the moving mind,"
Or even—"mere nothing,"
Thus resembling many women, and children,
Or unseeing the dull persons.

VI

Devotion to that Glorious Presence,
Infinite Instructor,
The real man,
Who,
Because of being ridden by maya,
Resembles the sun or the moon caught in an eclipse;
Yet, all the senses being withheld,
When he was in deep sleep,
Was constituted of pure being itself,
Which, at the time of waking,
Is confirmed by the knowledge,
"I was sleeping just before now."

VII

Devotion to that Glorious Presence,
Infinite Instructor,
Who,
By means of the auspicious hand-sign,
Makes clear to the worshippers
His own real nature
Always shining within as "I,"
Following into all the successive states—
Those beginning with childhood,
And those beginning with waking.

VIII

Devotion to that Glorious Presence,
Infinite Instructor,
This Real Man,

Who,
Being whirled about by maya,
In the dream or in the waking state,
Views the whole world brokenly,
Through relationships
Of effect and cause,
Of servant and master,
Of pupil and teacher,
Also of father and son,
And others of this nature.

IX

Devotion to that Glorious Presence,
Infinite Instructor,
Of whom this is an eight-fold form,
Including the animate and the inanimate,
Appearing as what we call earth, water, fire, air,
The sky-matter,
The sun and the moon,
And the life in man,
Beyond whose all-presence
There is naught else
To be found by any searchers.

X

Since, in this song of praise,
It has been made very clear that all is self,
Therefore from the hearing of it,
From the thinking on its meaning,
From meditation,
And from reciting it with devotion,
Arises, all by itself,
God-like independence,
And the knowledge of being at one with all,
Combined with great capacity for living.
Also, unimpeded divine power is attained
Unfolded in eight ways.

Translation by Ernest E. Wood

(6c) *Pluralistic Brahma Reasonings, by Ramanuja*

RAMANUJA (main accent on the first syllable, lesser accent on the third syllable) was born about 1050 or a little earlier. He was a preacher of Vaishnavism at Srirangam in South Madras. When persecuted by a local ruler who was an adherent of Shaivism, Ramanuja fled to Mysore, but he returned home after the death of the monarch and himself died in 1137.

Ramanuja felt no contradiction between his Vaishnavism and the school with which his name is generally associated, Pluralistic Vedantism. He wrote a commentary on the Brahma Sutras and one on the *Bhagavad Gita*, as well as a summary of Vedic doctrine, the *Vedarthasamgraha*. Selections from the latter work are reproduced below.

The terms which may require explanation have the following meanings:

Dharmas—Duties.
Karman—Burden of the moral consequences of one's conduct.
Narayana—A name of the Supreme Being, thought of as a
   personal God.
Samsara—The round of births and deaths.
Smrtis—Revealed teachings.
Srutis—Traditional teachings.
Yamuna—The teacher of Ramanuja's teachers.

1. Homage to the Principal to whom all spiritual and non-spiritual entities are accessory . . . Who is the treasury of immaculate and infinite beautiful qualities: Visnu.

2. May the Sage Yamuna prosper. He has dispelled the bewildering obscurity of ignorance which, albeit contrary to revelation and reason, has spread all over the world: such errors as the view that the Supreme Brahman, being nescient and afflicted with misconceptions, is implicated in samsara . . .

3. The only meaning which is to be found in the most important part of the whole body of srutis, which set forth what is blissful for the entire Universe, is as follows: True knowledge of the individual soul and of the Supreme Spirit, applied to the obligations imposed by the various dharmas pertaining to each stage and station of life, is to precede pious and humble acts of devotion for and meditation on the Supreme Spirit, acts held extremely dear

by the devotee, that ultimately result in the attainment of the Supreme Spirit.

4. In truth, all declarations of the Vedanta are meant to set forth the knowledge of the proper form and nature of the individual soul which are different from the body; the proper form and nature of the Supreme Spirit who is the inner Ruler of the soul; the worship of the Supreme Spirit; and the apprehension of Brahman as perfect boundless bliss . . . By setting forth all this the declarations of the Vedanta serve to remove the danger of rebirth which is inevitable since it results from the misconception of the individual soul that it is identical itself with that one of the four types of bodies—gods, from Brahma onwards; men; animals; inanimate beings—into which it has entered by the impulsion of the continuous flow of good or evil karman amassed during ageless ignorance.

6. The proper form of the inner Ruler is as follows: He is the sole cause of the cessation of samsara . . . His proper form is therefore distinct from all entities other than Himself, since He is absolutely opposed to all evil and comprises solely infinite perfection. His beautiful qualities are immeasurable, perfect and innumerable. He is known in the entire Veda under the various designations of Soul of all, the Supreme Brahman, Supreme Glory, Supreme Principle, Supreme Spirit, Real Being, etc.—all of which denote the Venerable Lord Narayana, the Supreme Person. . . .

7. Some philosophers contend that Brahman is . . . identical with the individual soul; this identity is concluded from . . . constructions such as *Thou art That*. Accordingly Brahman Itself . . . may be in bondage as well as released.

65. All the srutis . . . and smrtis propound that Brahman Himself is modified by all spiritual and non-spiritual entities . . .

66. In other words, the declaration that *Brahman is such* proves the reality—in subtle and gross phase alike—of the phenomenal world, consisting in a plurality of spiritual and non-spiritual entities, as the mode denoted by the word *such*. . . .

68. So, since the sum-total of all entities, animate and inanimate, constitute the Lord's body, their proper forms have real existence as the modes of the Lord. . . .

145. Considering that there must be people who are at once profound enough and without professional jealousy and who know

how to discriminate between what is of the essence and what not, I have written for them this Summary of the Meaning of the Veda.

Translation by J. A. B. van Buitenen

(6d) *Pluralistic Brahma Reasonings, by Anandatirtha Madhva*

MADHVA was born about 1200. He was named Vasudeva by his parents, but his given name is usually recorded as Anandatirtha. He is also known as Purnaprajna (one whose knowledge is complete).

Madhva wrote commentaries on various Upanishads, on the *Bhagavad Gita*, and on the Brahma Sutras, and he composed an independent treatise, *Srimad Vishnu-Tattva-Vinirnaya* (Supremacy of the Chief Diety, Here Called Vishnu), in which he defended pluralism. The selection printed here is from that treatise.

The following terms or passages in the selection may require explanation:

"Become one in the supreme unperishable atman"—Presumably a quotation from a text on union with the world soul ("atman" means soul).

Brahman—The supreme deity.

"Not so, not so"—A quotation from the Brihadaranyaka Upanishad, pointing out that one can only say of God that He is "not this, not that."

Purusa—Soul.

Quotation from "the Lord"—A quotation from Krishna in the *Bhagavad Gita*.

72. Experience itself establishes the difference between the individual self and God whose existence is supposed to be proved by inference. For it is a matter of everyone's experience that he is not the author of all. The scripture can have no validity if it contradicts experience.

73. Otherwise even the experience of the truth of the scripture becomes false.

75. It is a matter of experience that what is testified to by many and is also a fact of observation, becomes a strongly established principle.

112. Love is particularly seen to arise towards an individual who

acknowledges the superiority in qualities in one and it is not seen to arise in response to the affirmation of identity.

113. In fact those who excel develop the opposite of love towards their inferiors, if the latter assert identity with them.

114. Kings put down a subject if he claims, "I am the king." If, on the other hand, he praises the superior qualities of the king, the king grants him all his objects of desire.

116. The Lord himself has indicated that he develops overflowing love towards one who acknowledges his surpassing excellences, in the passage, "He who understands me undeluded as the highest purusa in this manner, is one who knows all and he serves me in all ways."

133. In the text, "Not so, not so," the difference of Brahman from all else is asserted . . .

134. Surely the difference from jars is not the same as the difference from cloth. Such a position would violate the verdict of experience.

137. In reality what has been cognised through valid modes of knowledge cannot be refuted by mere logic, for it is the universal principle that logic which runs against valid modes of knowledge is fallacious.

138. The perception of things like a piece of shell as silver is determined to be an illusion only because it contradicts very strong perceptual evidence and not by mere logic.

139. If mere logic could refute perception, as the other four elements like water do not have the characteristics of earth, it would be arguable that even earth does not have them, which is absurd.

140. Therefore, on the strength of mere logical quibbles, facts of observation cannot be explained away as illusions.

181. Surely there is no identity between the bird and the rope, no identity among the juices of many trees, between the rivers and the sea . . . the finest essence and the seed, the salt and the water . . . the ignorant man and the controller of the life-breath etc., and the thief and the stolen property.

207. The individual self cannot be the ultimate sustainer of life.

244. We know the world when we know it is the creation of Brahman.

299. The words of the text, "become one in the supreme un-

perishable atman," enunciating that Brahman is the seat of the process of becoming one, intimate difference.

300. Otherwise, the statement ought to have been that they become the supreme atman itself.

Translation by S. S. Raghavachar

LAWS, PROVERBS,
AND RHAPSODIES

INCLUDED AMONG THE PHILOSOPHICAL EPITOMES OF ANCIENT AND medieval India are several law codes, works embodying proverbial wisdom, and rhapsodies glorifying God.

Laws of Manu (Excerpts)

TRADITIONAL RULES of private and civic behavior were codified into about twenty codes which, according to tradition, were compiled by Manu (who was ancient enough to be mentioned in the Vedas), Kautilya (about 300 B.C.), Yajnavalkya (about 300 to 400 in the Christian era), and others.

The Code of Kautilya (also called Kautalya, Canakya, and Vishnugupta) was known only through references in other works prior to the present century. A manuscript copy of it was discovered in Mysore Province in 1905; it has since been translated twice into English. This work, written for the monarch Chandra Gupta Maurya, has been compared with Machiavelli's *The Prince*, by virtue of its teaching that the advantage of the sovereign is the criterion of what should be done. Kautilya's general theme is: Discipline, including political order and self-discipline, results in material and spiritual advantage.

Typical injunctions in Yajnavalkya's Code are the following, taken from Book 2 (on positive law), Chapter 1 (on rules of procedure):

"1. The king, divested of anger and avarice, should . . . administer justice, along with learned Brahmanas (members of the caste of Brahman), conformably to the precepts of law.

"2. Those should be made assessors (counselors) by the king who have studied the Vedas and Sastras (law codes), who know the law, who speak the truth, and who look to friends and foes with the same feelings.

"6. That which the plaintiff relates should be recorded in the presence of the defendant, marked with the year, the month, the fortnight, the day, the name, the caste, and the like."

Translation by V. N. Mandlik

The Code of Manu, presented below in excerpts, was probably edited between 200 B.C. and 200 in the Christian era in the form in which we have it. The terms in the excerpts which may require explanations have the following meanings:

Brahma—The supreme god.
Rishis—Saints.
Smriti—Revealed teachings.

BOOK I

58. Brahma, having framed this system of laws himself, taught it fully to me in the beginning.

59. I then taught it to Marici and the nine other sages, my off-spring. Of these, Bhrigu is deputed by me to declare the Code to you from beginning to end, for he has learned from me to recite the whole of it.

60. Then the great sage, Brighu, having been thus appointed by Manu to promulgate his laws, addressed all the Rishis with a pleased mind, saying "Listen!"

107. In this Code appears the whole system of law, with defini-tions of good and bad actions, and the traditional practices of the four classes, which usages are held to be eternal.

108. Traditional practice is equivalent to supreme law, since it is so pronounced by the Veda and by Smriti.

BOOK II

14. When there is contradiction of two precepts in the Veda, both are declared to be law; both have been justly promulgated by ancient sages as valid law.

15. Thus, there is a Vedic precept, calling for the oblation to fire when the sun has risen, and before it has risen, and when neither sun nor stars are visible. Wherefore the oblation to fire may be made at all times.

87. A Brahman becomes fit for beatitude by simple repetition of the Veda, whether he perform other rites or not; of this there is no doubt.

121. A youth who habitually salutes and constantly reveres the aged, prospers in four things, knowledge, reputation, fame, and strength.

161. Wound not another, though by him provoked,
Do no one injury by thought or deed,
Utter no word to pain thy fellow-creatures.

226. Even though wronged, treat not with disrespect
Thy father, mother, teacher, elder brother.

228. Think constantly, O son, how thou mayest please
Thy father, mother, teacher—these obey.
By deep devotion seek thy debt to pay.
This is the highest duty and religion.

233. By reverencing his mother, he gains this terrestrial world; by reverencing his father, the middle world; by constant attention to his spiritual master, the celestial world of Brahma.

238. From poison thou mayest take the food of life,
The purest gold from lumps of impure earth,
Examples of good conduct from a foe,

239. Sweet speech and gentleness from e'en a child,
Something from all; from men of low degree
Lessons of wisdom, if thou humble be.

BOOK III

8. Let him not marry a girl with reddish hair, nor one with a superfluity of limbs (for instance, six fingers), nor one who is sickly, nor one with either too little or too much hair, nor one who talks too much, nor one who is red-eyed.

9. Nor one named after a constellation, a tree, or a river, nor one with a barbarous name, or the name of a mountain, a bird, a snake, a slave, or any frightful object.

10. But let him marry a woman without defective or deformed

limbs, having an agreeable name, whose gait is like that of a flamingo or elephant, whose hair and teeth are moderate in quantity, and whose whole body is soft.

105. Let the householder not eat anything himself till he has made his guest eat.

106. The honouring of a guest confers wealth, reputation, life, and heaven.

BOOK IV

43. Let not a husband eat with his wife, nor looking at her.

138. Say what is true, speak not agreeable falsehood.

173. Iniquity once practised, like a seed,
　　　 Fails not to yield its fruit to him who wrought it,
　　　 If not to him, yet to his sons and grandsons.

236. Pride not thyself on thy religious works;
　　　 Give to the poor, but talk not of thy gifts.

237. By pride, religious merit melts away;
　　　 The merit of thy alms, by ostentation.

BOOK V

154. A husband must continually be revered as a god by a virtuous wife.

155. No sacrifice is permitted to women separately from their husbands, no religious observance, no fasting. As far as a wife obeys her husband, so far is she exalted in heaven.

160. A virtuous wife who remains unmarried after the death of her husband goes to heaven, even though she have no son.

BOOK VI

4. Having taken up his sacred fire and all the domestic utensils for making oblations to it, and having gone forth from the town to the forest, let him dwell there with all his organs of sense well restrained.

43. Let him remain without fire, without habitation; let him resort once a day to the town for food, regardless of hardships, resolute, keeping a vow of silence, fixing his mind in meditation.

47. Treat no one with disdain, with patience bear
　　　 Reviling language.

48.   With an angry man
Be never angry; blessings give for curses.

52. With hair, nails, and beard well clipped, carrying a bowl, a staff, and a pitcher, let him wander about constantly, intent on meditation and avoiding injury to any being.

81. In this manner, having little by little abandoned all worldly attachments, and freed himself from all concern about pairs of opposites (joy and sorrow, praise and blame, etc.), he obtains absorption into the universal Spirit.

84. This Veda is the refuge of those who do not understand it as well as those who do, of those who seek heaven and of those who seek immortality.

BOOK VII

8. A king, even though a child, must not be treated with contempt, as if he were a mortal; he is a great divinity in human shape.

130. A sixth, an eighth, or a twelfth part of grain may be taken by the king. Of cattle and gold and silver added to the capital stock, a fiftieth part may be taken by the king.

131. Moreover, he may take a sixth part of the annual increase of trees, meat, honey, clarified butter, perfumes, medicinal herbs, liquids, flowers, roots, and fruits.

132. Of leaves, pot-herbs, grass, wicker-work, hides, earthenware vessels, and all articles made of stone.

BOOK IX

2. Day and night must women be made to feel their dependence on their husbands. But if they are fond of worldly amusements, let them be allowed to follow their own inclinations.

12. Even if confined at home by faithful guardians they are not guarded; but those women who guard themselves by their own will are well guarded.

18. Women have no business to repeat texts of the Veda; thus is the law established.

40. Thou canst not gather what thou didst not sow;
As thou dost plant the tree, so will it grow.

96. Domestic rites are to be performed in common with a wife; so it is ordained in the Veda.

Translation by Sir Monier Monier-Williams

Maxims, by Tiruvalluvar

PROVERBIAL LORE in India is found most significantly in the two great epics (the *Mahabharata* and the *Ramayana*) and in a frankly didactic poem written by Tiruvalluvar.

Illustrative of the proverbial wisdom in the *Mahabharata* is the following passage from Book III:

> "The principles of duty lie
> Enveloped deep in mystery.
> On what can men their conduct found?
> For reasonings lack all solid ground;
> The Veda with itself conflicts,—
> One text another contradicts."

Also the following passages from Book XII:

> "How strange, to all her course who mark,
> Must Fortune's ways appear, how dark! . . .
> The man who strongest seems to be
> Is vexed by some infirmity.
> Oft rich men pine from lack of health,
> And gain scant good from all their wealth. . . .
> And men whom study, deep and long,
> Has taught the rules of right and wrong,
> By women lured, misled by knaves,
> Of vice are often found the slaves."

> "Death spares no class, no rank, nor age;
> He carries off the fool, the sage,
> The knave, the saint, the young, the old,
> The weak, the strong, the faint, the bold."

> "Seek, therefore, knowledge; wheresoe'er
> Thou seekest, thou shalt find it there."

> "With ceaseless care amass that wealth
> Which neither thieves can filch by stealth,
> Nor greedy tyrants snatch away,
> Which even in death shall with thee stay. . . .
> When mortals leave behind them here
> Their wealth, their friends, their kinsmen dear,
> Have they no comrades on the road
> Which leads to Yama's dread abode?
> Yes, all the deeds that men have done,
> In light of day, before the sun,

> Or veiled beneath the gloom of night,
> The good, the bad, the wrong, the right,
> These, though forgotten, reappear,
> And travel, silent, in their rear."

And the following passage from Book XIII:

> "A man, until his time arrives,
> Though pierced by hundred darts, survives,
> While he whose hour of death is nigh,
> Touched only by a straw, will die."

Proverbial wisdom in the *Ramayana* is illustrated by the following passage from Book VI:

> "My brother dear, thy life is pure;
> Thou spurnest every sensual lure;
> Thy conduct all is noble, just;
> The world, secure, thy word can trust.
> Yet what does all this virtue boot?
> To thee it brings no meed, no fruit;
> For thou art crushed by ills: I deem
> That virtue is a baseless dream. . . .
> I learn by demonstration strong
> That wrong is right, and right is wrong;
> I see,—it needs no insight nice,—
> That vice is virtue, virtue vice.
> The righteous pine, the wicked thrive;
> Why vainly after virtue strive?"

The foregoing translations are by John Muir.

Tiruvalluvar (whose name means "devotee of the Valluva caste," the caste of pariahs who proclaim the king's commands) was a weaver in Mylapore, Madras, at some time between 100 B.C. and 300 in the Christian era. His long didactic poem, the *Kural* (the name of a metrical scheme), was written in the Tamil tongue. Tiruvalluvar's people, the Tamils, belong to the Dravidian race, which inhabited southern India before the coming of the Aryans. Excerpts from the *Kural* are presented below.

CHAPTER 3

Behold the men who have renounced sense-enjoyments and live a life of discipline. The scriptures exalt their glory above every other good.

Thou canst not measure the greatness of the men of renunciation. Thou canst as well count the number of the dead.

Behold the men who have weighed this life with the next and have renounced the world. The earth is made radiant by their greatness.

Behold the man whose firm will controlleth his five senses even as the goading hook controlleth the elephant. He is a seed fit for the fields of heaven.

Dost thou desire to know the power of the saint who hath quenched the cravings of his five senses? Look on the King of the Gods, Indra. His one example is enough. . . .

The scriptures proclaim the greatness of the men of the mighty word.

It is impossible to support even for a moment the wrath of those who stand on the rock of renunciation.

CHAPTER 4

Righteousness leadeth unto heaven and it bringeth wealth also. Then what is there that is more profitable than righteousness?

There is no greater good than righteousness, nor no greater ill than the forgetting of it.

Be thou unremitting in the doing of good deeds. Do them with all thy might and by every means.

Be pure in heart. All righteousness is contained in this one commandment. All other things are nought but empty display. . . .

Say not in thy heart, "I shall be righteous by and by," but begin to do good works without delaying. For it is righteousness that will be thy undying companion on the day of thy death. . . .

That action alone is worth doing which is based on righteousness. And all action must be shunned which will subject thee to the reproof of the wise.

CHAPTER 7

We know of no blessing so great as the begetting of children that are endowed with understanding. . . .

The touch of children is the delight of the body. The delight of the ear is the hearing of their speech. . . .

Great is the joy of the mother when a man child is born unto her. But greater far is her delight when she heareth him called worthy.

What is the duty of the son to his father? It is to make the world ask, "For what austerities of his hath he been blessed with such a son?"

CHAPTER 10

The speech that is truly kind is the speech of the righteous man which is full of tenderness and free from dissimulation.

Better even than a generous gift are sweet speech and a kind and gracious look.

Behold the sweet and gracious look and the kind speech that cometh from the heart. Righteousness hath its dwelling place there.

Behold the man who always speaketh sweet words whosoever it be to whom he speaketh. Poverty, the increaser of sorrow, will never come near him. . . .

Sinfulness will wane away and righteousness will increase if thy thoughts are good and thy speech is kind.

The word that is serviceable and kind createth friends and bringeth forth benefits.

Words that are kind and are removed from all littleness yield good in this life and in the next also.

CHAPTER 32

The man who is pure in heart would not injure others even if he could obtain a princely estate thereby.

Even when another hath injured him in his hate, the man who is pure in heart returneth not the injury. . . .

How shall a man punish them that have injured him? Let him do them a good turn and make them ashamed in their hearts.

Of what avail is intelligence to a man if he doth not feel as his very own the pain suffered by other beings, and so feeling doth not abstain from injuring any?

When a man hath felt a pain for himself, let him take care that he inflicteth it not on others.

It is a great thing if thou injure not knowingly any man, at any time, and in any degree. . . .

If a man injureth his neighbour in the forenoon, evil will come to him in the afternoon of its own accord.

CHAPTER 92

Behold the women that desire a man for the sake of his gold and not for the sake of love. Their cajoleries will lead only to misery.

Behold the women who pretend love, but whose thoughts are ever fixed on their own profit. Consider their ways and keep them at a distance.

The prostitute pretendeth love when she embraceth her lover. But in her heart she feeleth even as one who hath touched a stranger's dead body in a dark room.

Behold the men whose hearts are inclined to deeds of purity. They defile themselves not with the touch of harlots.

Behold the men who add deep study to a clear understanding. They defile themselves not with the touch of women whose charms are free to all.

Behold the men that have a regard for their own good. They touch not the hand of wantons who put up their lewd charms for sale. . . .

The soft arms of the well-decked harlot are the infernal pit wherein contemptible fools drown themselves.

Translation by V. V. S. Aiyar

Great Liberation Tantra (Excerpts)

RHAPSODIES glorifying God in mystic, esoteric language were produced by various Hindu sects. While ritualistic sectarianism is a phenomenon not so much of Indian philosophy as of Indian religion, it is nevertheless relevant to a survey of Indian philosophy, because a man's religion reflects, or is a reflection of, his *Weltanschauung*.

Hinduism—interpreted strictly, as excluding Buddhism, Jainism, Islam, Parseeism, and other "non-Hindu" religions practiced in India—consists mainly of Vaishnavism (the worship of Vishnu as the chief diety), Shaivism (the worship of Shiva as the chief diety), and Shaktism (the worship of Shakti as the divine mother). Each of these sects has its esoteric scriptures, which supplement the Vedic hymns, the Upanishads, and the other Vedic documents common to all the Hindu sects.

Shaktism is perhaps of special interest as being the most occult of the three denominations. Its scriptures, known as "tantras," include passages (at one extreme) which teach universalistic theism, and some (at the other extreme) which teach necromancy.

The early chapters of the Mahanirvana Tantra (Tantra of the Great Nirvana, known more often as the Great Liberation Tantra) teach a modified form of universalistic theism. This document was probably written between 500 and 1400. Because the terms in this selection which require explanation are numerous, they are explained in parentheses where they occur.

CHAPTER I

Questions Relating to the Liberation of Beings

The enchanting summit of the Lord of Mountains (Mount Kailasa), resplendent with all its various jewels, clad with many a tree and many a creeper, melodious with the song of many a bird, scented with the fragrance of all the season's flowers, most beautiful, fanned by soft, cool, and perfumed breezes, shadowed by the still shade of stately trees; where cool groves resound with the sweet-voiced songs of troops of Apsara (beauteous maidens), and in the forest depths flocks of Kokila (Indian cuckoos) maddened with passion sing; where Spring, Lord of the Seasons, with his followers ever abides; peopled by troops of Siddha (miracle workers), Charana (celestial singer-dancers), Gandharva (sons of Brahma), and Ganapta (a class of heavenly spirits).

It was there that Parvati (daughter of the Himalayan Mount Parvata), finding Shiva (the supreme god), Her gracious Lord, in mood serene, with obeisance bent low and for the benefit of all the worlds questioned Him, the Silent Deva (luminous god), Lord of all things movable and immovable, the ever Beneficent and ever Blissful One, the nectar of Whose mercy abounds as a great ocean, Whose body is Pure Sattva Guna (having the attribute of existence), He Who is white as camphor and the jasmine flower, the Omnipresent One, Whose raiment is space itself, Lord of the poor and the beloved and loving Master of all Yogis (ascetic followers of the Yoga doctrine), Whose coiled and matted hair is wet with the spray of Gamga (the Ganges River) and of Whose naked body ashes are (or perhaps a halo is) the adornment only; the passionless One Whose neck is garlanded with snakes and skulls of men, the three-eyed One (the symbolical third eye, the inner eye of wisdom, being thought of as located in the forehead), Lord of the three worlds (heaven, earth, and the underworld), with one hand wielding the trident and with the other bestowing blessings; easily appeased, Whose very substance is unconditioned Knowledge; the Bestower of eternal Liberation, unconditioned, from Whom comes no fear, Changeless, Stainless, One without defect, the Benefactor of all, and the Deva of all Devas.

Shri (Madam) Parvati said:

O Deva of the Devas, Lord of the world, Jewel of Mercy, my Husband, Thou art my Lord, on Thee I am ever dependent and to Thee I am ever obedient. Nor can I say ought without Thy word. If Thou hast affection for me, I crave to lay before Thee that which passes in my mind. Who else but Thee, O Great Lord, in the three worlds is able to solve these doubts of mine, Thou Who knowest all and all the Scriptures?

Shri Sadashiva (Master Auspicious Shiva) said:

What is that Thou sayest, O Thou Great Wise One and Beloved of My heart? I will tell Thee anything, be it ever so bound in mystery, even that which should not be spoken of before Ganesha (elephant-headed son of Shiva), Commander of the Hosts of Heaven. What is there in all the three worlds which should be concealed from Thee? For Thou, O Devi (luminous goddess), art My very Self. There is no difference between Me and Thee. Thou too art omnipresent. What is it then that Thou knowest not that Thou questionest like unto one who knoweth nothing?

The pure Parvati, gladdened at hearing the words of the Deva, bending low made obeisance and thus questioned Shangkara (the Protector).

Shri Adya (Madam Primordial) said:

O Bhagavan (Celestial)! Lord of all, Greatest among those who are versed in Dharma (law), Thou in former ages in Thy mercy didst through Brahma reveal the four Vedas which are the propagators of all Dharma and which ordain the rules of life for all the varying castes of men and for the different stages of their lives.

In the First Age, men by the practice of Yoga and Yajna (worship) prescribed by Thee were virtuous and pleasing to Devas and Pitris (patriarchs). By the study of the Vedas, by Dhyana (meditation) and Tapas (austerities), and the conquest of the senses, by acts of mercy and charity men were of exceeding power and courage, industry, and prowess, adherents of the true Dharma, good and truthful, and, mortals though they were, they were yet like Devas and went to the abode of the Devas.

Kings then were faithful to their engagements and were ever concerned with the protection of their people, upon whose wives they were wont to look as if upon their mothers, and whose children they regarded as their very own. The people, too, did then look upon a neighbour's property as if it were mere lumps of clay, and, with devotion to their Dharma, kept to the path of righteousness.

There were then no liars, none who were selfish, thievish, malicious, foolish, none who were evil-minded, envious, wrathful, gluttonous, or lustful, but all were good of heart and of ever blissful mind. Land then yielded in plenty all kinds of grain, clouds showered seasonable rains, cows gave abundant milk, and trees were weighted with fruits. No untimely death there was, nor famine nor sickness.

Men were ever cheerful, prosperous and healthy, and endowed with all qualities of beauty and brilliance. Women were chaste and devoted to their husbands, Brahmanas, Kshatriyas, Vaishyas, and Shudras (members of the four castes) kept to and followed the Dharma of their respective castes in their worship and attained the final Liberation.

After the Krita (original) Age had passed away, Thou didst in the Treta (succeeding) Age perceive Dharma to be in disorder, and that men were no longer able by Vedic rites to accomplish their desires. For men, through their anxiety and perplexity, were unable to perform these rites in which much trouble had to be overcome, and for which much preparation had to be made. In constant distress of mind they were neither able to perform nor yet were willing to abandon the rites.

Having observed this, Thou didst make known on earth the Smriti (revealed) Scripture which explains the meaning of the Vedas, and thus delivered from sin, which is cause of all pain, sorrow, and sickness, men too feeble for the practice of Tapas and the study of the Vedas. For men in this terrible ocean of the world, who is there but Thee to be their Cherisher, Protector, Saviour, their fatherly Benefactor, and Lord? . . .

Now the sinful Kali Age (age of worship of the Divine Mother) is upon them, when Dharma is destroyed, an Age full of evil customs and deceit. . . .

Say, O Lord of all the distressed! in Thy mercy how without great pains men may obtain longevity, health, and energy, increase of strength and courage, learning, intelligence, and happiness; and how they may become great in strength and valour, pure of heart, obedient to parents, devoted to their wives, mindful of the good of their neighbour, reverent to the Devas and to their Gurus (spiritual teachers), cherishers of their children and kinsmen, possessing the knowledge of the Brahman (Brahma, the supreme god), learned in the lore of, and ever meditating on, the Brahman. Say, O Lord! for the good of the world, what men should or should not do according to their different castes and stages of life. For who but Thee is their Protector in all the three worlds?

CHAPTER II

Introduction to the Worship of Brahman

Having heard the words of the Devi, Shangkara, Bestower of happiness on the world, great Ocean of Mercy, thus truly spoke. Sadashiva said: . . .

None before has ever questioned Me as Thou hast done for the advantage of all mankind—nay, for the benefit of all that breathes, and that, too, in such detail and with reference to the needs of the present age. Therefore, out of My affection for Thee, O Parvati! I will speak to Thee of the supreme Essence of essences. . . .

Should good be done to the universe, the Lord of the universe is pleased, since He is its Self, and it depends on Him. He is One. He ever is. He is the Truth. He is the Supreme Unity without a second. He is Ever-full and Self-manifest. He is Eternal Consciousness and Bliss. He is without change, self-existent, and ever the same, serene, above all attributes. He beholds and is the Witness of all that is, Omnipresent, the Self of everything that is. He, the Eternal and Omnipresent, is hidden and pervades all things.

Though Himself devoid of senses, He is the Illuminator of all the senses and their powers. The Cause of all the three worlds, He is yet beyond them and the mind of men. Ineffable and Omniscient, He knows the universe, yet none know Him. He sways this incomprehensible universe, and all that has movement and is motionless in the three worlds depend on Him . . .

We too have come from Him as our Cause. He, the One Supreme Lord, is the Cause of all beings, the Manifestation of Whose creative Energy in the three worlds is called Brahma. . . .

It is He who destroys Time at the Great Dissolution, of whom even Fear and Death itself are afraid. . . . O Adored of the Devas! all the Devas and Devis—nay, the whole universe, from Brahma to a blade of grass—are His forms. If He be pleased, the Universe is pleased. If ought be done to gratify Him, then the gratification of All is caused. . . .

Oh, what use is it to say more before Thee, O my Beloved? There is none other but Him, to meditate upon, to worship, to pray to, for the attainment of Liberation with such delight or ease. Need there is none to trouble, to fast, to torture one's body, to follow rules and customs, to make large offerings . . .

Translation by Sir John G. Woodroffe

V

"The Life Divine": Modern Mysticism

MODERN MYSTICISM IN INDIA BEGAN ABOUT 1400 OR A LITTLE earlier. One of the first names worthy of note in this field is that of Lal (or Lalla) of Kashmir, who died about 1400. She is sometimes called Lal Ded (or Diddi), i.e., Grandmother Lal. She combined the doctrines of Yoga with the worship of Vishnu. Verses from the *Lallavakyani* (Sayings of Lalla), such as:

> "Keep clean the garden of thy heart,
>   So lilies there may be,
> And give good answer for thy part,
>   When Death doth question thee,"

are said to be often on the lips of today's Kashmiris.

Another significant figure in the beginnings of modern mysticism is Kabir, who flourished about 1450 or 1500. He was brought up by a Moslem weaver, probably in the Benares area, but he was drawn to Hinduism. He became a weaver himself, married, and had two sons. His poetic pronouncements, in Hindi, are preserved in a document called the *Bijak*, which is the scripture of the Kabir Panth (a religious sect), and, in different form, in a collection

entitled the *Adi-Granth*, which was compiled by the Sikh Arjun
and is revered by the Sikhs.

Rabindranath Tagore, with the assistance of Evelyn Underhill,
prepared and published an English translation of *One Hundred
Poems of Kabir*, apparently based on a Bengali version of the
Hindi originals. As the Bengali version for the most part does not
correspond to either the *Bijak* or the *Adi-Granth*, some Hindu
literary scholars, while valuing the Tagore translations from the
Bengali as reflecting the spirit of Kabir's teaching, have questioned
whether the poems translated by Tagore are actually poems by
Kabir.

Modern mysticism in India is represented in the present volume
through (1) some early Sikh documents, (2) passages from the
writings of two mystics of the nineteenth century, and (3) passages from the writings of two mystics of the twentieth century.

EARLY SIKHISM

SIKHISM IS SOMETIMES REFERRED TO AS REFORMED HINDUISM, and the Sikhs as the Protestants of India. The Sikh religion emphasizes mystic monotheism, the dignity of labor, the equality of all men, and the subservience of rituals to ethical conduct.

Psalms and Devotions, by Nanak

NANAK, founder of the Sikh religion, was born in Talwandi, Punjab, in 1469; was married at the age of fourteen; engaged in frequent religious devotions; and aspired to produce a religion which would be acceptable to Hindus and to Moslems. He traveled for twelve years in eastern India with a servant, preaching and composing hymns; returned to the Punjab, where he renounced his married life; traveled again, westward to Medina, southward to Ceylon, and northward to the Himalayas; returned to the Punjab; and died in 1538.

Of the six selections printed here, the first is a general psalm which he composed; the second is the prologue of his *Japji* (Spiritual Message); and the third, fourth, fifth, and sixth are the first, second, third, and twelfth stanzas of the *Japji*.

Of the unfamiliar terms used, some have been explained earlier, but for the convenience of those who may be reading this selection before earlier ones the following explanations may be useful:

Brahma, Vishnu, or Shiv—Top gods of the Indian pantheon.
Brahman or Khatri—Member of the top castes.

1

In the beginning there was indescribable darkness.

Then was not earth or heaven, naught but God's unequalled order.

Then was not day, or night, or moon, or sun; God was meditating on the void.

Then were not continents, or hells, or seven seas, or rivers, or flowing streams.

Nor was there paradise, or a tortoise, or nether regions; or the hell or heaven of the Muhammadans, or the Destroyer Death; or the hell or heaven of the Hindus, or birth or death; nor did any one come or go.

Then was not Brahma, Vishnu, or Shiv; no one existed but the One God.

Then was not female, or male, or caste, or birth; nor did any one feel pain or pleasure.

There was no caste or religious garb, no Brahman or Khatri. . . .

The Imperceptible God was Himself the speaker and preacher; Himself unseen He was everything.

When He pleased He created the world; without supports He sustained the sky. . . .

He issued His order and watched over all.

Translation by Max A. Macauliffe

2

There is One Reality, the Unmanifest-Manifested. Ever-existent, He is Naam (Conscious Spirit), the Creator; pervading all.

Without fear; without enmity; the Timeless; the Unborn and the Self-existent; complete within Itself.

Through the favour of His true Servant, the Guru, He may be realized.

He was when there was nothing; He was before all ages began; He existeth now, O Nanak, and shall exist forevermore.

3

One cannot comprehend Him through reason, even if one reasoned for ages.

One cannot achieve inner peace by outward silence, not though one sat dumb for ages.

One cannot buy contentment with all the riches of the world, nor reach Him with all mental ingenuity.

How may one know the Truth and break through the cloud of falsehood?

There is a Way, O Nanak, to make His Will our own, His Will which is already wrought in our existence.

4

All things are manifestations of His Will; but His Will is beyond description.

By His Will is matter quickened into life; by His Will is greatness obtained; by His Will some are born high and others low. By His Will are men's joys and sorrows ordained; by His Will the pious obtain salvation; by His Will the impious wander in endless transmigration.

All exist under His Will, and nothing stands outside.

One attuned with His Will, O Nanak, is wholly freed from ego.

5

Some sing of His greatness, but only according to the power bestowed upon them.

Some sing of His bounties, taking them as His signs.

Some sing of Him as incomprehensible.

Some sing of Him as transmuting dust into life, and life into dust again: Creator and Destroyer, the Giver of life and its Withdrawer.

Some sing of Him as at once the nearest and the most remote.

There is no end to His description.

Countless have tried to describe Him, but He still stands beyond all description.

His recipients may tire, but His bounty is untiring. Ages upon ages, man has fed upon it.

His Will directs the world; and yet, O Nanak, He dwells beyond concern or care.

6

None can describe the condition of one who has made God's Will his own. Whoever tries to do so must realise his folly.

No supply of paper, pen or scribe can ever describe the state of such a one.

O, great is the power of the Word; but few there be that know it.

Translation by Kirpal Singh

The Psalm of Peace, by Arjun (Excerpt)

ARJUN (1563–1606) was the fifth in the succession of Sikh gurus (teachers), of whom Nanak was the first. Residing at Amritsar in West Punjab, he gave away his wealth but, while devoting himself to religion, also took part in social projects, including the establishment of a leper colony. He was burned to death by the Moslem ruler of the area when he refused to accept the Moslem faith.

His *Sukhmani* (Psalm of Peace) consists of twenty-four cantos, each containing a prologue and eight stanzas. The selection printed here is the first canto. The following explanations may be useful to some readers:

Puranas—Ancient narratives of cosmology, legend, and history, mostly in poetic form.

Smritis—Revealed teachings.

PROLOGUE

I bow to the Divine Enlightener who was before anything else; who existed when time began its rounds; who is still the True Enlightener guiding the world even now; who is always the light of the world.

1

I think in love of my Lord, and as I do so, a peace dawns on my soul, erasing all worries of the body and mind from the tablet of my life.

I think of the goodness of Him who fills all things with His presence; whose Name is on the lips of countless various beings.

The Vedas, the Puranas and the Smritis, whose texts are preserved with so much care, were created out of a single letter of God's Name.

A particle of that Name coming to reside in the heart of a man gives him a glory beyond all praise.

But he who with a single mind yearns to have a sight of Him sheds a divine influence which is enough to save all men.

This Psalm of Peace is the joy-raining nectar; it is the Name of God which dwells in the hearts of His lovers. Meditate upon it.

2

If a man meditates on the Name, he will not go the round of births, he will be immune from the torture of Death, and will shed off all mortality.

His enemies will keep away from him, and he will be safe from all harm.

His mind will be always on the alert, and will not be affected by fear, or troubled by pain.

This meditation is learnt in the company of the holy.

All riches in abundance for him who is God-intoxicated!

3

In the joy of thinking of God is contained all wealth of earthly goods, of mental powers and the . . . sources of aesthetic enjoyment.

In the illumination got from His thought are contained all knowledge, all devotion and the essence of all wisdom. . . .

By the practice of the presence of the Lord all sense of duality is lost, and we see nothing but Him everywhere.

By thinking of Him we feel as steeped in His holiness as if we had bathed in all the waters of pilgrimage; we feel honoured in the court of God, and nothing but good emanates from us. Our lives become extremely fruitful.

They alone think of Him who are induced to do so by Him. I wish to attach myself to the feet of them.

4

The praising of His Name is the highest of all practices. It has upraised many a human soul.

It slakes the desire of the restless mind, and imparts an all-seeing vision.

To a man of praise Death loses all its terrors; he feels all his hopes fulfilled; his mind is cleared of all impurities and is filled with the ambrosial Name.

God resides in the tongue of the good. O that I were the slave of their slaves!

5

They alone are rich who love the Name; they alone are honourable.

They get acceptance in the eye of God, and are held as presiding geniuses in the councils of men.

The possession of the Name places them beyond all want, and makes them kings of men.

They live in eternal bliss, and enjoy everlasting life.

Who give themselves to the Name?—whom God brings under His grace. I pray for the dust of such men's feet.

6

The men of God lead lives of public good. All homage to them!

Their faces irradiate charm, and they live in constant peace.

Theirs is a life of self-control, and they follow the way of righteousness.

They command sources of manifold joy, because they live in the presence of God.

By the aid of such holy men, remain always wakeful: because who knows when the hour of fortune may strike, and you may be called into His presence!

7

The dear Remembrance ensures to man success in all undertakings, and leaves him nothing to worry about.

His tongue is busy with the praise of God, and his mind is fixed on the steady vision. Nothing can shake it.

The bloom of the lotus is on his heart, and the music of the spheres is in his ear.

There is no end to the joy that comes from singing God's Name. Who sing it but those to whom God is kind?

8

It was the quest of the Name that brought forth saints. The same quest led to the creation of Vedas, and inspired men to be hermits, celibates and donors of charity.

The practice of the Name has turned obscure men into luminaries of the world. It was for the glorification of the Name that the world was made.

Think, O think of the Lord as the cause of all causes! The Name has brought all forms into being.

Himself the Formless One lives in the utterance of the Name.

When by His grace He imparts this understanding to a man, he learns to practice the Name through the Guru.

Translation by Teja Singh

NINETEENTH CENTURY

A FTER THE TWO GREAT SIKH PREACHERS, THERE APPEARED NO giants in Indian mysticism until the nineteenth century. One notable figure in the interim was Ramaprasada Sena (1718–1775), a Tantric poet who taught that, at the moment of death, one should strive to retain in consciousness the name of the Great Mother, the goddess Kali. He wrote: "When Death shall seize me by the hair, then, Mind, do thou cry 'Kali, Kali,' and vain will be Death's purposes." But in the nineteenth and twentieth centuries a renaissance of religious philosophy occurred in India. Two historic features of the revival, aside from the work of the thinkers represented here, are:

(1) The establishment in 1828 of the Brahmo-Samaj, a movement aimed at reform in Hindu society and in the Hindu religion, which in later years had Rabindranath Tagore among its followers, and

(2) The establishment in India in 1882 of the headquarters of the worldwide Theosophical Society, led at first by Elena P. Blavatsky and later by Annie Besant, which, stressing the immanence of God, published for the first time many important texts in Indian philosophy having a bearing on that doctrine.

Spiritual Teachings, by Ramakrishna

RAMAKRISHNA (1836–1886), whose real name was Gadadhar Chatto-padhaya, was a priest at the temple of Kali (worshiped as the mother of the universe) in a community near Calcutta. In a tumultuous trance, he had a vision of Kali. Successively he embraced the worship of Rama (deified hero of the epic poem *Ramayana*) and then Krishna (major figure in the *Bhagavad Gita*) as the spirit of the universe, had a vision of each, and adopted the name Ramakrishna; he became a Moslem, worshiped Allah, and had a vision of God as Allah; and he studied Christianity, was deeply affected by a painting of Jesus and Mary, and had a vision of Jesus.

In his preaching, he stressed the unity of the aim of all religions.

Ramakrishna's preaching was recorded verbatim by a disciple, Mahendra Nath Gupta. Mahendra first published his notes in the original Bengali and then provided an English version to Swami Abhedananda of New York, who revised the English version and published it as *The Gospel of Ramakrishna*. Christopher Isherwood, writer and American Vedantist, declared concerning *The Gospel of Ramakrishna* that anybody who reads it with an open mind "will have to admit that here is one of the greatest teachers and saints the world has ever known."

Of the special terms and references appearing in the selection presented here, some are explained in parentheses by the translators. The meanings of some others, which may not be self-explanatory, are as follows:

Jagannath—Literally, Lord of the Universe. The term may refer here to the annual "car festival" at Puri, India, in which may be seen the wheeled representation known in English as the "Juggernaut."

Kavira—Founder of a Vaishnava sect. He lived from 1488 to 1512.

Puranas—Ancient narratives of cosmology, legend, and history, mostly in poetic form.

Tantras—Sacred writings mainly of the Shaiva and Sakta sects.

When there is true devotion and love, one can reach God by any of the sectarian religions. The Vaishnavas, the worshippers of Krishna, will attain God in the same way as the Saktas, the worshippers of the Divine Mother or the followers of Vedanta. Those who belong to the Brahmo-Samaj, the Mahometans and Christians, will also realize God through their respective religions.

If you follow any of these paths with intense devotion, you will reach Him. If there be any mistake in the path chosen, He will correct the mistake in the long run. The man who wishes to see Jagannath may go towards the South instead of towards the North, but some one will sooner or later direct him in the right way and he will surely visit Jagannath in the end. The one thing necessary for realization is whole-hearted and whole-souled devotion to God.

Vaishnavas, Mahometans, Christians and Hindus are all longing for the same God; but they do not know that He who is Krishna is also Shiva, Divine Mother, Christ and Allah. God is One, but He has many names. The Substance is one, but is worshipped under different names according to the time, place and nationality of His worshippers. All the different Scriptures of the world speak of the same God. He who is described in the Vedas as Absolute Existence-Intelligence, Bliss or Brahman, is also described in the Tantras as Shiva, in the Puranas as Krishna, in the Koran as Allah, and in the Bible as Christ.

Yet the various sects quarrel with one another. The worshippers of Krishna, for instance, say that nothing can be achieved without worshipping Krishna; those who are devoted to the Divine Mother think that the worship of the Divine Mother is the only way to salvation; similarly, the Christians say that no one can reach heaven except through Christ; He is the only way and Christianity is the only religion, all other religions are false. This is narrow-mindedness. "My religion is true while that of others is false,"— this kind of belief is not right. It is not our business to correct the errors of other religions. He who has created the world will correct them in time. Our duty is in some way or other to realize Him.

God can be reached through many paths; each of these sectarian religions points out a path which ultimately leads to Divinity. Yes, all religions are paths, but the paths are not God. I have seen all sects and all paths. I do not care for them any more. People belonging to these sects quarrel so much! After trying all religions, I have realized that God is the Whole and I am His part; that He is the Lord and I am his servant; again I realize, He is I; I am He.

People dispute among themselves, saying: "God is personal, with form. He cannot be impersonal and formless,"—like the Vaishnavas who find fault with those who worship the Impersonal Brahman. When realization comes, then all these questions are settled. He who has seen God can tell exactly what He is like. As Kavira said: "God with form is my Mother, God without form is my Father. Whom shall I blame, whom shall I praise? The balance is even." He is with form, yet He is formless. He is personal, yet He is impersonal, and who can say what other aspects He may have! . . .

The Sat-chit-ananda (the Absolute Existence-Intelligence-Bliss) likewise has many forms. The devotee who has seen God in one aspect only, knows Him in that aspect alone. But he who has seen Him in manifold aspects is alone in a position to say with authority: "All these forms are of one God and God is multiform." He is formless and with form, and many are His forms which no one knows.

God is not only personal and with form but He can take the form of Krishna, Christ or any other Incarnation. It is true that He manifests Himself in infinite forms to fulfil the desires of His devotees. It is also true that He is formless Indivisible Existence-Intelligence-Bliss Absolute. The Vedas have described Him to be both personal, with form and attributes, and impersonal, beyond all form and attributes. Do you know how this is? He is like the infinite ocean of Absolute Existence-Intelligence-Bliss.

As in the ocean intense cold will freeze a portion of the water into ice which may float in various forms on the water, similarly intense devotion (Bhakti) may condense a portion of Divinity and make it appear in different forms. The Personal God with form exists for the sake of His Bhaktas (dualistic devotees). When the sun of wisdom rises, the block of ice melts and becomes water once more; above, below, and on every side the Infinite Being pervades. Therefore there is a prayer in the Scriptures: "O Lord, Thou art personal with form. Thou art also impersonal and formless. Thou hast manifested Thyself in a human form and hast lived in our midst, but in the Vedas Thou art described as beyond speech and mind, Unspeakable, Imperceptible and Unthinkable." But it can be said that for a certain class of Bhaktas He is eternally personal and always with form. There are places where the ice never melts; it becomes crystallized. . . .

Know that God resides in all things animate and inanimate.

Hence everything is an object of worship, be it men, beasts or birds, plants or minerals. In our relation with men all that we can do is to take heed to ourselves that we mix with good people and avoid bad company. It is true, however, that God resides in bad people also, yes, even in a tiger; but surely it does not follow that we should embrace a tiger. It may be asked: Why should we run away from a tiger when God is dwelling in that form? To this the answer is that God abiding in our hearts directs us to run away from the tiger. Why should we not obey His will? . . .

A person living in society should have a little Tamas (the spirit of resisting evil) for purposes of self-protection. But this is necessary only for outward show, its object being to prevent the wicked from doing harm to you. At the same time you should not do actual injury to another on the ground that he has done injury to you. . . . Resist not evil by causing evil in return.

Translation by Mahendra Nath Gupta and Abhedananda

Hinduism, by *Vivekananda* *(Excerpts)*

VIVEKANANDA (1863–1902), whose real name was Narendranath Datta, became a disciple of Ramakrishna. On a three-year visit to the United States and Europe, he made a profound impression with his doctrine of combined spiritual consciousness and social responsibility. Especially significant were his talks at the Parliament of Religions in Chicago in 1893.

During his travels, he founded the Vedanta movement (now active especially in California), visited William James, and lectured before the Graduate Philosophical Society of Harvard University; at about this time, he adopted the name Vivekananda (accented on the "ka" syllable), which means "Bliss Discernment."

In India, he influenced many political leaders of the emerging nation.

Vivekananda's writings in prose and poetry, as well as his addresses and reports of interviews with him, including what he said or wrote in English and translations into English of what he said or wrote in Bengali or Sanskrit, were collected and published at Mayavati, India, in seven volumes plus an index volume, in 1924–1932. The selection presented here is from the talk which Vivekananda gave on September 19, 1893, at the Parliament of Religions. Although most of the

allusions in the talk are self-explanatory, some readers may find the
following explanations useful:

Akbar—Mogul emperor (1542–1605) who conquered most of
  India.
Asoka—Emperor of India (273 to about 232 B.C.).
Sanpo—A river in Tibet, tributary of the Brahmaputra, which is
  a great river of India. Sometimes spelled "Tsanpo."

Three religions now stand in the world which have come down
to us from time prehistoric—Hinduism, Zoroastrianism and Judaism. They have all received tremendous shocks and all of them
prove by their survival their internal strength. But while Judaism
failed to absorb Christianity and was driven out of its place of
birth by its all-conquering daughter, and a handful of Parsis is all
that remains to tell the tale of their grand religion, sect after sect
arose in India and seemed to shake the religion of the Vedas to its
very foundations, but like the waters of the seashore in a tremendous earthquake it receded only for a while, only to return in an
all-absorbing flood, a thousand times more vigorous; and when
the tumult of the rush was over, these sects were all sucked in,
absorbed and assimilated into the immense body of the mother
faith.

From the high spiritual flights of the Vedanta philosophy, of
which the latest discoveries of science seem like echoes, to the low
ideas of idolatry with its multifarious mythology, the agnosticism
of the Buddhists and the atheism of the Jains, each and all have
a place in the Hindu's religion.

Where then, the question arises, where is the common centre to
which all these widely diverging radii converge? Where is the
common basis upon which all these seemingly hopeless contradictions rest? And this is the question I shall attempt to answer.

The Hindus have received their religion through revelation, the
Vedas. They hold that the Vedas are without beginning and without end. It may sound ludicrous to this audience, how a book can
be without beginning or end. But by the Vedas no books are
meant. They mean the accumulated treasury of spiritual laws
discovered by different persons in different times. Just as the law
of gravitation existed before its discovery, and would exist if all
humanity forgot it, so is it with the laws that govern the spiritual

world. The moral, ethical, and spiritual relations between soul and
soul and between individual spirits and the Father of all spirits,
were there before their discovery, and would remain even if we
forgot them.

The discoverers of these laws are called Rishis, and we honour
them as perfected beings. I am glad to tell this audience that some
of the very greatest of them were women.

Here it may be said that these laws as laws may be without
end, but they must have had a beginning. The Vedas teach us
that creation is without beginning or end. Science is said to have
proved that the sum total of cosmic energy is always the same.
Then, if there was a time when nothing existed, where was all this
manifested energy? Some say it was in a potential form in God.
In that case God is sometimes potential and sometimes kinetic,
which would make Him mutable. Everything mutable is a compound, and everything compound must undergo that change
which is called destruction. So God would die, which is absurd.
Therefore there never was a time when there was no creation.

If I may be allowed to use a simile, creation and creator are two
lines, without beginning and without end, running parallel to each
other. God is the ever-active providence, by whose power systems
after systems are being evolved out of chaos, made to run for a time
and again destroyed. This is what the Brahmin boy repeats every
day: "The sun and the moon, the Lord created like the suns and
moons of previous cycles."

Here I stand and if I shut my eyes, and try to conceive my
existence, "I," "I," "I," what is the idea before me? The idea of
a body. Am I, then, nothing but a combination of material substances? The Vedas declare "No." I am a spirit living in a body.
I am not the body. The body will die, but I shall not die. Here
am I in this body; it will fall, but I shall go on living. I had also a
past. The soul was not created, for creation means a combination
which means a certain future dissolution. If then the soul was
created, it must die. Some are born happy, enjoy perfect health,
with beautiful body, mental vigour, and all wants supplied. Others
are born miserable, some are without hands or feet, others again
are idiots, and only drag on a wretched existence. Why, if they are
all created, why does a just and merciful God create one happy
and another unhappy, why is He so partial? Nor would it mend

matters in the least to hold that those who are miserable in this life will be happy in a future one. Why should a man be miserable even here in the reign of a just and merciful God?

In the second place, the idea of a creator God does not explain the anomaly, but simply expresses the cruel fiat of an all-powerful being. There must have been causes, then, before his birth, to make a man miserable or happy and those were his past actions.

Are not all the tendencies of the mind and the body accounted for by inherited aptitude? Here are two parallel lines of existence—one of the mind, the other of matter. If matter and its transformations answer for all that we have, there is no necessity for supposing the existence of a soul. But it cannot be proved that thought has been evolved out of matter; and if a philosophical monism is inevitable, spiritual monism is certainly logical and no less desirable than a materialistic monism; but neither of these is necessary here.

We cannot deny that bodies acquire certain tendencies from heredity, but those tendencies only mean the physical configuration through which a peculiar mind alone can act in a peculiar way. There are other tendencies peculiar to a soul caused by his past actions. And a soul with a certain tendency would by the laws of affinity take birth in a body which is the fittest instrument for the display of that tendency. This is in accord with science, for science wants to explain everything by habit, and habit is got through repetitions. So repetitions are necessary to explain the natural habits of a new-born soul. And since they were not obtained in this present life, they must have come down from past lives.

There is another suggestion. Taking all these for granted, how is it that I do not remember anything of my past life? This can be easily explained. I am now speaking English. It is not my mother tongue, in fact no words of my mother tongue are now present in my consciousness, but let me try to bring them up, and they rush in. That shows that consciousness is only the surface of the mental ocean, and within its depths are stored up all our experiences. Try and struggle, they would come up and you would be conscious even of your past life.

This is direct and demonstrative evidence. Verification is the perfect proof of a theory, and here is the challenge thrown to the

world by the Rishis. We have discovered the secret by which the
very depths of the ocean of memory can be stirred up—try it and
you would get a complete reminiscence of your past life.

So then the Hindu believes that he is spirit. Him the sword
cannot pierce—him the fire cannot burn—him the water cannot
melt—him the air cannot dry. The Hindu believes that every soul
is a circle whose circumference is nowhere, but whose centre is
located in the body, and that death means the change of this
centre from body to body. Nor is the soul bound by the conditions
of matter. In its very essence, it is free, unbounded, holy, pure,
and perfect. But somehow or other it finds itself tied down to
matter, and thinks of itself as matter.

Why should the free, perfect, and pure being be thus under the
thraldom of matter, is the next question. How can the perfect soul
be deluded into the belief that it is imperfect? We have been told
that the Hindus shirk the question and say that no such question
can be there. Some thinkers want to answer it by positing one or
more quasi-perfect beings, and use big scientific names to fill up
the gap. But naming is not explaining. The question remains the
same. How can the perfect become the quasi-perfect; how can the
pure, the absolute, change even a microscopic particle of its nature?
But the Hindu is sincere. He does not want to take shelter under
sophistry. He is brave enough to face the question in a manly
fashion; and his answer is: "I do not know. I do not know how
the perfect being, the soul, came to think of itself as imperfect, as
joined to and conditioned by matter." But the fact is a fact for
all that. It is a fact in everybody's consciousness that one thinks
of oneself as the body. The Hindu does not attempt to explain
why one thinks one is the body. The answer that it is the will of
God is no explanation. This is nothing more than what the Hindu
says, "I do not know."

Well, then, the human soul is eternal and immortal, perfect and
infinite, and death means only a change of centre from one body
to another. The present is determined by our past actions, and the
future by the present. The soul will go on evolving up or reverting
back from birth to birth and death to death. But here is another
question: Is man a tiny boat in a tempest, raised one moment on
the foamy crest of a billow and dashed down into a yawning
chasm the next, rolling to and fro at the mercy of good and bad
actions—a powerless, helpless wreck in an ever-raging, ever-rush-

ing, uncompromising current of cause and effect; a little moth placed under the wheel of causation which rolls on crushing everything in its way and waits not for the widow's tears or the orphan's cry? The heart sinks at the idea, yet this is the law of Nature. Is there no hope? Is there no escape?—was the cry that went up from the bottom of the heart of despair. It reached the throne of mercy, and words of hope and consolation came down and inspired a Vedic sage, and he stood up before the world and in trumpet voice proclaimed the glad tidings: "Hear, ye children of immortal bliss! even ye that reside in higher spheres! I have found the Ancient One, who is beyond all darkness, all delusion: knowing Him alone you shall be saved from death over again."

"Children of immortal bliss"—what a sweet, what a hopeful name! Allow me to call you, brethren, by that sweet name—heirs of immortal bliss—yea, the Hindu refuses to call you sinners. Ye are the Children of God, the sharers of immortal bliss, holy and perfect beings. Ye divinities on earth—sinners! It is a sin to call a man so; it is a standing libel on human nature. Come up, O lions, and shake off the delusion that you are sheep; you are souls immortal, spirits free, blest and eternal; ye are not matter, ye are not bodies; matter is your servant, not you the servant of matter.

Thus it is that the Vedas proclaim not a dreadful combination of unforgiving laws, not an endless prison of cause and effect, but that at the head of all these laws, in and through every particle of matter and force, stands One, "By whose command the wind blows, the fire burns, the clouds rain, and death stalks upon the earth."

And what is His nature?

He is everywhere, the pure and formless One, the Almighty and the All-merciful. "Thou art our father, Thou art our mother, Thou art our beloved friend, Thou art the source of all strength; give us strength. Thou art He that beareth the burdens of the universe; help me bear the little burden of this life." Thus sang the Rishis of the Veda. And how to worship Him? Through love. "He is to be worshiped as the one beloved, dearer than everything in this and the next life."

This is the doctrine of love declared in the Vedas, and let us see how it is fully developed and taught by Krishna, whom the Hindus believe to have been God incarnate on earth.

He taught that a man ought to live in this world like a lotus leaf, which grows in water but is never moistened by water; so a man ought to live in the world—his heart to God and his hands to work.

It is good to love God for hope of reward in this or the next world, but it is better to love God for love's sake, and the prayer goes: "Lord, I do not want wealth, nor children, nor learning. If it be Thy will, I shall go from birth to birth, but grant me this, that I may love Thee without the hope of reward—love unselfishly for love's sake." One of the disciples of Krishna, the then Emperor of India, was driven from his kingdom by his enemies and had to take shelter with his queen, in a forest in the Himalayas, and there one day the queen asked him how it was that he, the most virtuous of men, should suffer so much misery. Yudhishthira answered: "Behold, my queen, the Himalayas, how grand and beautiful they are: I love them. They do not give me anything, but my nature is to love the grand, the beautiful, therefore I love them. Similarly, I love the Lord. He is the source of all beauty, of all sublimity. He is the only object to be loved; my nature is to love Him, and therefore I love. I do not pray for anything; I do not ask for anything. Let Him place me wherever He likes. I must love Him for love's sake. I cannot trade in love."

The Vedas teach that the soul is divine, only held in the bondage of matter; perfection will be reached when this bond will burst, and the word they use for it is therefore Mukti—freedom, freedom from the bonds of imperfection, freedom from death and misery.

And this bondage can only fall off through the mercy of God, and this mercy comes on the pure. So purity is the condition of His mercy. How does that mercy act? He reveals Himself to the pure heart; the pure and the stainless see God, yea even in this life. Then and then only all crookedness of the heart is made straight; then all doubt ceases. He is no more the freak of a terrible law of causation. This is the very centre, the very vital conception of Hinduism. The Hindu does not want to live upon words and theories. If there are existences beyond the ordinary sensuous existence, he wants to come face to face with them. If there is a soul in him which is not matter, if there is an all-merciful universal Soul, he will go to Him direct. He must see Him, and that alone can destroy all doubts. So the best proof a Hindu sage gives about the soul, about God, is—"I have seen the soul; I have seen

God." And that is the only condition of perfection. The Hindu religion does not consist in struggles and attempts to believe a certain doctrine or dogma, but in realising—not in believing, but in being and becoming.

Thus the whole object of their system is by constant struggle to become perfect, to become divine, to reach God and see God, and this reaching God, seeing God, becoming perfect even as the Father in Heaven is perfect, constitutes the religion of the Hindus.

And what becomes of a man when he attains perfection? He lives a life of bliss infinite. He enjoys infinite and perfect bliss, having obtained the only thing in which man ought to have pleasure, namely God, and enjoys the bliss with God.

So far all the Hindus are agreed. This is the common religion of all the sects of India; but then perfection is absolute, and the absolute cannot be two or three. It cannot have any qualities. It cannot be an individual. And so when a soul becomes perfect and absolute, it must become one with Brahman, and it would only realise the Lord as the perfection, the reality, of its own nature and existence, the existence absolute, knowledge absolute, and bliss absolute. We have often and often read this called the losing of individuality and becoming a stock or a stone.

"He jests at scars that never felt a wound."

I tell you it is nothing of the kind. If it is happiness to enjoy the consciousness of this small body, it must be greater happiness to enjoy the consciousness of two bodies, the measure of happiness increasing with the consciousness of an increasing number of bodies, the aim, the ultimate of happiness being reached when it would become a universal consciousness.

Therefore, to gain this infinite universal individuality, this miserable little prison-individuality must go. Then alone can death cease when I am one with life, then alone can misery cease when I am one with happiness itself, then alone can all errors cease when I am one with knowledge itself; and this is the necessary scientific conclusion. Science has proved to me that physical individuality is a delusion, that really my body is one little continuously changing body in an unbroken ocean of matter, and Advaita (unity) is the necessary conclusion with my other counterpart, Soul. . . .

This, brethren, is a short sketch of the religious ideas of the

Hindus. The Hindu may have failed to carry out all his plans, but if there is ever to be a universal religion, it must be one which will have no location in place or time; which will be infinite, like the God it will preach, and whose sun will shine upon the followers of Krishna and of Christ, on saints and sinners alike; which will not be Brahminic or Buddhistic, Christian or Mohammedan, but the sum total of all these, and still have infinite space for development; which in its catholicity will embrace in its infinite arms, and find a place for, every human being, from the lowest grovelling savage not far removed from the brute, to the highest man towering by the virtues of his head and heart almost above humanity, making society stand in awe of him and doubt his human nature. It will be a religion which will have no place for persecution or intolerance in its polity, which will recognise divinity in every man and woman, and whose whole scope, whose whole force, will be centred in aiding humanity to realise its own true, divine nature.

Offer such a religion and all the nations will follow you. Asoka's council was a council of the Buddhist faith. Akbar's, though more to the purpose, was only a parlour-meeting. It was reserved for America to proclaim to all quarters of the globe that the Lord is in every religion.

May He who is the Brahman of the Hindus, the Ahura-Mazda of the Zoroastrians, the Buddha of the Buddhists, the Jehovah of the Jews, the Father in Heaven of the Christians, give strength to you to carry out your noble idea! The star arose in the East; it travelled steadily towards the West, sometimes dimmed and sometimes effulgent, till it made a circuit of the world, and now it is again rising on the very horizon of the East, the borders of the Sanpo, a thousandfold more effulgent than it ever was before.

Hail, Columbia, motherland of liberty! It has been given to thee, who never dipped her hand in her neighbour's blood, who never found out that the shortest way of becoming rich was by robbing one's neighbours, it has been given to thee to march at the vanguard of civilisation with the flag of harmony.

TWENTIETH CENTURY

CONTEMPORARY INDIAN MYSTICISM IS CHARACTERIZED BY A continuance of the sophistication and cosmopolitanism introduced by Vivekananda at the end of the nineteenth century. For example, *The Aryan Path*, an influential periodical inaugurated in Bombay in 1930, contains, amid theosophical meditations, discussions of existentialist concepts, of problems in aesthetics, and of developments in psychiatry.

The two best-known twentieth-century Indian mystics are Aurobindo Ghose and Jiddu Krishnamurti.

Sonnets of Cosmic Consciousness, by Aurobindo Ghose

AUROBINDO GHOSE, born in 1872, was educated at Cambridge, returned to India in 1893, taught French and English, married in 1900 a fourteen-year-old girl (who died about twenty years later), was tried for sedition in connection with his work for Indian independence and was acquitted, and became the first major advocate of passive resistance as a national political measure.

During his year of detention (1908–1909) while awaiting trial, he practiced spiritual meditation (yoga) and achieved a mystic consciousness of the presence of God. From 1910 to his death in 1950 he lived at Pondicherry, then a French port on the east coast of southern India (now Indian territory), writing voluminously on the life of the spirit.

He established there an ashram (spiritual center) which attracted thinkers and devotees from around the world.

At various times in his life, his name was spelled in alternative ways by friends and relatives, including "Aravinda" for the given name and "Ghosh" for the family name. His followers came to refer to him as Sri Aurobindo ("Sri" is a title of deference).

His co-leader of the ashram, a Paris-born devotee known as "the Mother," was thought by many, including Aurobindo, to have supernatural powers. Aurobindo also believed that he himself had more than natural knowledge.

In 1934 Sarvepalli Radhakrishnan wrote: "Among the present-day Indian thinkers, Sri Aurobindo Ghosh is perhaps the most accomplished."

Aurobindo's principal work is *The Life Divine,* in which he taught that the mystic consciousness is open to all who are willing to persist in the proper psychological exercises. His other works include essays short and long, plays, two epics, and many short poems. The selections printed here are taken from *Last Poems,* published in 1952.

THE INDWELLING UNIVERSAL

I contain the whole world in my soul's embrace:
  To me Arcturus and Belphegor burn.
  To whatsoever living form I turn
I see my own body with another face.

All eyes that look on me are my sole eyes;
  The one heart that beats within all breasts is mine.
  The world's happiness flows through me like wine,
Its million sorrows are my agonies.

Yet all its acts are only waves that pass
  Upon my surface; inly for ever still
  Unborn I set, timeless, intangible:
All things are shadows in my tranquil glass.

My vast transcendence holds the cosmic whirl;
I am hid in it as in the sea a pearl.

THE HIDDEN PLAN

However long night's hour, I will not dream
  That the small ego and the person's mask
Are all that God reveals in our life-scheme,
  The last result of Nature's cosmic task.

A greater Presence in her bosom works;
    Long it prepares its far-epiphany:
Even in the stone and beast the godhead lurks,
    A bright Persona of eternity.

It shall burst out from the limit traced by Mind
    And make a witness of the prescient heart;
It shall reveal even in this inert blind
    Nature, long veiled in each inconscient part,

Fulfilling the occult magnificent plan,
The world-wide and immortal spirit in man.

LIBERATION

I have thrown from me the whirling dance of mind
    And stand now in the spirit's silence free;
Timeless and deathless beyond creature-kind,
    The centre of my own eternity.

I have escaped and the small self is dead;
    I am immortal, alone, ineffable;
I have gone out from the universe I made,
    And have grown nameless and immeasurable.

My mind is hushed in a wide and endless light,
    My heart a solitude of delight and peace,
My sense unsnared by touch and sound and sight,
    My body a point in white infinities.

I am the one Being's sole immobile Bliss:
No one I am, I who am all that is.

COSMIC CONSCIOUSNESS

I have wrapped the wide world in my wider self
    And Time and Space my spirit's seeing are.
I am the god and demon, ghost and elf,
    I am the wind's speed and the blazing star.

All Nature is the nursling of my care,
    I am its struggle and the eternal rest;
The world's joy thrilling runs through me, I bear
    The sorrow of millions in my lonely breast.

I have learned a close identity with all,
　Yet am by nothing bound that I become;
Carrying in me the universe's call
　I mount to my imperishable home.

I pass beyond Time and life on measureless wings,
Yet still am one with born and unborn things.

LIFE-UNITY

I housed within my heart the life of things,
　All hearts athrob in the world I felt as mine;
I shared the joy that in creation sings
　And drank its sorrow like a poignant wine.

I have felt the anger in another's breast,
　All passions poured through my world-self their waves;
One love I shared in a million bosoms expressed.
　I am the beast man slays, the beast he saves.

I spread life's burning wings of rapture and pain;
　Black fire and gold fire strove towards one bliss:
I rose by them towards a supernal plane
　Of power and love and deathless ecstasies.

A deep spiritual calm no touch can sway
Upholds the mystery of this Passion-play.

THE GOLDEN LIGHT

Thy golden Light came down into my brain
　And the grey worms of mind sun-touched became
A bright reply to Wisdom's occult plane,
　A calm illumination and a flame.

Thy golden Light came down into my throat,
　And all my speech is now a tune divine,
A paean-song of thee my single note;
　My words are drunk with the Immortal's wine.

Thy golden Light came down into my heart
　Smiting my life with Thy eternity;
Now has it grown a temple where Thou art
　And all its passions point towards only Thee.

Thy golden Light came down into my feet;
My earth is now Thy playfield and Thy seat.

THE SELF'S INFINITY

I have become what before Time I was.
  A secret touch has quieted thought and sense:
All things by the agent Mind created pass
  Into a void and mute magnificence.

My life is a silence grasped by timeless hands;
  The world is drowned in an immortal gaze.
Naked my spirit from its vestures stands;
  I am alone with my own self for space.

My heart is a centre of infinity,
  My body a dot in the soul's vast expanse.
All being's huge abyss wakes under me,
  Once screened in a gigantic Ignorance.

A momentless immensity pure and bare,
I stretch to an eternal everywhere.

THE GUEST

I have discovered my deep deathless being:
  Masked by my front of mind, immense, serene,
It meets the world with an Immortal's seeing,
  A god-spectator of the human scene.

No pain and sorrow of the heart and flesh
  Can tread that pure and voiceless sanctuary.
Danger and fear, Fate's hounds, slipping their leash
  Rend body and nerve,—the timeless Spirit is free.

Awake, God's ray and witness in my breast,
  In the undying substance of my soul
Flamelike, inscrutable the almighty Guest.
  Death nearer comes and Destiny takes her toll;

He hears the blows that shatter Nature's house:
Calm sits he, formidable, luminous.

THE MIRACLE OF BIRTH

I saw my soul a traveller through Time;
  From life to life the cosmic ways it trod,
Obscure in the depths and on the heights sublime,
  Evolving from the worm into the god.

A spark of the eternal Fire, it came
  To build a house in Matter for the Unborn.
The inconscient sunless Night received the flame,
  In the brute seed of things dumb and forlorn.

Life stirred and Thought outlined a gleaming shape
  Till on the stark inanimate earth could move,
Born to somnambulist Nature in her sleep,
  A thinking creature who can hope and love.

Still by slow steps the miracle goes on,
The Immortal's gradual birth mid mire and stone.

SELF

He said, "I am egoless, spiritual, free,"
  Then swore because his dinner was not ready.
I asked him why. He said, "It is not me,
  But the belly's hungry god who gets unsteady."

I asked him why. He said, "It is his play.
  I am unmoved within, desireless, pure.
I care not what may happen day by day."
  I questioned him, "Are you so very sure?"

He answered, "I can understand your doubt.
  But to be free is all. It does not matter
How you may kick and howl and rage and shout,
  Making a row over your daily platter.

To be aware of self is liberty,
Self I have got and, having self, am free."

The Pool of Wisdom, by Jiddu Krishnamurti (Excerpts)

In "Jiddu Krishnamurti," the given name is Krishnamurti and the family name is Jiddu. Nevertheless, this thinker is regularly known as Krishnamurti.

He was born in 1895. At the age of twelve he was already steeped in religious devotion, and he came to the attention of Annie Besant, president of the Theosophical Society, who was living in India. She helped to found the Order of the Star of the East, based on the expected coming of a great spiritual leader, and Krishnamurti, while yet in his teens, was appointed head of the order.

He spent the years of the First World War in Europe, and a part of the 1920s in the United States and other countries. He dissolved the order in 1929, at its headquarters in the Netherlands, because of the exaggerated expectations of its more impressionable members.

He presented talks in Latin America in the 1930s; in California in the 1940s; in India, Ceylon, Europe, and California in the 1950s; and in India, Europe, and California in the early 1960s. Between trips, he resides at Ojai, California.

Krishnamurti's chief message is a call to awaken to the supreme value of spiritual self-realization.

The selection printed here is taken from a talk given by him at Ommen in the Netherlands in 1926. Of the special terms used in the talk, "Nirvana" is by this time familiar to the reader of the present volume. "Moksha" means liberation.

I

What is the Kingdom of Happiness, where does it exist and how can we attain it? What does it mean, and in what manner can we conquer it? By what thoughts and by what feelings, by what control and by what steady straining, shall we attain that perfection of eternal Happiness, and enter that garden where there are many shadows that give peace, where there is beauty, tranquillity, where there is destruction of the separate self?

I want from the very outset to say that I speak in all humility, though I may perhaps use strong phrases, that I do not want you to obey blindly or listen without thought, that I speak in the sincerity which I feel and that you must listen likewise if you would properly understand. It is, as it were, that I am looking through a larger opening at the same sky that is seen by each one of you. You are perhaps looking through a smaller opening and perceiving only a part of the firmament, while perhaps I may be looking through a wider window which shows me the beauty and glory of that sky. In all friendship, in all sincerity, I invite you to my window and I ask you to quit your small opening, to come and look through a bigger opening at a more beautiful view. In that spirit only do I speak.

I would ask you to look at it, not emotionally, not sentimentally, not mesmerised by words, but with your minds, not to be carried away by mass hypnotism, not to act as one of a crowd, but to use your minds individually and think the problem out for yourselves. Where there are large crowds gathered, we find people all thinking alike; when their feelings are stirred, they are apt to be forced along a particular line laid down by the speaker who is for the moment on the platform. You will be doing a great injury, a great injustice, to yourselves if you do that. If you are carried along by the mass, you will fail to understand even that which is very simple.

The mind is the true ruler, the true helper, the true guide; but the mind is also the destroyer, if misused. The mind, when properly used, should be the guiding force for the majority of us. Though we may not be intellectual giants, we have ordinary intelligence, ordinary perception and the power to balance things. When you use the mind in this manner, you have a tremendous helper, a great power to build, to create. It gives power to direct, to control, as do the reins of a fast-running horse; and for this reason you must use your mind and not be merely emotional, if you would understand the subject that I want to put before you. . . .

To understand gives you a power, a sense of tremendous vitality. It is always necessary, essential and important to understand and not merely to feel. You must use your intelligence from the very beginning, from the very first step of the ladder, from the very lowest slopes of that mountain which we are all going to climb.

My ambition is to gain the Kingdom of Happiness, that Kingdom which must be attained by each one of us, which must be part of us, in which we must dwell eternally. It is not to be found in a particular country, or along the shores of the sea, or in some secluded spot away from humanity, or to be found on a beautiful still evening. Like the generations of old who went out to seek treasures, you must go forth in search of this Happiness. You must apply your mind and your heart to discover this hidden garden, this Kingdom of Happiness, which lies within each one of us.

It is not a Kingdom that lies far off, nor an abode for which we need make a voyage to the ends of the earth. You must find the key that opens all the gates of Heaven, all the gardens of ecstasy; and that key is your own inner Voice, that key is your intuition, and with that key you can enter and live everlastingly in that garden. If you have that Voice, clear, perfect and well-trained—the Voice that is born of many experiences, many sorrows, many ecstasies, many pleasures and many pains—if you have that Voice perfected and cultivated, and if that Voice is the only tyrant that you obey, then that Kingdom of Happiness is within the reach of every one of you.

As the river dances down to the sea—every rock causing the waters to give forth music, every pebble making a new song—at every bend of the shore there is a new enjoyment and at every fall there is a roar. As the river dances down to the sea, enjoying, having ecstasies on its way, it has but one aim, but one purpose. Though meandering, it is always sedulously seeking the shortest course to the ocean, to that sea of infinity where there is no individuality, no sense of separation, no sense of solitude and loneliness. Until that river enters into the sea, it is always an individual stream, having its own ecstasies, its own troubles, its own songs. As the river, so must you be.

As the tremendous roar of a great river is enticing, beautiful and magnificent, so is the Voice of him who is struggling towards that sea of Infinity, of Nirvana, or Moksha, of Heaven, where there is no separate self. Though you may have many experiences in going towards the sea, for you must have experiences, you, like the river, should have but one thought, one purpose, one determination—to reach that vast ocean.

So each one of us must seek, so each one of us must dance through life, must have tremendous ecstasies, great sorrows and pains and great pleasures; and the greater and stronger they are, the more quickly shall we arrive at that stage of Nirvana, that absolute oneness with Life.

When once you have drunk at the fountain of all knowledge, of all wisdom, which is Happiness, nothing else in the world will ever satisfy you. Every one who is struggling, who is living, who is dancing through life, has that Happiness in store for him. But every one who seeks that Happiness must obey that Voice whose dominion, whose power, whose authority he alone can recognise.

For many years I have searched for that Happiness, I have wandered through many climes, I have read many books, I have perhaps suffered a little; but I have always desired that Vision, that Happiness, which no pleasures of this earth can ever give. And for some months past, I have found it; for some months past I have lived in that Kingdom and that Kingdom has become real.

For this reason, I would have you breathe that scented air, that air of divinity, that scent of perfection. I would urge you to come with me, and would make you enjoy and sport yourselves in the shadows of that garden, and then it will not matter what you are, whether you are a Sannyasi—the man who has given up the world— or whether you have great possessions and live in a palace. You are then detached from everything, but you are at the same time interested in all things.

For this reason, it is important, essential that you should understand with your mind. It is so easy to weep, so easy to cry, so easy to be emotional over such things, but if you once understand with your mind, it gives you the strength to guide yourself. You are the Absolute, you are the Path, you are in every tree in that garden, in every plant, in every creature.

If you would understand, you must obey only that Voice within each one of you. If you would see that Vision, you must obey that Voice, absolutely and completely. But you must take care that that Voice is the Real Voice, that has become purified and ennobled through great experiences, great sorrows, great pains and great pleasures. That Voice will have such power, such dominion, such authority over you, that you can but obey its commands. And then you will enter that garden, enter that Kingdom of Happiness; and when once you have tasted its delights, when once you have seen the vision within, you need not be held down by anything on earth, you are at the source of eternal Happiness.

II

All wise people, all people who are searching after knowledge, must look about them and contemplate. All things, whether living or non-living, are transient. Nothing is lasting, nothing is permanent. There is birth and death; there is a rush and a jostle; there is a passing pain and a passing joy; there are cravings, unsatisfied desires, desires that can never be satisfied; there is an immense ocean of nothingness. Affections and love fade as the delicate flower of a secluded valley; there is rejoicing at birth and sorrow at death. A day of glory is as a passing cloud. All things, whether living or non-living, are subject to decay and they perish; all go down to the grave, and hence to the dust.

Wherever we look, there is this chaos, this vast unrest, this something that cannot be satisfied. And the contemplative mind that seeks the reason of things must ask, must demand, must search out and find if there is anything lasting, anything permanent, anything enduring, any resting-place.

Is there not an abode where we can be free from desires, from those desires that are unsatisfiable, where the mind can be tranquil, peaceful and composed? Is there no Eternity where nothing changes, nothing decays, nothing can fade? The wise mind contemplates, looks around, sees these transient things, and then asks: Is there not something that will last, something which is Eternal?

Those who have not found that Eternity cannot answer; and those who have found it can but answer vaguely, for each must find that which he seeks according to his evolution, according to his stage of thought and of feeling. But we can all have the same vision, we can see the same beauty, though our lips may translate it into words which convey different meanings.

Those who are wise, those who are full of age—not necessarily of the body, but full of age that comes through experience, through many sorrows, through many pains, through many pleasures and through many ecstasies—those can say, if they have once seen that vision, that there is Eternity, that it is beyond the possibility of doubt.

What then is this Vision? It is Truth. Truth is permanent, everlasting. It has no beginning and no end, it is changeless and immortal. And when you ask: "Where does it abide, where can I find it?"—I say: "You will find it only in that Kingdom of Happiness."

If you would find it, you must apply your mind and your heart to know, to seek, and to search out that Pool of Heaven which is Wisdom, which is Truth. For there, in that Kingdom, in the Holy of Holies, we must learn, we must experience, we must grow mentally and emotionally, and find that image which is the incarnation, which is the embodiment of Truth, which is Eternal. And like all people who are not satisfied by the mere world of passing glories ... by the flatteries of friends, you must seek, must brush aside the undergrowth in the forest, if you would see the clear skies of heaven. You must cut away the dead branches of life, before you can see the stars by which you can guide your way out of the forest of transient things.

In such a way must we set about it. In such a way I set about it. I saw my Eternity. I saw the source of all things, the beauty, the perfection, and the joy of all things. I tasted Immortality. What I saw can be described only from my point of view, can be given only in words that may seem to mean very little. But when you have longed for it and it has come; when once you have seen it for yourself, when once it is the very breath of your life, then you will understand, then you will know that you have tasted Immortality, that you have seen the permanent, the lasting and unchangeable.

There is nothing in the world that can give satisfaction, that can satisfy your cravings, except that Immortality, that finding of Truth. But he who would seek that Pool of Wisdom, that Kingdom of Happiness where Truth abides, must first learn to destroy self. He must first learn to appreciate and to feel the greatness of real friendship, the friendship that comes when you feel one with all things, when you have no existence apart from others; when in everything about you, through the transient, you see the Eternal; when every word, when every person, when every passing cloud and all things of earth give a new meaning, have a different song, a different pleasure, and a different Happiness. Then you will be able to enter into that Kingdom of Happiness, where there is the freshness of many breezes.

VI

"The Men of the Great Soul":
Twentieth-Century Popular
Philosophy

THE TWO MOST INFLUENTIAL NON-ACADEMIC PHILOSOPHERS OF INDIA in the twentieth century, aside from the avowed mystics, are Tagore and Gandhi. Their principal contributions consist in formulations of the bearing of soul force upon reality, in the case of Tagore; of the bearing of soul force upon conduct, in the case of Gandhi.

SOUL FORCE AND
REALITY

R ABINDRANATH TAGORE (1861–1941) WAS BORN IN CALCUTTA,
studied in London, returned to India, married in 1883,
founded a school at Bolpur in Bengal (now the Visva Bharati, a
university, at Santiniketan, near Bolpur), became India's most
popular poet, won the Nobel Prize for literature in 1913, and was
knighted in 1915. He had two sons and three daughters. His wife
died in 1902.

Tagore visited and lectured in Canada, the United States, and
South America; England and several countries of Europe, including the Soviet Union; and Turkey, Iran, Ceylon, China, and
Japan. He was in personal contact with Bergson, Croce, Einstein,
Russell, and other renowned thinkers of his period, including some
of the twentieth-century Indian thinkers represented in the present
volume.

He wrote about one hundred books of verse (mostly in Bengali,
and partly translated by himself from his own Bengali version into
English), about fifty plays (in some of which he acted the main
role when they were staged), about forty works of fiction, and
about fifteen books of essays. His best-known poems appear in
Gitanjali (Song Offerings), with an introduction by W. B. Yeats
(1913); *The Crescent Moon* (1913); and *Fruit-Gathering* (1916).
He produced some drawings and paintings, beginning about his
seventieth year, and planned and produced ballets.

Tagore's main essays and philosophical contributions available in English appear in *Sadhana, The Realisation of Life* (1913), *Personality* (1917), *Creative Unity* (1922), *The Religion of Man* (1931), and *Man* (1937).

His basic philosophical position is that of mediation. Thus, he combined the best insights not only of those who hold that God is immanent and those who hold that He is transcendent; but also of humanists, who exalt man, and of the otherworldly, who belittle man; of naturalists, who deny spirit, and of extreme partisans of spirit, who cut man off from nature; of individualists and universalists; of determinists and defenders of free will; of hedonists and ascetics; and of romanticists and realists.

Romain Rolland, referring to the Orient and the Occident, said that Tagore contributed more than anyone else toward "the union of these two hemispheres of spirit." Radhakrishnan called Tagore "the greatest figure of the Indian Renaissance."

Soul Consciousness, by Rabindranath Tagore (Excerpts)

TAGORE'S BOOK *Sadhana, The Realisation of Life*, published in 1913, was a reworking by him in English of the discourses which he had given in Bengali to the students of his school at Bolpur. The English version was used by Tagore as the basis of his lectures of 1912–13 at Harvard University. "Soul Consciousness" is the title of the second chapter of the book.

"Sadhana" has the accent on the first syllable; the "a" in that syllable is pronounced like the "a" in "far."

Facts are many, but the truth is one. The animal intelligence knows facts, the human mind has power to apprehend truth. The apple falls from the tree, the rain descends upon the earth—you can go on burdening your memory with such facts and never come to an end. But once you get hold of the law of gravitation you can dispense with the necessity of collecting facts *ad infinitum*. You have got at one truth which governs numberless facts.

This discovery of a truth is pure joy to man—it is a liberation of his mind. For, a mere fact is like a blind lane, it leads only to itself—it has no beyond. But a truth opens up a whole horizon, it leads us to the infinite.

That is the reason why, when a man like Darwin discovers some simple general truth about Biology, it does not stop there, but like a lamp shedding its light far beyond the object for which it was lighted, it illumines the whole region of human life and thought, transcending its original purpose. Thus we find that truth, while investing all facts, is not a mere aggregate of facts—it surpasses them on all sides and points to the infinite reality.

As in the region of knowledge so in that of consciousness, man must clearly realise some central truth which will give him an outlook over the widest possible field. And that is the object which the Upanishad has in view when it says, Know thine own Soul. Or, in other words, realise the one great principle of unity that there is in every man.

All our egoistic impulses, our selfish desires, obscure our true vision of the soul. For they only indicate our own narrow self. When we are conscious of our soul, we perceive the inner being that transcends our ego and has its deeper affinity with the All. . . .

To understand anything is to find in it something which is our own, and it is the discovery of ourselves outside us which makes us glad. This relation of understanding is partial, but the relation of love is complete. In love the sense of difference is obliterated and the human soul fulfils its purpose in perfection, transcending the limits of itself and reaching across the threshold of the infinite. Therefore love is the highest bliss that man can attain to, for through it alone he truly knows that he is more than himself, and that he is at one with the All.

This principle of unity which man has in his soul is ever active, establishing relations far and wide through literature, art, and science, society, statecraft, and religion. Our great Revealers are they who make manifest the true meaning of the soul by giving up self for the love of mankind. They face calumny and persecution, deprivation and death in their service of love. They live the life of the soul, not of the self, and thus they prove to us the ultimate truth of humanity. We call them *Mahatmas*, "the men of the great soul."

It is said in one of the Upanishads: It is not that thou lovest thy son because thou desirest him, but thou lovest thy son because thou desirest thine own soul. The meaning of this is, that whomsoever we love, in him we find our own soul in the highest sense. The final truth of our existence lies in this. *Paramatma*, the supreme soul, is in me, as well as in my son, and my joy in my son is the realisation of this truth. It has become quite a common-place fact, yet it is wonderful to think upon, that the joys and sorrows of our loved ones are joys and sorrows to us—nay, they are more. Why so? Because in them we have grown larger, in them we have touched that great truth which comprehends the whole universe. . . .

According to the Upanishads, the key to cosmic consciousness, to God-consciousness, is in the consciousness of the soul. To know our soul apart from the self is the first step towards the realisation of the supreme deliverance. We must know with absolute certainty that essentially we are spirit. This we can do by winning mastery over self, by rising above all pride and greed and fear, by knowing that worldly losses and physical death can take nothing away from the truth and the greatness of our soul. . . .

I have already warned my hearers, and must once more warn them against the idea that the teachers of India preached a re-nunciation of the world and of self which leads only to the blank emptiness of negation. Their aim was the realisation of the soul, or, in other words, gaining the world in perfect truth. When Jesus said, "Blessed are the meek, for they shall inherit the earth," he meant this. He proclaimed the truth that when man gets rid of his pride of self then he comes into his true inheritance. No more has he to fight his way into his position in the world; it is secure for him everywhere by the immortal right of his soul. Pride of self interferes with the proper function of the soul which is to realise itself by perfecting its union with the world and the world's God. . . .

The doctrine of deliverance that Buddha preached was the freedom from the thraldom of *Avidya*. *Avidya* is the ignorance that darkens our consciousness, and tends to limit it within the boundaries of our personal self. It is this *Avidya*, this ignorance, this limiting of consciousness that creates the hard separateness of the ego, and thus becomes the source of all pride and greed and cruelty incidental to self-seeking. When a man sleeps he is shut up within the narrow activities of his physical life. He lives, but he knows not the varied relations of his life to his surroundings,— therefore he knows not himself. So when a man lives the life of *Avidya* he is confined within his self. It is a spiritual sleep; his

consciousness is not fully awake to the highest reality that sur-
rounds him, therefore he knows not the reality of his own soul.
When he attains *Bodhi*, i.e. the awakenment from the sleep of
self to the perfection of consciousness, he becomes Buddha. . . .

Man's history is the history of his journey to the unknown in
quest of the realisation of his immortal self—his soul. Through the
rise and fall of empires, through the building up of gigantic piles
of wealth and the ruthless scattering of them upon the dust;
through the creation of vast bodies of symbols that give shape to
his dreams and aspirations, and the casting of them away like the
playthings of an outworn infancy; through his forging of magic
keys with which to unlock the mysteries of creation, and through
his throwing away of this labour of ages to go back to his workshop
and work up afresh some new form; yes, through it all man is
marching from epoch to epoch towards the fullest realisation of
his soul,—the soul which is greater than the things man accumu-
lates, the deeds he accomplishes, the theories he builds; the soul
whose onward course is never checked by death or dissolution.

Man's mistakes and failures have by no means been trifling or
small, they have strewn his path with colossal ruins; his sufferings
have been immense, like birth-pangs for a giant child; they are the
prelude of a fulfilment whose scope is infinite. Man has gone
through and is still undergoing martyrdoms in various ways, and
his institutions are the altars he has built whereto he brings his
daily sacrifices, marvellous in kind and stupendous in quantity. All
this would be absolutely unmeaning and unbearable if all along
he did not feel that deepest joy of the soul within him, which
tries its divine strength by suffering and proves its exhaustless
riches by renunciation. Yes, they are coming, the pilgrims, one
and all—coming to their true inheritance of the world, they are
ever broadening their consciousness, ever seeking a higher and
higher unity, ever approaching nearer to the one central Truth
which is all-comprehensive.

The Four Stages of Life, by Rabindranath Tagore (Excerpts)

In may 1930 Tagore delivered the Hibbert Lectures at Oxford. In the
following year the lectures were published in expanded form as a book,

The Religion of Man. "The Four Stages of Life" is the book's next-to-the-last chapter.

Manu, mentioned near the end of the chapter, is the legendary (and perhaps historical) author of a law code.

The tendency of the Indian mind has ever been towards that transcendentalism which does not hold religion to be ultimate but rather to be a means to a further end. This end consists in the perfect liberation of the individual in the universal spirit across the furthest limits of humanity itself.

Such an extreme form of mysticism may be explained to my Western readers by its analogy in science. For science may truly be described as mysticism in the realm of material knowledge. It helps us to go beyond appearances and reach the inner reality of things in principles which are abstractions; it emancipates our mind from the thraldom of the senses to the freedom of reason. . . .

The final freedom which India aspires after . . . is beyond all limits of personality, divested of all moral or aesthetic distinctions; it is the pure consciousness of Being, the ultimate reality, which has an infinite illumination of bliss. . . . In India it has been said by the yogi that through an intensive process of concentration and quietude our consciousness does reach that infinity where knowledge ceases to be knowledge, subject and object become one—a state of existence that cannot be defined.

We have our personal self. It has its desires which struggle to create a world where they could have their unrestricted activity and satisfaction. While it goes on we discover that our self-realization reaches its perfection in the abnegation of self. This fact has made us aware that the individual finds his meaning in a fundamental reality comprehending all individuals—the reality which is the moral and spiritual basis of the realm of human values. This belongs to our religion. As science is the liberation of our knowledge in the universal reason, which cannot be other than human reason, religion is the liberation of our individual personality in the universal Person who is human all the same.

The ancient explorers in psychology in India who declare that our emancipation can be carried still further into a realm where infinity is not bounded by human limitations, are not content with advancing this as a doctrine; they advocate its pursuit for the attainment of the highest goal of man. And for its sake the path of discipline has been planned which should be opened out across our life through all its stages, helping us to develop our humanity to perfection, so that we may surpass it in a finality of freedom. . . .

Our teachers in ancient India realized the soul of man as something very great indeed. They saw no end to its dignity, which found its consummation in Brahma himself. Any limited view of man would therefore be an incomplete view. He could not reach his finality as a mere Citizen or Patriot, for neither City nor Country, nor the bubble called the World, could contain his eternal soul. . . .

India has not advised us to come to a sudden stop while work is in full swing. It is true that the unending procession of the world has gone on, through its ups and downs, from the beginning of creation till to-day; but it is equally obvious that each individual's connection therewith does get finished. Must he necessarily quit it without any sense of fulfilment?

So, in the division of man's world-life which we had in India, work came in the middle, and freedom at the end. As the day is divided into morning, noon, afternoon and evening, so India had divided man's life into four parts, following the requirements of his nature. The day has the waxing and waning of its light; so has man the waxing and waning of his bodily powers. Acknowledging this, India gave a connected meaning to his life from start to finish.

First came *brahmacharya*, the period of discipline in education; then *garhasthya*, that of the world's work; then *vanaprasthya*, the retreat for the loosening of bonds; and finally *pravrajya*, the expectant awaiting of freedom across death.

We have come to look upon life as a conflict with death—the intruding enemy, not the natural ending—in impotent quarrel with which we spend every stage of it. When the time comes for youth to depart, we would hold it back by main force. When the fervour of desire slackens, we would revive it with fresh fuel of our own devising. When our sense organs weaken, we urge them to keep up their efforts. Even when our grip has relaxed we are reluctant to give up possession. We are not trained to recognize the inevitable as natural, and so cannot give up gracefully that which has to go, but needs must wait till it is snatched from us. The truth comes as conqueror only because we have lost the art of receiving it as guest. . . .

The flower must shed its petals for the sake of fruition, the fruit must drop off for the re-birth of the tree. The child leaves the refuge of the womb in order to achieve the further growth of body and mind in which consists the whole of the child life; next, the soul has to come out of this self-contained stage into the fuller life, which has varied relations with kinsman and neighbour, together with whom it forms a larger body; lastly comes the decline of the body, the weakening of desire. Enriched with its experiences, the soul now leaves the narrower life for the universal life, to which it dedicates its accumulated wisdom and itself enters into relations with the Life Eternal, so that, when finally the decaying body has come to the very end of its tether, the soul views its breaking away quite simply and without regret, in the expectation of its own entry into the Infinite.

From individual body to community, from community to universe, from universe to Infinity—this is the soul's normal progress.

Our teachers, therefore, keeping in mind the goal of this progress, did not, in life's first stage of education, prescribe merely the learning of books or things, but *brahmacharya*, the living in discipline, whereby both enjoyment and its renunciation would come with equal ease to the strengthened character. Life being a pilgrimage, with liberation in Brahma as its object, the living of it was as a spiritual exercise to be carried through its different stages, reverently and with a vigilant determination. And the pupil, from his very initiation, had this final consummation always kept in his view. . . .

After the period of such training comes the period of world-life—the life of the householder. Manu tells us: "It is not possible to discipline ourselves so effectively if out of touch with the world, as while pursuing the world-life with wisdom." That is to say, wisdom does not attain completeness except through the living of life; and discipline divorced from wisdom is not true discipline, but merely the meaningless following of custom, which is only a disguise for stupidity. . . .

The second stage of life having been thus spent, the decline of the bodily powers must be taken as a warning that it is coming to its natural end. This must not be taken dismally as a notice of dismissal to one still eager to stick to his post, but joyfully as maturity may be accepted as the stage of fulfilment.

After the infant leaves the womb, it still has to remain close to its mother for a time, remaining attached in spite of its detachment, until it can adapt itself to its new freedom. Such is the case in the third stage of life, when man though aloof from the world still remains in touch with it while preparing himself for the final stage of complete freedom. He still gives to the world from his store of wisdom and accepts its support; but this interchange is not of the same intimate character as in the stage of the householder, there being a new sense of distance.

Then at last comes a day when even such free relations have their end, and the emancipated soul steps out of all bonds to face the Supreme Soul. . . .

For this fourfold way of life India attunes man to the grand harmony of the universal, leaving no room for untrained desires of a rampant individualism to pursue their destructive career unchecked, but leading them on to their ultimate modulation in the Supreme.

SOUL FORCE AND
CONDUCT

MOHANDAS KARAMCHAND GANDHI (1869–1948) WAS BORN IN Porbandar in western India, studied at Cambridge, practiced law briefly in India, went to South Africa in 1893 in connection with litigation there, became aroused over the discrimination practiced against Indians, and remained in South Africa about twenty years campaigning, through passive resistance and civil disobedience, with eventual marked success, against the injustices suffered by the Indians.

Gandhi returned to India in 1914, and after the war promoted campaigns of passive resistance and civil disobedience against the British, aimed at the goal of Indian independence, which was achieved following World War II. Meanwhile, his wife Kasturbai, whom he had married in 1882 and who had borne him four sons, died while she was in prison with him in 1944.

In his later years, he was better known as Mahatma (Great-Soul) Gandhi than as M. K. Gandhi. He was assassinated by a Hindu who opposed his efforts to reconcile the Hindus and the Moslems.

Gandhi's writings include *Hind Swaraj or Indian Home Rule*; editorial essays published in the periodical *Young India* in the 1920s and in the periodical *Harijan* (Children of God, i.e., the Untouchables) in the 1930s and 1940s; and an autobiography, *The Story of My Experiments with Truth*.

His chief teachings were: Non-violence is the best means to

overcome oppression. Self-restraint, or non-injury, is not only a negative principle; as soul force, it entails love of neighbors. Untouchables should be liberated from their social disabilities. Sharing with those in need can provide a moral basis for the economic order. God is immanent and transcendent, the compassionate source of good.

Statements on the Nature of God, by M. K. Gandhi

IN THE ISSUES of *Young India* dated March 5, 1925, January 21, 1926, and October 11, 1928, Gandhi discussed the nature of God.

I

To me God is Truth and Love; God is ethics and morality; God is fearlessness. God is the source of Light and Life and yet He is above and beyond all these. God is conscience. He is even the atheism of the atheist. For in His boundless love God permits the atheist to live. He is the searcher of hearts. He transcends speech and reason. He knows us and our hearts better than we do ourselves. He does not take us at our word for He knows that we often do not mean it, some knowingly and others unknowingly.

He is a personal God to those who need His personal presence. He is embodied to those who need His touch. He is the purest essence. He simply Is to those who have faith. He is all things to all men. He is in us and yet above and beyond us. . . .

He cannot cease to be because hideous immoralities or inhuman brutalities are committed in His name. He is long suffering. He is patient but He is also terrible. He is the most exacting personage in the world and the world to come. He metes out the same measure to us as we mete out to our neighbours—men and brutes. With Him ignorance is no excuse. And withal He is ever forgiving for He always gives us the chance to repent.

He is the greatest democrat the world knows, for He leaves us "unfettered" to make our own choice between evil and good. He is the greatest tyrant ever known, for He often dashes the cup from our lips and under cover of free will leaves us a margin so wholly inadequate as to provide only mirth for Himself at our expense. Therefore it is that Hinduism calls it all His sport (Lila), or calls it all an illusion (Maya). We are not, He alone Is. And if we will be, we must eternally sing His praise and do His will. Let us dance to the tune of his bansi (flute), and all would be well.

II

I talk of God exactly as I believe Him to be. I believe Him to be creative as well as non-creative. This too is the result of my acceptance of a doctrine of the manyness of reality. From the platform of the Jains I prove the non-creative aspect of God, and from that of Ramanuja the creative aspect. As a matter of fact we are all thinking of the Unthinkable, describing the Indescribable, seeking to know the Unknown, and that is why our speech falters, is inadequate and even often contradictory. That is why the Vedas describe Brahman as "not this," "not this." But if He or It is not this, He or It is. If we exist, if our parents and their parents have existed, then it is proper to believe in the Parent of the whole creation. If He is not, we are nowhere. . . .

He is one and yet many; He is smaller than an atom, and bigger than the Himalayas. He is contained even in a drop of the ocean, and yet not even the seven seas can compass Him. Reason is powerless to know Him. He is beyond the reach or grasp of reason. But I need not labour the point. Faith is essential in this matter. My logic can make and unmake innumerable hypotheses. An atheist might floor me in a debate. But my faith runs so much faster than my reason that I can challenge the whole world and say, "God is, was and ever shall be."

But those who want to deny His existence are at liberty to do so. He is merciful and compassionate. He is not an earthly king needing an army to make us accept His sway. He allows us freedom, and yet His compassion commands obedience to His will. But if any one of us disdain to bow to His will, He says: "So be it. My sun will shine no less for thee, my clouds will rain no less for thee. I need not force thee to accept my sway." Of such a God let the ignorant dispute the existence. I am one of the millions of wise men who believe in Him and am never tired of bowing to Him and singing His glory.

III

There is an indefinable mysterious Power that pervades everything. I feel it, though I do not see it. It is this unseen Power which makes itself felt and yet defies all proof, because it is so unlike all that I perceive through my senses. It transcends the senses.

But it is impossible to reason out the existence of God to a limited extent. Even in ordinary affairs we know that people do not know who rules or why, and how he rules. And yet they know that there is a power that certainly rules. . . .

Law and the Law-giver are one. I may not deny the Law or the Law-giver, because I know so little about It or Him. Even as my denial or ignorance of the existence of an earthly power will avail me nothing, so will not my denial of God and His Law liberate me from its operation; whereas humble and mute acceptance of divine authority makes life's journey easier even as the acceptance of earthly rule makes life under it easier.

I do dimly perceive that whilst everything around me is ever changing, ever dying, there is underlying all that change a living power that is changeless, that holds all together, that creates, dissolves and recreates. That informing power or spirit is God. And since nothing else I see merely through the senses can or will persist, He alone is.

And is this power benevolent or malevolent? I see it is purely benevolent. For I can see that in the midst of death life persists, in the midst of untruth truth persists, in the midst of darkness light persists. Hence I gather that God is Life, Truth, Light. He is Love. He is the Supreme Good.

But He is no God who merely satisfies the intellect, if He ever does. God to be God must rule the heart and transform it. He must express Himself in every smallest act of His votary. This can only be done through a definite realization more real than the five senses can ever produce. Sense perceptions can be, often are, false and deceptive, however real they may appear to us. Where there is realization outside the senses it is infallible. It is proved not by extraneous evidence but in the transformed conduct and character of those who have felt the real presence of God within.

Such testimony is to be found in the experiences of an unbroken line of prophets and sages in all countries and climates. To reject this evidence is to deny myself.

This realization is preceded by an immovable faith. He who would in his own person test the fact of God's presence can do so by a living faith. And since faith itself cannot be proved by extraneous evidence, the safest course is to believe in the moral government of the world and therefore in the supremacy of the moral law, the law of truth and love. Exercise of faith will be the safest where there is a clear determination summarily to reject all that is contrary to Truth and Love.

I cannot account for the existence of evil by any rational method. To want to do so is to be coequal with God. I am therefore humble enough to recognize evil as such. And I call God long suffering and patient precisely because He permits evil in the world. I know that He has no evil. He is the author of it and yet untouched by it.

I know too that I shall never know God if I do not wrestle with and against evil even at the cost of life itself. I am fortified in the belief by my own humble and limited experience. The purer I try to become, the nearer I feel to be to God. How much more should I be, when my faith is not a mere apology as it is today but has become as immovable as the Himalayas and as white and bright as the snows of their peaks? . . .

Statements on Non-violence, by M. K. Gandhi

IN THE ISSUES of *Young India* dated August 8, 1920, March 9, 1922, and May 29, 1924, Gandhi discussed non-violence.

The meanings of three terms which may not be clear in the context are as follows:

Rishis—Holy men.
Satyagraha—Self-restraint, or soul force.
Swaraj—Independence.

I

I am not a visionary. I claim to be a practical idealist. The religion of non-violence is not meant merely for the rishis and saints. It is meant for the common people as well. Non-violence is the law of our species as violence is the law of the brute. The spirit lies dormant in the brute and he knows no law but that of physical might. The dignity of man requires obedience to a higher law—to the strength of the spirit.

I have therefore ventured to place before India the ancient law of self-sacrifice. For Satyagraha and its offshoots, non-co-operation and civil resistance, are nothing but new names for the law of suffering. The rishis, who discovered the law of non-violence in the midst of violence, were greater geniuses than Newton. They were themselves greater warriors than Wellington. Having themselves known the use of arms, they realized their uselessness and taught a weary world that its salvation lay not through violence but through non-violence.

Non-violence in its dynamic condition means conscious suffering. It does not mean meek submission to the will of the evil-doer, but it means the pitting of one's whole soul against the will of the tyrant. Working under this law of our being, it is possible for a single individual to defy the whole might of an unjust empire to save his honour, his religion, his soul and lay the foundation for that empire's fall or its regeneration.

And so I am not pleading for India to practise non-violence because it is weak. I want her to practise non-violence being conscious of her strength and power. No training in arms is required for realization of her strength. We seem to need it because we seem to think that we are but a lump of flesh. I want India to recognize that she has a soul that cannot perish and that can rise triumphant above every physical weakness and defy the physical combination of a whole world. . . .

If India takes up the doctrine of the sword, she may gain momentary victory. Then India will cease to be the pride of my heart. I am wedded to India because I owe my all to her. I believe absolutely that she has a mission for the world. She is not to copy Europe blindly. India's acceptance of the doctrine of the sword will be the hour of my trial. I hope I shall not be found wanting. My religion has no geographical limits. If I have a living faith in it, it will transcend my love for India herself. My life is dedicated to the service of India through the religion of non-violence which I believe to be the root of Hinduism.

II

When a person claims to be non-violent, he is expected not to be angry with one who has injured him. He will not wish him harm; he will wish him well; he will not swear at him; he will not cause him any physical hurt. He will put up with all the injury to which he is subjected by the wrong-doer. Thus non-violence is complete innocence. Complete non-violence is complete absence of ill-will against all that lives. It therefore embraces even sub-human life not excluding noxious insects or beasts. They have not been created to feed our destructive propensities. If we only knew the mind of the Creator, we should find their proper place in His creation. Non-violence is therefore in its active form goodwill towards all life. It is pure love. I read it in the Hindu Scriptures, in the Bible, in the Quran.

Non-violence is a perfect state. It is a goal towards which all mankind moves naturally though unconsciously. Man does not become divine when he personifies innocence in himself. Only then does he become truly man. In our present state we are partly men and partly beasts and in our ignorance and even arrogance say that we truly fulfil the purpose of our species, when we deliver blow for blow and develop the measure of anger required for the purpose. We pretend to believe that retaliation is the law of our being, whereas in every scripture we find that retaliation is no-where obligatory but only permissible. It is restraint that is obligatory. Retaliation is indulgence requiring elaborate regulating. Restraint is the law of our being. For, highest perfection is unattainable without highest restraint. Suffering is thus the badge of the human tribe.

The goal ever recedes from us. The greater the progress, the greater the recognition of our unworthiness. Satisfaction lies in the effort, not in the attainment. Full effort is full victory.

III

My claim to Hinduism has been rejected by some, because I believe and advocate non-violence in its extreme form. They say that I am a Christian in disguise. I have been even seriously told that I am distorting the meaning of the *Gita*, when I ascribe to that poem the teaching of unadulterated non-violence. Some of my Hindu friends tell me that killing is a duty enjoined by the *Gita* under certain circumstances.

My religion is a matter solely between my Maker and myself. If I am a Hindu, I cannot cease to be one even though I may be disowned by the whole of the Hindu population. I do however suggest that non-violence is the end of all religions.

But I have never presented to India that extreme form of

non-violence, if only because I do not regard myself fit enough to deliver that ancient message. Though my intellect has fully understood and grasped it, it has not as yet become part of my whole being. My strength lies in my asking people to do nothing that I have not tried repeatedly in my own life.

I am then asking my countrymen today to adopt non-violence as their final creed, only for the purpose of regulating the relations between the different races, and for the purpose of attaining Swaraj. Hindus and Mussulmans, Christians, Sikhs and Parsis must not settle their differences by resort to violence, and the means for the attainment of Swaraj must be non-violent. This I venture to place before India, not as a weapon of the weak, but of the strong. . . .

A nation of three hundred million people should be ashamed to have to resort to force to bring to book one hundred thousand Englishmen. To convert them, or, if you will, even to drive them out of the country, we need, not force of arms, but force of will. If we have not the latter, we shall never get the former. If we develop the force of will we shall find that we do not need the force of arms.

Acceptance of non-violence, therefore, for the purposes mentioned by me, is the most natural and the most necessary condition of our national existence. It will teach us to husband our corporate physical strength for a better purpose, instead of dissipating it, as now, in a useless fratricidal strife, in which each party is exhausted after the effort. And every armed rebellion must be an insane act unless it is backed by the nation. But almost any item of non-co-operation fully backed by the nation can achieve the aim without shedding a single drop of blood.

VII

Twentieth-Century Theories of Value, the Self, and God

TWENTIETH-CENTURY PHILOSOPHERS OF INDIA ARE ACTIVELY concerning themselves with, and are making significant contributions to, the standard technical problems which have perplexed philosophers all over the world. The problems on which contemporary Indian thinkers are especially productive are (1) God and the self and (2) value.

Outstanding thinkers in addition to those represented in this chapter include P. T. Raju, of the University of Rajasthan in Jaipur; T. M. P. Mahadevan, of Madras University; and (counting as an Indian philosopher a teacher in Pakistan, just as we herein count as an Indian philosopher A. K. Coomaraswamy, who was Ceylonese) H. D. Bhattacharya, of Dacca University.

GOD AND THE SELF

God as Ultimate Reality, by S. Radhakrishnan (Excerpts)

SARVEPALLI RADHAKRISHNAN WAS BORN IN A SMALL TOWN IN Madras Presidency in 1888 and was educated in India. From 1909 to 1949 he taught philosophy at five Indian colleges or universities and at Oxford University in England, with time out from 1931 to 1936 to serve as vice-chancellor, i.e., head, of Andhra University in what is now the State of Madras. From 1939 to 1948 he was honorary vice-chancellor of Banaras Hindu University. From 1949 to the present he has held public office: as Indian ambassador to the Soviet Union, as vice-president of India, and (since May 1962) as president of India.

In 1926 and in later years he was special lecturer at various American and British universities and in China. In 1927 he was president of the Indian Philosophical Congress. He was knighted in 1931. In the 1930s he was a member of the League of Nations International Committee on Intellectual Cooperation, and in the late 1940s and the 1950s he was active in UNESCO, serving at various times as chairman of UNESCO's executive board and as president of its General Conference. Since 1953 he has been chancellor of Delhi University.

Radhakrishnan's writings include *The Reign of Religion in Contemporary Philosophy* (1920), *Indian Philosophy* (2 volumes, 1923–1927), *The Philosophy of the Upanishads* (1924), *The Hindu View of Life* (1927), and *An Idealist View of Life* (1932), as well as two contributions (an intellectual autobiography and a reply to critics) in *The Philosophy of Sarvepalli Radhakrishnan*, edited by Paul A. Schilpp (1952), which contains descriptive and critical essays on Radhakrishnan's thought by twenty-three experts, including two who are represented in this volume (Datta and Wadia).

Radhakrishnan has, moreover, translated into English various documents included in the present volume, namely, the principal Upanishads, the *Dhammapada*, the *Bhagavad Gita*, and the Brahma or Vedanta Sutras. His translations, however, are marked by the indicia of scientific scholarship, and they have therefore been passed over in favor of more intentionally literary translations for the benefit of the presumed general readers of this volume.

Among the valuable collections which Radhakrishnan has edited is one somewhat paralleling the present volume: *A Source Book of Indian Philosophy*, edited by Radhakrishnan and Charles A. Moore (1957). Like Radhakrishnan's own translations, those selected by him and Moore for the *Source Book* are intended for the scientific scholar.

Radhakrishnan's philosophy may be summarized in four hierarchical propositions:

1. Twentieth-century man has, in large measure, lost his sense of spiritual value.

2. It is an important task of philosophy to restore to man his sense of spiritual value.

3. This is to be done by showing that science, technology, and formal religion (in all of which spiritual value seems to have sunk from view) not only are not incompatible with spiritual value, but indeed they support it.

4. That science, technology, and formal religion support spiritual value may be seen by reflecting that, in the evolution of man, modern civilization is only a way station: the next stage would seem to be a stage of spiritual consciousness, of spiritual liberation.

Professor D. S. Sarma has said of Radhakrishnan what Radhakrishnan said of Tagore: he is one of the greatest figures of the modern Hindu Renaissance. Sarma declares: "As far as the exposition of Hinduism is concerned, no teacher since the appearance of Swami Vivekananda on the platform of the World Congress of Religions at Chicago in 1893 has attracted so much attention as Professor Radhakrishnan."

The selection printed here consists of the closing sections of *An Idealist View of Life*. The allusions in this selection which are perhaps not self-explanatory may be explained as follows:

Brahma—Radhakrishnan distinguishes between Brahma, the Creator-God, and Brahman, the Absolute Spirit.

Karma—The burden of the consequences of one's past moral conduct.

RgVeda—Rig Veda. ("R" serves as a vowel in the original
Sanskrit word.)

. . . the world process with its order and creativity requires for
its explanation a creative power. For however far we may travel
backwards in space or time, we cannot jump out of space or time,
and we cannot account for space-time structure. The rationality
of the universe suggests that the creative power is mind or spirit.
There is no reason why we should identify it with vital force or
life, as Bergson suggests, and not with spirit, for spirit is the
highest we know. . . . God is not the cause in the ordinary sense,
for that would be to make him an event within the series of
events. The cause of the world creation lies in a sense outside
itself. God is prior to the world, but not in any temporal sense.
He is the logical *prius* of the world.

The ultimate creative energy of the universe is one and not
many, for nature is too closely knit to be viewed as a scene of
conflict between two or more powers. The first principle of the
universe possesses unity, consciousness and priority of existence.

The teleological argument suggests that it is creative will and
purpose. . . . In spite of signs of lack of design, there is a general
trend in evolution towards specific forms not yet realised. The
immanent purposiveness of the world is not inconsistent with the
presence of evil, ugliness and error. They are not, as McTaggart
says, "too bad to be true" or actual. Possibly they are necessary
for the greater good of the reign of law in the universe.

The overwhelming goodness of the universe requires its ordered-
ness, and that may mean acute suffering and such other facts of
experience which are seemingly irreconcilable with the purposiveness of the universe. If what we see of man's life is all there is to
see, if there is no life before the cradle or beyond the grave, possibly we may not be able to establish the preponderant goodness
of the world achieved at the cost of intense suffering and intoler-
able evil. The principles of Karma and rebirth suggest to us that
the value of the world is not in any way affected by the actuality
of evil, error and ugliness. The universe is one where these elements are transmuted into their opposites through a gradual
process. . . .

God as the universal mind working with a conscious design, who is at once the beginning of the world, the author of its order, the principle of its progress and the goal of its evolution, is not the God of religion unless we take into account the facts of religious consciousness. Our moral life tells us that God is not only the goal but the spring and sustainer of moral effort. Our spiritual experience reveals to us the fact of the supreme all-comprehensive one.

There is an affinity between the structure of the world and the mind of man. Our sense perceptions, our logical concepts, our intuitive apprehensions are not forms superinduced on reality, but are determinate forms of reality itself. From the beginning we are in the presence of givenness, something experienced. . . .

The conception of God as wisdom, love and goodness is not a mere abstract demand of thought but is the concrete reality which satisfies the religious demand. If we combine the ideas we are led to posit from the different directions of metaphysics, morals and religion, we obtain the character of God as the primordial mind, the loving redeemer and the holy judge of the universe. The Hindu conception of God as Brahma, Visnu and Siva illustrates the triple character.

Brahma is the primordial nature of God. He is the "home" of the conditions of the possibility of the world, or of the "eternal objects" in Whitehead's phrase. . . . But the thoughts of Brahma, or the primordial mind, should become the things of the world. This process of transformation of ideas into the plane of space-time is a gradual one which God assists by his power of productive and self-communicating life. . . .

God as Visnu is sacrifice. He is continuously engaged in opposing every tendency in the universe which makes for error, ugliness and evil, which are not mere abstract possibilities, but concrete forces giving reality to the cosmic strife. God pours forth the whole wealth of his love to actualise his intentions for us. He takes up the burden of helping us to resist the forces of evil, error and ugliness, and transmute them into truth, beauty and goodness. . . .

Hindu Mythology looks upon God as an eternal beggar waiting for the opening of the door that he may enter into the darkness and illumine the whole horizon of our being as with a lightning flash. It is not so much man seeking God as God seeking man. . . . God so loves the world that he gives himself to it. In communicating his nature to us, he makes us sharers in his creative power.

Human co-operation is an essential condition of the progress of the world, and the freedom of man introduces an element of uncertainty. The struggle is not a parade, nor is history a mere pageant. . . .

The sovereignty of God is indicated in the character of Siva. God acts according to fixed laws. He does not break or suspend his own laws. . . . God cannot forgive the criminal, even when he repents, for the moral order which is conceived in love and not in hatred requires that wrongdoing should have its natural consequences. . . .

The one God creates as Brahma, redeems as Visnu, and judges as Siva. These represent the three stages of the plan, the process, and the perfection. The source from which all things come, the spring by which they are sustained, and the good into which they enter are one. God loves us, creates us, and rules us. Creation, redemption and judgment are different names for the fact of God.

So far as the world is concerned, God is organic with it. It is impossible to detach God from the world. The Hindu theologian Ramanuja regards the relation of God to the world as one of soul to body. He brings out the organic and complete dependence of the world on God. . . . Life eternal which carries us beyond the limits of temporal growth may take us to the Absolute, but God is essentially bound up with the life in time. . . .

The process of the world is not a mere unfolding of what is contained in the beginning. It is not a question of mere preformation. The end of the world is not contained in the beginning, such that God might retire from the process altogether. . . . The world is in the making, and is being created constantly, and the reality of change means a plastic world and not a block universe. . . .

A God who has arranged everything at the beginning of the world and can change nothing, create nothing new is not a God at all. If the universe is truly creative, God works as a creative genius does. The end grows with the process and assumes a definite shape through the characteristics of the parts of the process. . . . God the planner acts with real genius when confronted by actual situations. . . .

While the character of God as personal love meets certain religious needs, there are others which are not fulfilled by it. In the highest spiritual experience we have the sense of rest and fulfilment, of eternity and completeness. These needs provoked from the beginning of human reflection conceptions of the Absolute as pure and passionless being which transcends the restless turmoil of the cosmic life. If God is bound up with the world, subject to the category of time, if his work is limited by the freedom of man and the conditions of existence, however infinite he may be in the quality of his life, in power, knowledge and righteousness, he is but an expression of the Absolute.

But man wants to know the truth of things in itself, in the beginning—nay, before time and before plurality, the one "breathing breathless," as the Rg Veda has it, the pure, alone and unmanifest, nothing and all things, that which transcends any definite form of expression, and yet is the basis of all expression, the one in whom all is found and yet all is lost. The great problem of the philosophy of religion has been the reconciliation of the character of the Absolute as in a sense eternally complete with the character of God as a self-determining principle manifested in a temporal development which includes nature and man. . . .

While the Absolute is pure consciousness and pure freedom and infinite possibility, it appears to be God from the point of view of the one specific possibility which has become actualised. While God is organically bound up with the universe, the Absolute is not. The world of pure being is not exhausted by the cosmic process which is only one of the ways in which the Absolute reality which transcends the series reveals itself. The Absolute is the foundation and *prius* of all actuality and possibility.

This universe is for the Absolute only one possibility. Its existence is an act of free creation. Out of the infinite possibilities open to it, this one is chosen. When we analyse our sense of freedom we find that it consists in accepting or rejecting any one of a number of possibilities presented to us. The Absolute has an infinite number of possibilities to choose from, which are all determined by its nature. It has the power of saying yes or no to any of them.

While the possible is determined by the nature of the Absolute, the actual is selected from out of the total amount of the possible, by the free activity of the Absolute without any determination whatsoever. It could have created a world different in every detail from that which is actual. If one drama is enacted and other possible ones postponed, it is due to the freedom of the Absolute. . . .

The Indian figure of lila makes the creation of the universe an

act of playfulness. Play is generally the expression of ideal possibilities. It is its own end and its own continuous reward. . . .
Though the creation of the world is an incident in the never-ending
activity of the Absolute, it satisfies a deep want in God. . . .

The Absolute is the pre-cosmic nature of God, and God is the
Absolute from the cosmic point of view.

The Meanings of "Does God Exist?" by D. M. Datta (Excerpts)

DHIRENDRA MOHAN DATTA was born in East Bengal in 1892, was edu-
cated in India, became a social worker, and taught philosophy at
Patna University and elsewhere. In 1952 he was president of the
Indian Philosophical Congress. He is now retired.

Datta is the author of *The Six Ways of Knowing* (1932), *The
Chief Currents of Contemporary Philosophy* (1950), and *The Philosophy of Mahatma Gandhi* (1953), and co-author with S. C. Chatterjee of *An Introduction to Indian Philosophy* (fifth edition, 1954).

The present selection was Datta's contribution to a volume of essays
published in 1954 in honor of A. R. Wadia. The terms in it which
may require explanation have the following meanings:

Advaita Vedanta—Non-dualistic (i.e., monistic) Vedanta, that
wing of the Vedanta philosophy which views all things as
basically of one kind.
Fallacy of composition—Fallacy in which an attribute of the
parts of something is wrongly ascribed to the whole of it
(e.g., ascribing lightness to a whole machine because each of its
parts is light).
Gautama—Author of the Nyaya Sutras (not Gautama Buddha).

It is possible to discuss a question rationally only when the
participants agree to take the words composing the question in
some fixed and identical senses. What happens, however, in
ordinary and often even in philosophical discussions, is that the
meanings of the words concerned are not explicitly stated and
agreed upon. Discussion proceeds on some vague assumption of
agreement regarding meanings. The result often is that the words
are not used in the same senses throughout the discussion. No
wonder, then, if no agreement is reached by the parties as to the
answer to the question discussed. In India we find as early as
Gautama's *Sutras* elaborate rules laid down to prevent these and

other causes of futile discussion. Later Nyaya and other systems influenced by its methods developed the very sound practice of analysing the meanings of the question to be discussed, and analysed an apparently simple question into many alternative questions, treating them separately, one by one. Contemporary Western philosophy has also begun to stress the necessity of such analysis. It is proposed to show here how important analysis of meaning is in respect of even such a simple question as "Does God exist?"

Each of the two key words in the question, namely, "God" and "exist," has many meanings. The number of possible meanings of the question is the product of the number of meanings given to the two words. If, for example, each of the two words, "God" and "exist," has three different meanings, then the question will admit to nine different interpretations, and, if all of them are formally consistent, the apparently simple question will be found to conceal nine different questions. Such analysis will reveal many instructive and interesting phenomena underlying the common arguments, agreement, and disagreement among disputants regarding the existence of God.

Different concepts of God representing the many meanings of the word can be found by comparing the notions of the important thinkers who have written in English and who have used the word. But the word has also been used as a translation of many corresponding, but not always identical, concepts expressed by words of Hebrew, Greek, Latin, Arabic, Sanskrit, Zend, Chinese, and other languages. The word "God" has thus acquired a bewildering multiplicity of meanings which cannot be exhaustively enumerated. We can select here some of the more important ones for our present purpose.

The most common meaning of God found in different religious traditions is "creator of the world." But "creation" itself means for some (e.g., Christian theologians) "making out of nothing" (i.e., making without pre-existing materials) and for others (e.g., Indian thinkers like the Naiyayikas) it means "construction out of pre-existing material." . . . In Indian philosophy, God as creator is found, from another angle, to imply either "a real active maker possessed of the creative will" (as in Nyaya and Vaisnava thought), or "a necessary spiritual factor devoid of will and change

but capable of initiating change in matter by its mere presence"
(as in Yoga), or even "a merely apparent role attributed to the
Indeterminate Reality by human ignorance for understanding the
world of appearance" (as in Advaita Vedanta).

Before proceeding further to the other important meanings of
God, let us try to understand in the light of this meaning (e.g.,
"the creator") the significance of our question, "Does God exist?"

Now, to understand this question we have to understand the
meaning of the other key word, "exist." At once we find that this
word, too, is used in many different senses in ordinary discussion,
as well as in the history of Western philosophy. English usage has
made this word a highly elastic one. In its widest sense, it may
apply, like the copula "is," to every conceivable entity. For example, we say, "A table exists in the room," "A hope or fear or
even the illusory object exists in the mind," "Non-being may exist
only in thought and not in reality," "A relation may exist between
two terms or two propositions," "Roundness exists only in round
objects," and so on. Taken in this widest sense, the question of the
"existence" of God, the creator, is of very little consequence, since
the status of God according to this meaning of "existence" may
be anything from a figment of the imagination to a real entity in
space and time.

In a narrower sense, "existence" is sometimes used as synony-
mous with "being," thus excluding "non-being." But "being" is
also a wide category within which fall the possible and the actual,
the mental and the non-mental, the subjective and the objective,
etc., and the question as to whether God, the creator, has a status
of any of these kinds would be frivolous and unimportant. In a
large number of still narrower senses (which partly overlap and
therefore are not clearly distinguishable) "existence" means something actual (as distinguished from "possible"), something having
some accidents (as distinguished from "essence"), something belonging to space or time or both (as distinguished from subsistence), something perceptible (as distinguished from the "imag-
inary"), something real (as distinguished from the "illusory"),
and the like. . . .

So far we have tried to understand the meaning of the question
"Does God exist?" by relating the . . . chief senses of "existence"
to only one sense of "God," namely, "creator of the world." But

in addition to this there are many other meanings of God . . . Allied to the idea of God as creator there are the ideas of God as the cause, the ground, and the substance of the world. . . .

Another group of allied meanings in which "God" has been used in the history of Western philosophy consists of the concepts of the Infinite (Descartes), the Most Perfect (Anselm), and the Absolute (Hegel). . . .

We may briefly consider, lastly, another group of allied conceptions of God entertained by some philosophers who frankly admit that no objective status can be claimed for such an entity, though its great value and utility cannot be denied. God is conceived by Kant, for example, as a regulative "Idea of Reason," with the help of which we can unify and organize all our empirical experiences but which cannot be said to belong to the empirical world. The question of the existence of such a God does not arise in any empirical sense of existence in the space-time world. But this does not take away the value of the idea of, and belief in, God for thought and practical life. Though devoid of empirical and objective existence, such a God may still be a proper subject for philosophical enquiry regarding its existence, in the senses of "actuality" (in so far as God may be an active principle in thought and life) and "reality" (in so far as belief in such an entity may be said to be based on uncontradicted evidence, if we find that we cannot explain our empirical experiences satisfactorily without it).

William James, again, conceives God, rather similarly, as that entity belief in which supplies man with the most perfect object that can satisfy his thought, emotion, and will in a manner that nothing else can. Pragmatically, God is also, therefore, the greatest reality for us. The question of the existence of God from this point of view would be mainly a demand for enquiring into the practical utility claimed for the idea of God. There are a few other similar ideas of God (namely, as the best principle for the organization of life, the ultimate goal of all human striving, etc.) which will have similar bearings on the question of existence.

We may conclude the discussion now with a summary of the results of this analytical investigation into the question of the existence of God: The first thing to be noted is the baffling complexity of this apparently simple question, which cannot be answered by a simple "yes" or "no" without exposing oneself to serious objections. Lest it should be thought that this hopeless situation about God paves the way for materialism, it would be well to point out that analysis of the simple question "Does matter exist?" would also be found to reveal a similarly baffling situation, since "matter" also has been conceived and used in many different ways by scientists and laymen down through the ages. The present examination shows that ordinary theism and atheism are both vague and superficial.

The second thing to note is that our ordinary notion of existence (i.e., being in space and time) is incompatible with many of the concepts of God, which latter, however, are quite consistent with other notions of existence. So, it would follow that it is wrong to demand, for example, that God must be shown to exist like tables and chairs in space and time and that otherwise God cannot be said to exist at all.

The third point worthy of notice here is that there are some senses (e.g., absolute reality) in which the existence of God would be extremely difficult to deny. The fourth thing we should note is that what makes the decision of the question of existence of God difficult is that too many of the different senses distinguished above are often combined and what is to be proved is God possessed of all such attributes. It would be easier, for example, to prove the existence of God conceived as the ultimate reality, but very difficult to show that he is also omniscient, omnipotent, benevolent, and possessed of personality. Popular notions of God combine, in different ages and countries, different sets of aspects and attributes of God. The inability to maintain any part of these composite notions does not wholly disprove the existence of God, just as the inability to demonstrate that there is a round, brown, wooden table in a room does not imply that there is no table at all in the room.

Lastly, we should note, about the advantages of this analytical method of enquiry, that it helps philosophy to remove much vagueness, ambiguity, and misconception and to avoid the waste of time that would result from the discussion of vague and meaningless questions. A clear understanding of the meaning of the question of the existence of God helps us to understand what kind of evidence would be relevant. But at the same time it must also have been evident from the above discussion that there is no end to the process of analysis of meanings. When "existence," for example, is analysed into its various alternative meanings, we cannot guarantee that these are all that is meant by the word. Besides, each of the words standing for the different meanings admits of further analysis, since there is scarcely any univocal word in any living language—scientific or non-scientific.

Moreover, it should also be realized that there is ultimately a circular process involved in analysis, since, for analysing the meanings of a given word (say *a*) we have to use other words (say, *b, c* and *d*) and, while analysing one of the latter (say *c*), we may have to use the first (i.e., *a*), and so on. Still more important, without a synthetic grasp of the total situation and its meaning analysis is apt to give only a disjointed view of things and may even lead to the fallacy of composition. These limitations of the method of analysis would disprove the exaggerated claims made by some modern Western logical empiricists who think that analysis should be the sole business of philosophy.

While philosophy should and can employ analysis to a certain extent to remove popular misconceptions, it cannot altogether avoid the background of the peoples' languages, meanings, and beliefs on which it has to draw ever and again even to carry on its own purifying mission. Even the greatest sceptics in the history of philosophy have tacitly accepted, for their destructive work, the words, meanings, and beliefs of society. It is too much, therefore, to expect that philosophy will ever be able to eliminate all confusion and solve all problems to the satisfaction of all people at all times. But what limited clarity and certainty philosophy can achieve has always been a source of benefit to the life and thought of the individual as well as of society. Analytical philosophy can very well be proud of this modest achievement.

The Concept of Liberation in Indian Philosophy, by S. C. Chatterjee (Excerpts)

Satischandra chatterjee (1876–   ), of Calcutta University, contributed this paper to a volume of essays published in 1954 in honor of A. R. Wadia. Chatterjee was president of the Indian Philosophical

Congress in 1953. His first name is sometimes given in two parts, and he is sometimes therefore listed as S. C. Chatterjee.

His books include *The Nyaya Theory of Knowledge* (1939), *The Problems of Philosophy* (1949), *The Fundamentals of Hinduism* (1950), and the book which he wrote jointly with D. M. Datta, *An Introduction to Indian Philosophy* (fifth edition, 1954).

Of the technical terms which appear in this selection, most are explained in the text. For some, the context provides an adequate clarification. A few are explained earlier in the present volume.

Indian philosophy has often been criticized as other-worldly and, therefore, pernicious in its influence on man's practical life in this world. It is said to be a philosophy of world-negation, instead of world-affirmation. It prevents the Indian mind from taking an abiding interest in the affairs of this world and keeps it dwelling incessantly on the prospect of man's liberation from bondage to the world. How far this criticism is justified in its scope and how far Indian philosophy is justifiable in its outlook on life will appear in the course of this paper.

Generally speaking, Indian philosophy recognizes four ends of human life and activity, namely, wealth (*artha*), enjoyment (*karma*), virtue (*dharma*), and liberation (*moksa*). It is only in the materialist system of the Carvakas that the last two ends have been discredited and discarded as false and fictitious. The other systems of Indian philosophy seem to agree in accepting all the four, although with some difference in the distribution of emphasis upon them. They agree, further, in holding that liberation is the highest end of man's life. While the first three ends, wealth, enjoyment and virtue, are, after all, limited and short-lived values of life, liberation is believed to be an infinite and eternal good which surpasses them all. Hence, they should be subordinated to the highest end, liberation, and a man should so regulate the pursuits of wealth, enjoyment, and virtue that they may ultimately lead to the attainment of liberation. The contrast between the Carvaka and the other main systems of Indian philosophy would thus seem to be a difference between a this-worldly materialistic philosophy and an other-worldly spiritualist philosophy, a philosophy of world-affirmation and that of world-negation.

Now, the very fact that almost all the Indian systems recognize the material values of wealth and enjoyment, and the moral value of righteousness goes to show that they are not altogether other-worldly and negativistic in their attitude to this life. It is true that they subordinate these values to liberation, which is the highest of all values for them. But is this a fair and sufficient ground for depreciating them as other-worldly and negativistic philosophy? Or, is it not a just ground for appreciating them as a more rational and balanced philosophy, in which both the physical and spiritual sides of man's life have been recognized and properly related and wisely adjusted? Any satisfactory answer to these questions requires a careful examination of the concept of liberation in Indian philosophy.

The idea of liberation is relative to that of bondage, for to be liberated means to be delivered from a previous state of bondage. Now, by bondage we generally mean an individual's subjection to such limitations as cause pain and suffering to him. For Indian thinkers the process of birth and rebirth means such limitations for an individual, for once an individual is born in this world he cannot but be liable to pain and misery, such are the very conditions of life in this world. Hence, by "bondage" Indian thinkers commonly mean the process of birth and rebirth and the consequent miseries to which an individual is subject. Accordingly, liberation means for them the stoppage of this process, or freedom from the limitations that are imposed on an individual by life in the body. It will be seen here that the body is taken to imply certain limitations for the individual, because the self of the individual is regarded as different from the body, the senses, and the mind. It is this idea that the reality of an individual being is not to be found in his body and mind that lies at the basis of the Indian systems of philosophy which aim at liberation. There is thus a general agreement among these systems with regard to the nature of the individual self and its bondage and liberation. But they differ, and sometimes widely, from one another in their specific ideas and views regarding all these matters. So, we propose to consider them more fully, one after another, and try to form a correct idea of their respective attitudes to practical life in the world.

In the Jaina philosophy the individual soul (*jiva*) is regarded as a conscious substance which is inherently perfect and has infinite potentialities within. It has the potentiality of infinite knowledge, infinite faith, infinite power, and infinite bliss. But it cannot realize its infinite potentialities and attain perfection because it is overlaid heavily with *karma*-matter which obstructs the manifestation of its omniscience and other perfections. The limitations that we find in any individual soul are thus due to the material body with which the soul has identified itself and by which its natural qualities are overpowered. These limitations mean bondage for the soul. The causes which bring about its bondage are its own past deeds done under the influence of the low passions like anger, pride, infatuation, and greed. These act like a sticky fluid and make matter-particles stick to the soul. Bondage, in the Jaina philosophy, therefore, means the fact that the individual soul, affected and infected with passions, takes up matter in accordance with its *karma* and is thereby robbed of its native perfections.

The conception of liberation in the Jaina philosophy centres round three main points, namely, right faith, right knowledge, and right conduct. The passions of anger, vanity, infatuation, and greed, which forge the fetters of the soul, spring from our ignorance about the real nature of the soul and of the world. Hence, the necessity of right knowledge or the knowledge of reality is stressed by the Jainas. Right knowledge can be obtained only by studying carefully the teachings of the omniscient teachers (*tirthankaras*) who have already attained liberation and are, therefore, qualified to lead others out of bondage. But, for a fruitful study of their teachings one should have the right attitude of faith in, and respect for, them. With an implicit faith in the competence of the teachers one should study their teachings and gain right knowledge about the soul and other things. But mere knowledge is useless unless one reforms his life in its light. Right conduct is regarded by the Jainas, therefore, as the third indispensable condition for liberation.

For the regulation of the conduct of the spiritual aspirant after liberation, Jaina philosophy elaborates a moral code which is meant for both the householder and the monk, though with different degrees of rigorousness. Even a man who lives the life of a householder in this world will attain liberation, if with perfect faith and knowledge he lives a perfectly moral life. To this end, he should observe the five great vows, and abstain, in thought, deed, and word, from intentional injury to any living being, from untruth, and from theft, self-indulgence, and greed for worldly possessions. When a person, through the harmonious development of right knowledge, faith, and conduct, succeeds in overcoming the forces of all passions and *karmas*, the soul becomes free from its bondage to matter and attains liberation. The liberated soul thus attains its inherent perfection in this life and in this world. It lives in the world a life of infinite peace and bliss, unfettered by debasing passions and evil propensities.

Of all the Indian systems, it is the Buddhist philosophy that seems to be most liable to the charge of being pessimistic and world-negating. It not only emphasizes most the evil and suffering in man's life in this world, but declares that the essential conditions of life, human and subhuman, are fraught with misery. It is man's very birth in this world that makes him subject to sufferings like disease, old age, and death. To end suffering, therefore, we are to stop the wheel of birth and death by extinguishing all the causes and forces which keep it moving on and on. It is the delusion of a separate, permanent soul in man and of a permanent substance in things and the desire to enjoy them that are responsible for his birth in the world with all its inevitable miseries. To be liberated from suffering one must extinguish his individual self and extirpate all his desires to enjoy objects of the world. Liberation, in Buddhist philosophy, thus comes to mean extinction of the individual self and of the will to live and enjoy life in any world. This is called *nirvana* and is regarded as the highest end of life for the Buddhist.

The conception of liberation in Buddhist philosophy would, on the face of it, appear as life-negating and, therefore, pernicious in its influence on practical life. Yet, a closer and more detailed examination of it may lead one to a different view. Buddhist philosophy, from of old, is divided into two main schools, namely the Hinayana and the Mahayana. The conceptions of *nirvana* which one finds in the two schools are also different in their content and in their practical bearings. This has been noted by many authoritative writers on Buddhist philosophy. Junjiro Takakusu observes: "According to the general views of the Hinayana, the state without any special condition is Nirvana, because Nirvana is perfect freedom from bondage. The Realistic School (the Sarvastivada), belonging to the Hinayana, goes a step further and assumes that selflessness, impermanence and Nirvana (flamelessness) are the true state of all things. The Nihilistic School (the Satyasiddhi) holds that all things, matter and mind, are void or unreal and that nothing exists even in Nirvana."

The Mahayana school, however, he points out, is not satisfied with the negative descriptions of the Hinayana and "explains Nirvana in affirmative terms as permanency (against worldly impermanence), and bliss (against human suffering), as self (against the selflessness of all beings), and as purity (against the pollution of human life)." . . .

On either view, it is imperative for man to reform his moral life, and control and curb his natural passions and base propensities. But to demand moral reformation, to insist upon self-purification, is not to paralyze one's practical life but to make it worthier and nobler. In so far as the two major Buddhist schools recommend different kinds of moral discipline for man, and exhort him to make all right effort for attaining the goal of *nirvana*, they cannot be accused of being pessimistic and pernicious in their outlook on life. It may also be noted here that the Hinayana school insists on man's self-effort for self-perfection more than do some of the Mahayana schools which believe in transference of merit and salvation by grace. So, whatever may be the conception of *nirvana* attained after death, it would affect a man's life in this world for better, and not for worse.

. . . According to the Nyaya-Vaisesika, the soul is a substance which has the psychical and moral qualities of cognition, pleasure, pain, and merit and demerit. But the soul in itself has no such qualities. It acquires them only in its bodily setting. So long as it is associated with the mind-body, it is inevitably subject to pain and misery. When it stands completely dissociated from its present body, however, and is not liable to be embodied again, it abides in its pure essence as an unconscious substance. As such, it is neither subject to pain and misery nor capable of experiencing pleasure and happiness. . . .

Later Naiyayikas, like Bhasarvajna and others, however, reject the older negative concept of liberation and accept the positive idea of it as that state of freedom from suffering which is also connected with the experience of happiness. It is, no doubt, a state of the pure existence of the soul. But bliss and the experience of bliss belong to the very nature of the soul. In the state of bondage the soul has no experience of its inherent bliss because of the impediments produced by its bad deeds and thoughts. When liberated, its nature becomes free from all obstructions, and there is the manifestation of its bliss and also the experience of it. Hence, liberation is at once the absolute cessation of all suffering and the unhampered experience of bliss.

. . . On the Samkhya-Yoga view, the state of liberation can be attained by the self in this life and in this world. When, with perfect insight into the nature of the self, and with perfect control over the natural passions and impulses, one practises the discipline of *yoga*, perfect concentration, he realizes his self as a spiritual reality which is above the mind-body complex and is unaffected by their affections and afflictions. He thus attains liberation in this life. This kind of liberation is called *jivanmukti*, emancipation of the soul while living in this body. After the death of the body such a soul attains what is known as *videhamukti*, emancipation of the spirit from all bodies, gross or subtle. This ensures complete and absolute freedom from all suffering for all time to come. But in both cases liberation is only the absolute cessation of all kinds of misery and not a state of joy and happiness. Where there is no pain, there can be no pleasure, because the two are relative and inseparable.

. . . According to some Mimamsakas, such as Parthasarathi Misra, since in liberation the soul is freed from its connection with the body, the senses, and the mind, it cannot have any consciousness, nor can it, therefore, enjoy bliss. Liberation is the highest good, not as a state of bliss, but as the total cessation of all suffering. It is a state in which the soul exists in its intrinsic nature as a substance with the potentiality of consciousness, but no actual consciousness. It is, therefore, a state in which there is neither pain nor pleasure, nor any specific quality of the soul. But some other Mimamsakas, such as Bhattasarvajna and others, go further and hold that in liberation there is not only the cessation of all pain but also the manifestation of eternal bliss. Hence, liberation is an experience of eternal bliss for the individual self. These two different concepts of liberation in the Mimamsa correspond very closely to those in the Nyaya-Vaisesika philosophy. . . .

According to the Advaita Vedanta of Samkara and his followers, the individual soul is, in reality, identical with *Brahman*, the Absolute. It is *maya*, ignorance, that conceals this truth from his view and makes him appear as a small individual, an ego or "I," which is identical with the body and different from the Absolute. This means bondage for the individual soul and brings upon him all the miseries of the worldly life. . . .

Now, liberation, according to the Advaita Vedanta, does not mean merely the absence of all misery that arises from the illusory sense of distinction between self and *Brahman*. It is conceived here in accordance with the Upanisads as a state of positive bliss, for liberation means identity of the self with *Brahman*, and *Brahman* is infinite, eternal bliss. . . .

In the Vaisnava schools of the Vedanta, liberation is conceived as a state of positive bliss, but for them it does not consist in the identification of the individual soul with *Brahman*—the Absolute, independent reality. The soul of man is here regarded as a finite being which is somehow different from *Brahman* but absolutely dependent on Him. It is unthinkable that the finite and dependent individual can ever be identical with *Brahman*, who is infinite and independent. But although different from *Brahman* in these respects, the individual soul is similar to Him in so far as it possesses the qualities of existence, consciousness, and bliss in common with Him. The soul is a conscious reality which is utterly different from the body, the senses, and the mind. It also has the quality of bliss hidden in it. . . .

Now, we are in a position to judge how far and in what sense, if at all, Indian philosophy is other-worldly and world-negating. The basis of this charge, as already pointed out, is that most of the Indian systems of philosophy accept the idea of liberation as the highest goal of man's life and treat his other values, pleasure, wealth, and virtue, as subordinate to it. But, as we have seen, liberation is conceived in the Indian systems either as a state of perfect and blissful existence attainable in this life or as the cessation of all suffering for the individual when freed from life in the body. In all the systems, however, the present life and the present world have received due care and recognition. Nowhere do we find the attempt made or the advice given to dismiss the world or destroy our life in it. Even those schools of Buddhist and Vedanta philosophy which deny the ultimate reality of the ordinary world of experience have not failed to recognize its practical and empirical reality.

So, also, the ideal of liberation held before man does not require him to escape from life or to destroy it. What he should do for achieving this goal is to free his life from the defects and imperfections which lead to pain and misery in the long run. These are his base passions and impulses, selfish desires, and egoistic activities. What the Indian systems really aim at is not negation of the body or of life in the world, but of the limitations and imperfections of our bodily or worldly life. The life of the liberated man is a life of self-control and self-enlightenment, or renunciation, love, and service to all. If such a man be called other-worldly, we are to say simply that it is his privilege and prerogative to be so.

Man is not a mere animal. He is a self or spirit living in an animal body. As spirit he belongs to a higher order of existence than the physical world, although as body he is only a part of nature. He is a child of the earth, but an heir to heaven. What is distinctive of man is his divine heritage, the spirit in him, and not the body which he has in common with the brute. Hence, if man is to be true to his nature, he should be more spiritualistic than materialistic and, in this sense, more other-worldly than this-worldly. For him, conquest of the lower self through self-control is a higher achievement than conquest of the world through power. What avails a man, if he conquers the whole world but loses his own self?

Every man seeks freedom from bondage of every kind. But to be free from the chains of iron and remain fettered by one's impulses and passions is not the highest goal for man. If man is to attain the highest freedom of which he is capable, then he must control his lower nature, subdue the animal in him, and live and breathe in an atmosphere of spiritual freedom. The ideal of liberation in Indian philosophy creates this atmosphere, which by reason of its high rarefaction makes that philosophy appear to some as other-worldly and world-negating.

It is true that at certain periods of its long history and in the life of some of its followers, an exclusive emphasis was laid on the ideal of liberation at the cost of the other values of man's life. The criticism that Indian philosophy is other-worldly and world-negating may have some justification with reference to such phases of its development. But in so far as it presents a balanced view of life, in which all the major values and goals of man have been given their due place, order, and importance, it need not necessarily make us wholly unworldly or other-worldly. It only corrects the one-sided emphasis on man's physical life and material well-being—the shortsightedness and selfishness that extreme worldliness involves.

VALUES

Philosophy of Values, by M. Hiriyanna (Excerpts)

M YSORE HIRIYANNA (1871–1950), EDUCATED AT MYSORE AND AT
Madras, was professor of Sanskrit and Indian philosophy at
the University of Mysore from 1917 to 1927. He was the author of
several books, including *Outlines of Indian Philosophy* (1932), *The
Essentials of Indian Philosophy* (1949), and *The Quest After Perfection* (a collection of his essays, published in 1952).

The selection presented here consists of excerpts from his essay on
the philosophy of values, first published in *The Quest After Perfection*
but prepared for inclusion in a volume of essays by various authors on
the cultural heritage of India.

Radhakrishnan has characterized Hiriyanna as "one of the significant figures of our time in Indian thought."

One of the distinguishing features of Indian Philosophy is that,
as a consequence of the pragmatic view it takes of knowledge, it
has, throughout its history, given the foremost place to values.
Indeed, they form its central theme; and questions like those of
"being" and of "knowing" come in only as a matter of course.
It may, on this account, be described as essentially a philosophy
of values.

There are various problems connected with value. For instance,
it may be asked whether we desire things because they are of
value, or whether they are of value because we desire them. For

want of space, we cannot consider such general questions here, however important and interesting they may be. We shall confine our attention to the values included in the well-known group of four, viz., *dharma* ("virtue"), *artha* ("wealth"), *kama* ("pleasure") and *moksa* ("self-realisation"). We shall only observe, in passing, that values may be either instrumental or intrinsic. . . . That is, tho' the term "value" is primarily used for the ends that are sought, often the means to their attainment are also, by courtesy, called so.

Tho' all the above four are ordinarily reckoned as values of life, a distinction is sometimes made within them, according to which only the first three are regarded so, excluding the last one of *moksa*. Early works like the *Ramayana* and the *Mahabharata*, for example, often refer to them alone. But it would be wrong to conclude therefrom that the fourth value of *moksa* was not known at the time, for these epics and other early works themselves refer to it also. In fact, the ideal of *moksa* is, at least, as old as the Upanisads. The restriction of the name of "value" to the "aggregate of three" or the *tri-varga*, as this group is designated, probably only means that the writers of the works in question address themselves chiefly to the common people, for whom the final ideal of *moksa* is of little immediate interest. Whatever the reason for this inner distinction may be, it is a convenient one; and we shall adopt it in our treatment of the subject here.

I

To take up the *tri-varga* for consideration first: In this group of three, *artha* may be said to stand for economic value; *kama*, for psychological value; and *dharma*, for moral value. To speak in the main, *artha* is an instrumental value, for it is helpful in satisfying one or other of the diverse needs of life. Their satisfaction is *kama*, which is an intrinsic value, since it does not admit of the question of "why?" We may, for example ask why we seek food; but we cannot similarly ask what for we seek the satisfaction, arising from the partaking of it. We describe it as "psychological value," not in its usual sense of subjective value in general, but in that of an end which satisfies the natural impulses of an individual as such.

These two values of *artha* and *kama* are sought not only by man, but by all sentient creatures. The only difference is that, while man can seek them knowingly, the other creatures do so instinctively. In this distinction, we find the characteristic feature of *purusarthas* or "human values," viz., that they represent ends that are *consciously* pursued. When they are sought otherwise by him, as they sometimes are, they may remain values but cease to be *purusartha*. The possibility of his seeking them unconsciously is due to the fact that man combines in himself the character of an animal and that of a self-conscious agent—that he is not merely a spiritual but also a natural being. The wants which are common to man and the lower animals and whose urge is natural, rather than spiritual, are self-preservation and the propagation of off-spring, or, as it may otherwise be stated, race-conservation.

The case is quite different as regards *dharma*, for its appeal is restricted to man. While it is virtually unknown to the lower animals, man may be said to be innately aware of it. In this consists its uniqueness as compared with the other two values of *artha* and *kama*, and we shall presently see in what respect it is superior to them. We have rendered it as "moral value"; and some forms of Indian thought, like early Buddhism, will bear us out completely here. But in others, especially the so-called orthodox systems, the connotation of the term is much wider, for they include under it not only moral but also religious values, such as are detailed in the ritualistic portions of the Veda. . . .

What is the relation of *dharma* to *artha* and *kama*? Or as *artha* is ordinarily but a means to *kama*, we may narrow the scope of our question and ask: What is the relation of *dharma* to *kama*? If *kama* stands for pleasure, as stated above, we may say that it is desired by all, for pleasure is always welcome to every one. Indeed, we cannot help desiring our own felicity. But not every thing desired is necessarily *desirable*. A sick person may long for a certain kind of food, but it may not at all be advisable for him to partake of it from the standpoint of his physical well-being. That is, *kama*, while it may be an object of desire, may not always be desirable; and, though appearing to be a true value of life, it may not really be so or may even prove to be a disvalue. How then can we distinguish these two kinds of *kama*?

To speak with reference only to the *tri-varga* which we are now considering, *dharma* furnishes the necessary criterion. That variety

of *kama* is a true value, which is in accord with the requirements
of *dharma*, but not any other. In thus helping us to discriminate
between good and bad *kama* or in rationalising it, as we might put
it, consists the superiority of *dharma*; and it is accordingly
reckoned as the highest of the three values. This conception of
dharma as a regulative principle is so important in the philosophy
of conduct that all the *sastras* and all the higher literature of India
(the latter, though only impliedly) emphasise it. That is, for
example, what Sri Krishna means when he says in the Gita:
Dharmaviruddhah kamo'smi: "I am *kama*, not at strife with
dharma."

Having considered the general nature of *dharma* and its relation
to *kama*, and therefore also to *artha* which is commonly but a
means to it, we may ask whether its function is limited to regulating the pursuit of these two values or whether it has any purpose
of its own. There are two answers to be given to this question:

(1) The popular view, and probably also the older of the two,
is that it has a purpose of its own. In this view then, *dharma* is
conceived as an instrumental value. A steadfast pursuit of it, in its
double aspect of self-regarding and other-regarding virtues, results
in one's good here as well as elsewhere; and this good—whether it
stands for worldly happiness or heavenly bliss—is, as a whole,
designated *abhyudaya* or "prosperity." . . .

(2) The other view is that *dharma* is an intrinsic value and
therefore an end in and for itself. It is maintained by some
Mimamsakas, viz., those of the Prabhakara school. They ridicule
the idea that virtue should appeal to man's interest for being
practised. That would be to look upon man as a creature of
inclination and forget that he is a moral agent, who has the power
to do what he ought and to abstain from doing what he ought not.
Further, they allege that such a view makes *dharma* not only a
means, but also a means to the admittedly inferior value of *kama*,
by making it minister to the doer's felicity. However unexception-
able the *kama* pursued may be in its nature, and whatever altruistic
activity it may incidentally involve, it finally stands for a subjective
end or, in plainer terms, for self-love.

. . . Here we have the well-known principle of practising virtue
for its own sake; and the student of Western philosophy will see
in it a general kinship with Kant's teaching of the "categorical

imperative," that is, a command about which there is nothing contingent or conditional.

This will, no doubt, appear at first as a very exalted view of *dharma* or "duty," if we may use that term instead, worthy to evoke our admiration. But it is really untenable, because it is based upon unsound psychology. It assumes that voluntary activity is possible without any end in view or, to put the same in another way, that it forms its own end (*svayam-prayojanabhuta*). But how can anything be its own consequence? To accept such a view, as Samkara observes, changes what is put forward as a "gospel of duty" into a "gospel of drudgery." For, in that case, devotion to duty would mean present toil; and dereliction of it, future evil, so that whether a person does his duty or leaves it undone, he has only trouble as his lot in life. Hence this view of *dharma* has not come to prevail. It was once for all given up in India when Mandana, a contemporary of Samkara, enunciated the principle that "nothing prompts a man to acts of will, but what is a means to some desired end."

II

So much about *tri-varga*. When we shift our standpoint from the system of the three values to that of the four (*caturvarna*) including *moksa*, we find the conception of *dharma* undergoes a profound change, which makes it superior to that in either of the above views. It continues here to be regarded as an instrumental value, as in the first of them; but the end, which it is taken to serve, is not the agent's "prosperity." It is rather the purification of one's character or, as the term used for it in Sanskrit means, "the cleansing of one's mind" (*sattva-suddhi*) by purging it of all lower or selfish impulses. This cleansing is effected through the performance of the duties for which *dharma* stands in the manner taught in the Gita, that is, without any thought whatsoever of their fruit. . . .

But it may be said that moral purification or the conquest of the lower self is too negative in its nature to prompt voluntary activity. So it is necessary to add that actually, in this view, self-conquest is only the immediate end of *dharma*, while its final aim is *moksa* or self-realisation. This is the ultimate value; and its conception is quite positive, since it consists not in merely subjugating the lower self, but also in growing into the higher one. Or, to state the same otherwise, it implies gaining the larger life, and not merely leaving the narrow life behind. This change in the older view of *dharma* or its transvaluation, viz., that it is a means to *moksa*, is already made in the Upanisads. . . .

What is the exact nature of this ultimate ideal called *moksa*? It is held by some to be a state of absolute bliss; and by others, as one merely of absence of all pain and suffering. The distinction depends upon a difference in the conception of the self in the various systems. Bliss or joy is intrinsic to it, according to some, and it therefore naturally reveals itself when the self is released from bondage. According to others, neither bliss nor its opposite belongs to the self, and it is therefore without either in the condition of *moksa* when its true nature is restored to it.

Before describing this condition further, it is necessary to briefly refer to an objection that is sure to occur to the reader at the above characterisation of *moksa* in terms of pleasure and absence of pain, viz., that the ideal is hedonistic—a view which is now regarded as psychologically quite faulty. This is an objection which, on a superficial view, applies to the whole of the Indian theory of value; but whatever the answer to that general objection may be, the charge of hedonism does not, in the least, affect the conception of the ultimate value with which we are now concerned. For the pleasure for which it stands should be unmixed, and there should be no lapse from it when it is once attained—conditions which the kind of pleasure the hedonist has in view does not, and is not meant to, satisfy. In fact, *moksa* means absolute or unconditioned bliss (or, alternatively, absence of suffering), which is vastly different from the pleasure that hedonism holds to be the supreme end of life. . . .

We have mentioned two aids to the attainment of the goal, pursuing the good and acquiring a knowledge of the true self. Corresponding to these, the life of the knower, broadly speaking, will be characterised by two features. In the first place, it will be entirely free from the tyranny of the egoistic self, and therefore also free from the feverish activity for gratifying personal desires which can never be completely gratified. In the second place, it will be marked by an unshakable conviction in the unity of all, and consequently by love for others—love for them, not as equals but as essentially one with oneself. . . .

There is in this regard the magnanimous example of Buddha who, we may remark by the way, is only one instance among several that have appeared in the spiritual history of India. Hence, though the final aim of life or the ultimate value is here stated to be self-realisation, it is really very much more, for it also signifies doing one's utmost to secure universal good.

We have described the state of *moksa* from the standpoint of what is called *jivanmukti* or "liberation while one is still alive," for it is sure to make a better appeal to the modern mind. This ideal, however, is not accepted in all the systems, but only in some like the Advaita, Sankhya-Yoga and Buddhism. The others insist that spiritual freedom will not actually be attained until after physical death. It is known as *videhamukti*. But even these systems may be said to admit *jivanmukti* in fact, though not in name, for they postulate final release in the case of an enlightened person as soon as he leaves his physical body, implying thereby that there is nothing more to be done by him for attaining *moksa*. The distinction between the two views reduces itself finally to this: whether or not the discipline prescribed for the spiritual aspirant should as such (that is, under a sense of constraint) continue in the interval between the dawn of true knowledge and the moment of physical death. According to those who do not accept the ideal of *jivan-mukti*, it should continue, while according to the rest, it need not.

The question that now remains to ask is whether such an ideal can be achieved at all. In one sense, the question is not legitimate because *moksa*, standing as it does for a progressive attainment, is being realised at every stage. But it may be taken to mean whether the process of self-realisation is an endless one or has a culminating stage; and if it has such a stage, whether it is attainable. All the Indian systems, including the non-Vedic ones, are of *opinion* that this process is directed to a definite goal, and that that goal can assuredly be achieved. According to them, the evil of *samsara* or bondage carries with it the seeds of its own destruction, and it is sooner or later bound to be superseded by the good.

In other words, none of the Indian schools is finally pessimistic, and the present-day criticism that they are "gospels of woe" is entirely wrong. We have more than one interesting indication in the Sanskrit language of this faith of the Indian in the ultimate goodness and rationality of the world. The Sanskrit word *sat*, as noticed by Max Müller long ago, means not only "the real" but

also "the good." Similarly, the word *bhavya*, we may add, means
not only "what will happen in the future" but also "what is
auspicious," implying that the best is yet to be.

Intention in Art, by Ananda K. Coomaraswamy (Excerpts)

ANANDA KENTISH COOMARASWAMY (1877–1947) was born in Co-
lombo, Ceylon, and was educated in England. From 1917 to the time
of his death, he was Fellow for Research in Indian, Persian, and
Muhammadan Art at the Museum of Fine Arts in Boston. He married
D. Luisa Runstein, and they had one son. The name "Coomaraswamy"
is accented on the "ma" and "swa" syllables.

Coomaraswamy lectured widely on art in general and on Oriental
and Indian art in particular, as well as on more general subjects, both
political and social. He published more than a dozen books, including
The Indian Craftsman (1909), *Buddha and the Gospel of Buddhism*
(1916), *The Dance of Shiva* (1918, reprinted three times in the
1940s and 1950s, once with an introduction by Romain Rolland),
Introduction to Indian Art (1923), *A New Approach to the Vedas*
(1933), *The Transformation of Nature in Art* (1934), *Figures of
Speech or Figures of Thought* (1946), and *Am I My Brother's
Keeper?* (1947).

The selection printed here consists of excerpts from an open letter
to the authors of the article "Intention" in the *Dictionary of World
Literature* (New York: Philosophical Library, 1943), edited by Joseph
T. Shipley. The open letter appeared first in the *American Bookman*,
Volume I, Winter 1944, and was reprinted in *Figures of Speech or
Figures of Thought*. It is reproduced here from the latter source.

Messrs. Monroe C. Beardsley
and W. K. Wimsatt, Jr.

Gentlemen:

You, Sirs, in the *Dictionary of World Literature*, discussing
"Intention," do not deny that an author may or may not succeed
in his purpose, but do say that his success or failure, in this respect,
is indemonstrable. You proceed to attack the criticism of a work
of art in terms of the relation between intention and result; in the

course of this attack you say that to pretend "that the author's aim can be detected internally in the work even where it is not realised . . . is merely a self-contradictory proposition"; and you conclude the paragraph as follows: "A work may indeed fall short of what the critic thinks should have been intended, or what the author was in the habit of doing, or what one might expect him to do, but there can be no evidence, internal or external, that the author had conceived something which he did not execute."

In our subsequent correspondence you say that even if a criticism could be made in terms of the relation of purpose to result, this would be irrelevant, because the critic's main task is "to evaluate the work itself"; and you make it very clear that this "evaluation" has much more to do with "what the work ought to be" than with "what the author intended it to be." In the same connection you cite the case of a school teacher who proposes to correct a pupil's composition; the pupil maintains that what he wrote is what he "meant to say"; the teacher then says, "Well, if you meant to say so and so, all I can say is that you should not have meant it." You add that there are "good intentions and poor intentions," and that intention *per se* is no criterion of the *worth* of the poem.

I not only dissent from all but the last of these propositions, but also feel that you have not done justice to the principle of criticism that you attack; and, finally, that you confuse "criticism" with "evaluation," overlooking that "values" are present only in the end to which the work is ordered, while "criticism" is supposed to be disinterested. My "intention" is to defend the method of criticism in terms of the ratio $\dfrac{\text{intention}}{\text{result}}$, which I should also state as that of $\dfrac{\text{concept}}{\text{product}}$ or $\dfrac{\text{forma}}{\text{figura}}$ or $\dfrac{\text{art of the artist}}{\text{artifact}}$. If, in the following paragraphs, I cite some of the older writers, it is not so much as authorities by whom the problem is to be settled for us, as it is to make it clear in what established sense the word "intention" has been used, and to give to the corresponding method of criticism at least its proper historical place.

In the Western world, criticism that takes account of intention begins, I think, with Plato. He says: "If we are to be connoisseurs of poems we must know in each case in what respect they do not miss their mark. For if one does not know the essence of the work, what it intends, and of what it is an image, he will hardly be able to decide whether its intention (*boulesis*) has or has not found its mark. One who does not know what would be correct in it [but only knows what pleases him], will be unable to judge whether the poem is good or bad" (*Laws* 668 C, with parenthesis from B). . . .

You, Sirs, say in our correspondence, that you are "concerned only with poetic, dramatic and literary works." Whatever I say is intended to apply to such works, but also to works of art of any kind, since I hold with Plato that "the productions of all arts are kinds of poetry ('making'), and their craftsmen are all poets" (*Symposium* 205 C), and that the orator is just like all other craftsmen, since none of them works at random, but with a view to some end (*Gorgias* 503 E). I cannot admit that different principles of criticism are applicable to different kinds of art, but only that different kinds of knowledge are required if the common critical method is to be applied to works of art of different kinds.

The most general case possible of the judgment of a work of art in terms of the ratio of intention to result arises in connection with the judgment of the world itself. When God is said to have considered his finished work and found it "good," the judgment was surely made in these terms; what he had *willed*, that he had *done*. The ratio in this case is that of the *Kosmos noetos* to the *Kosmos aisthetikos*, invisible pattern to material imitation. In just the same way the human maker "sees within what he has to do without"; and if he finds his product satisfactory (Skr. *alam-krta*, "ornamental" in the primary sense of "complemented") it can be only because it seems to have fulfilled his intention. You, Sirs, in your article and our correspondence have agreed that "in most cases the author understands his own work better than anyone else, and in this sense the more the critic's understanding approximates the author's, the better his criticism will be," and thus essentially with my own assertion that the critic should "so place himself at the original author's standpoint as to see and judge with his eyes."

If, on the other hand, the critic goes about to "evaluate" a work that actually fulfills its author's intention and promise, in terms of what he thinks it "should have been," it is not the work but the intention that he is criticising. I shall agree with you that, in general, the critic has a right and even a duty to evaluate in this sense; it is, indeed, from just this point of view that Plato sets up his censorship (*Rep.* 379, 401, 607, etc.). But this is his right and duty, not as a critic of art, but as a critic of morals; for the present we are considering only the work of art as such, and must not confuse art with prudence. In criticising the work of art *as such*, the critic must not go behind it, to wish it had never been undertaken; his business as an art critic is to decide whether or not the artist has made a good job of the work he undertook to do. In any case, such a moral judgment is valid only if the intention is really open to moral objection, the critic being presumed to judge by higher standards than the artist. . . .

At this point it may be helpful to refer to some specific examples of authors' own statements of their "intentions." Avencebrol says, in his *Fons Vitae* (I. 9), Nostra *intentio* fuit speculari de materia universali et forma universali. Again (ib. II. i) he asks, Quae est *intentio* de qua debemus agere in hoc tractatu? and answers, Nostra *intentio* est invenire materiam et formam in substantiis simplicibus. On the other hand, the disciple (here, in effect the writer's "patron," critic and reader) says, Jam *promisisti* quod in hoc secundo tractatu loquereris de materia corporali. . . . *Ergo comple* hoc et apertissime explana (ib. II. i).

Hence the master's "promise" is surely adequate "external evidence" of his intention; and it is obvious that the master himself might either consider that he had actually fulfilled his promise in the extant work, or otherwise might have said, "I am afraid I come a little short of what I undertook." Or, in answer to some question put by the pupil, he might either say, "I have nothing to add, you must think it out for yourself," or "Perhaps I did not make myself quite clear on that point." In the latter case an amended statement would not, as you suggest, imply that "the author has thought of something better to say," but that he has found a better way of expressing what he had originally intended. On his part, the disciple might have justly complained if the master had actually failed to "fulfill his promise and very clearly set forth" the proposed matter.

In much the same way, when Witelo, introducing his *Liber de Intelligentiis*, says: Summa in hoc capitulo *nostrae intentionis est*, rerum naturalium difficiliora breviter colligere, etc., criticism will naturally be concerned, not with the propriety of the subject matter, but with the degree of the author's success in presenting it. . . .

Whenever, in fact, an author provides us with a preface, argument or preamble, we are given a criterion by which to judge his performance. On the other hand, he may tell us *post factum*, what was the intention of the work. When Dante says of the *Commedia* that "the purpose of the whole work is to remove those who are living in this life from the state of wretchedness and to lead them to the state of blessedness," or when Asvaghosa at the end of his *Saundarananda* tells us in so many words that the poem was "composed, not for the sake of giving pleasure, but for the sake of giving peace," such an advertisement is perfectly good "external evidence" of the author's meaning (unless we assume him to have been a fool or liar) . . .

You, Sirs, regard it as very difficult or even impossible to distinguish an author's intention from what he actually says. . . . and I say that we can never find fault unless we can distinguish what the author meant to say from what he actually said. We can certainly do that in a minor way if we detect a slip of the pen; just as, also, in the case of a misprint we can distinguish what the author meant to say from what he is made to say. Or suppose an Englishman writing in French; the intelligent French reader may see very well what the author meant to say, however awkwardly he says it; and if he cannot, he can very well be called undiscriminating or uncritical.

However, it is not only with such minor faults that we are concerned, but rather with the detection of real internal conflict or inconsistency as between the matter and the form of work. I assert that the critic cannot know if a thing has been well said if he does not know what was to be said. You, in correspondence, "deny that it is ever possible to prove from external evidence that the author intended the work to mean something that it doesn't actually mean." What then do we mean by "proof"? Outside of the field of pure mathematics, are there any "absolute proofs"? Do we know that the "laws of science" on which we rely so implicitly are only statements of statistical probability? We do not *know* that the sun will rise to-morrow, but have sufficient reason to expect that it will; our life is governed by assurances, never by "proofs." It is, then, quibbling to assert that there can be no external "proof" of an author's intention. . . .

I say, then, that the critic *can* know what was in the author's mind, if he wants to, and within the limits of what is ordinarily meant by certainty, or "right opinion." But this implies work, and not a mere sensibility. "Wer den Dichter will verstehen, muss in Dichters Lande gehen." What "land" is that? Not necessarily, though often advantageously, a physical territory, but still another world of character and another spiritual environment. To begin with, the critic must both know the author's subject and delight in it—*sine desiderio mens non intelligit*—, yes, and believe in it— *crede ut intelligas*. It is laughable if one who is ignorant of and indifferent to, if not scornful of, metaphysics, and unfamiliar with its figures of thought, proceeds to criticise "Dante as literature" or calls the Brahmanas "inane" or "unintelligible." Is it not inconceivable that a "good" translation of Plato could be made by any nominalist, or by anyone not so vitally interested in his doctrine as sometimes to be able even to "read between the lines" of what is actually said?

Is it not just this that Dante demands when he says,

> O voi che avete gl'intelletti sani,
> Mirate la dottrina che s'asconde
> Sotto il velame degli versi strani?
> *Inferno* IX. 61–63

I assert, from personal experience, that one can so identify oneself with a subject and point of view that one can foresee what will be said next, and even make deductions which one afterwards meets with as explicit statements in some other part of the book or in a work belonging to the same school of thought. If, in fact, one cannot do this, textual emendation would be possible only on grammatical or metrical grounds. I fully agree that interpretation in terms of what an author "must have thought" can be very dangerous. But when? Only if the critic has identified, not himself with the author, but the author with himself, and is really telling us, not what the author must have meant but what he would have liked the author to mean, i.e., what in his opinion the author "ought to have meant."

This last is a matter about which a literary critic, as such, can hold no views, because he is setting about to criticise an existing work, and not its antecedent causes. If the critic does presume to tell us what an author ought to have meant, this is a condemnation of the author's intentions, which existed before the work was made accessible to anyone. We can, and have a right to, criticise intentions; but we cannot criticise an actual performance *ante factum*. . . .

I fully agree with you that "intention *per se*" is no criterion of the worth of a poem (even if "worth" is to be taken amorally); in the same way that a good intention is no guarantee of actually good conduct; in both cases there must be, not only a will, but also the power to realise the purpose. On the other hand, an evil intention need not result in a poor work of art; if it miscarries, it can be ridiculed or ignored; if it succeeds, the artist (whether a pornographer or a skilful murderer) is liable to punishment. A Dictator's strategy or oratory is not necessarily bad as such merely because we disapprove of his aims; it may, in fact, be much "better" than ours, however excellent our own intentions; and if it is worse, we cannot call him a bad man on that account, but only a bad soldier or poor speaker.

All making or doing has reasons or ends; but in either case there may, for a great variety of reasons, be a failure to hit the mark. It would be absurd to pretend that we do not know what the archer intends, or to say that we must not call him a poor shooter if he misses. The "sin" (properly defined as "any departure from the order to the end") may be either artistic or moral. In the present discussion, I think, our common intention was to consider only artistic virtue or error. It is precisely from this point of view that I cannot understand your terms "what the work of art ought to be," or "should be" as an "ought" to be distinguished from the gerundive—*faciendum*—implied in the author's intention to produce a work that shall be as good as possible *of its kind*. He cannot have in view to produce a work that is simply "beautiful" or "good," because all making by art is occasional and can be directed only to particular and not to universal ends. The only possible literary criticism of an already existing and extant work is one in terms of the ratio of intention to result. No other form of criticism can be called objective, because there are no degrees of perfection, and we cannot say that one work of art, as such, is "worth" more than another, if both are perfect in their kind. We can, however, go behind the work of art itself, as if it were not yet extant, to enquire whether or not it "ought" ever to have been undertaken at all, and so also decide whether or not it is "worth" preserving. That may be, and I hold that it is, a very proper enquiry. But it is not literary criticism nor the criticism of any work of art *qua* work of art; it is a criticism of the author's intentions.

The Place of Philosophy in Modern Society, by A. R. Wadia (Excerpts)

ARDESHIR RUTTONJI WADIA, born in 1888, was educated in India and in England, taught philosophy at the University of Mysore and elsewhere, was president of the Indian Philosophical Congress in 1930, was principal of Victoria College at Gwalior in west central India from 1946 to 1949, has been active in Rotary International, and is now director of the Tata Institute of Social Sciences in Bombay. His writings include *The Ethics of Feminism* (1923); *The Life and Teachings of Zoroaster* (1946); *Religion as a Quest for Values* (1950); and *The Philosophy of Mahatma Gandhi, and Other Essays, Philosophical and Sociological* (1958).

The selection presented here, from the last-named book, was read before the Indian Philosophical Congress in 1950.

Of the terms appearing in this selection which are not self-explanatory or explained by the context, some are explained earlier in the present volume. The following explanations, partly repetitive, may be useful to some readers:

Gandhiji—An affectionate form of "Gandhi."
Harijans—Untouchables.
Maya—Illusion.
Sadhana—A trance in which, through deep meditation on the self, one realizes the unity of one's own self with all selves, or with the one world soul.
Sruti—Traditional scriptures.
Tat tvam asi—That art thou.

The very idea of discussing the place of the philosopher in modern society at the Silver Jubilee Session of the Indian Philosophical Congress may appear to be odd, for it implies that his place and his importance are both questionable, whereas in any cultured society, and most so in India with her hoary philosophical traditions, it should be taken for granted that without philosophy there can be no culture. Even to suggest that modern society can do without philosophy would be to cast doubt on the cultural value of our modern society. Yet in the fitness of things it may not be undesirable to take stock of what the philosophers may be presumed to have done in the space of twenty-five years, especially in India where life has been shaken to its foundations by her contact with the new virile ideas of the West and the impact of a personality like Gandhiji's, which while challenging the Western civilization has let loose forces which have transformed India from being a socially conservative and politically impotent country into a country pulsating with a new political vigour and a new social conscience, seeking to elevate her womanhood and the Harijans after the neglect of centuries.

One might expect that in such a great revolution the philosopher could not but have played his part, and yet in this very Congress last year in the symposium on *Philosophy and Sadhana* views were expressed which practically cold-storage philosophy. It was argued by Dr. Chubb that Truth could not be attained by reason, that philosophy was only an agitation of the mind, that philosophy had turned jailor and that "more and more intelligent persons should break out of the prison house of philosophy," and that the place of philosophy had to be taken by some mystic Silence, repudiating the claims of Reason. Professor Dandekar put forth substantially the same plea, though in a more temperate vein. He developed the paradox that "The truth is: we know it not, yet we know it," i.e., we know it not through reason, but through some mystic intuition. Both Dr. Chubb and Professor Dandekar do not mince words in their condemnation of the Western approach to philosophy or in their desire to revive the old Upaniṣadic way of learning Truth through the *Sruti* or the grace of some illumined teacher.

Surely in such a climate it is neither impertinent nor irrelevant to review the worth of philosophy from the standpoint of modern society. But in this review we cannot be blind to the fact that there is some fundamental difference in the way philosophic truth is approached and envisaged in India and in Europe-America. Both look upon philosophy as the search for Truth, but the Europeans from the Greeks downwards have looked upon it as knowledge, disinterested knowledge apart from any practical axe to grind, and they have looked to reason as its main, and even perhaps the only, instrument, though the very finitude of reason has put an inevitable limit to the attainment of knowledge whether in its totality or its fullness.

But this has led to a wonderful development of science, which superficially has led people to talk of Western philosophy and culture as materialistic without caring to probe a little deeper into the inner significance of the development of philosophy in the West. . . . there is a will to raise the lowest man to something better, to raise his standard of life, to make him immune from epidemics, to develop his mind and bring the treasures of literature and science to his door. This may be called materialism by those who despair of life here and now and seek compensation in dreaming of better worlds hereafter and elsewhere. But with greater justice it could be spoken of as the spiritualization of the material. In short, philosophy in the West has not sought to run away from the shortcomings of life, rather it has sought to overcome them.

In India on the other hand philosophy has developed on appreciably different lines. Apart from the joyousness of the Vedas, from the days of the earliest Upanisadic seers there has been a persistent consciousness of the ills of life and hence the attempt not merely to know the Ultimate but to realize it as a means to rid one's self of the cycle of births and deaths. . . .

So far as India is concerned Dr. Paul Brunton hazards an interesting theory: "A fiercely hot and depressingly humid country, whose climate causes everyone to shun physical effort, led man naturally to search for part of his satisfaction in contemplative thought and inward life." Many of us who have had an experience of the gruelling heat of our plains and have delighted in the cool night breezes, just lying flat and relaxed and gazing at the eternal beauty of the stars, are likely to accept Dr. Brunton's theory. And those of us who have not the energy even to open or close their eyelids may legitimately flatter themselves that they are at least on the lowest rung of the ladder which will lead them ultimately to *mukti* (liberation).

However reasonable such an explanation may appear to be on the surface, it does not justify this studied distrust of things of sense and looking only within and seeking knowledge only in Silence. So long as ideas of this type prevail there is sufficient justification for the contempt in which our younger generation holds philosophical studies and for the paucity of students in our philosophy classes. There is a widespread feeling that India has had too much of philosophy and it would be better to have less of it, if not nothing of it. Acharya P. C. Ray years ago said this to me and very recently a Rotarian in proposing a vote of thanks to a speaker on philosophy gently hinted that India should do without philosophy. For this reason too the subject of this symposium is justifiable.

Whatever may be the shortcomings of Western philosophy it has had at least one merit, that it has brought us back to solid earth and made us realize that philosophy must make us better, morally and metaphysically, here and now, and should not be merely an escape mechanism to get away from the responsibilities of life. Hunger for peace is legitimate, but it becomes illegitimate when it aims at securing peace by turning one's back on the crying evils of our society or by exploiting the resources of logic to prove that this world is an illusion or just a dream, and liberation comes smiling as soon as this is realized. What then can philosophy hope to do for our modern society?

There can be no doubt that philosophy, whatever *ism* it may propound, is a basic subject, giving a certain character to our cultural outlook. There was a time when philosophy compassed within its bosom the whole gamut of knowledge, but the growth in our knowledge of the various sciences has made it impossible for any person to master all knowledge, and yet if the palpable shortcomings of knowing more and more of less and less—and this is what specialization has come to mean—are to be overcome, we must have a science which can look at things as a whole, and that can only be metaphysics. It may be superior to science, but cannot be completely divorced from it, for what exists cannot be totally divorced from the Real. On the logical side of metaphysics all the categories of science have to be correlated into a synthesis, so that the ultimate unity of knowledge may not be dissipated in the conflicting demands of the different sciences.

In the nineteenth century it appeared as if the sciences would constitute the last word in knowledge, completely ousting metaphysics. This was a claim which few philosophers could venture to support, but the twentieth century has brought sobriety to the scientists themselves and the most towering of them have grown conscious of the limitations of science. No less a person than Sir Arthur Eddington writes in his *Time, Space and Gravitation*:

"All through the physical world runs that unknown content, which must surely be the stuff of our consciousness. Here is a hint of aspects deep within the world of physics, and yet unattainable by the methods of physics. And, moreover, we have found that where science has progressed the furthest, the mind has but regained from Nature that which the mind has put into Nature."

Similar passages are to be found in the writings of Sir James Jeans, Max Planck and other eminent scientists. The great Einstein has not allowed himself to be insensible to the many aspects of life over and above science; he is said to be "awed by the incredible beauty of nature." His love for music brings out the romantic in him and is perhaps responsible for his love of the mysterious when he says: "The most beautiful thing we can experience is the mysterious, the source of all true art, science and religion." Thus he is conscious of the oneness of the whole universe and is driven to accept the need for philosophy as the cementing force in the world of knowledge. In these days of extreme specialization and the resulting narrowness of head and heart, it is only to philosophy that modern society can turn to save itself.

If philosophy to-day cannot be the summation of all knowledge it can at least claim to be the completion of knowledge in the old Platonic sense of the term. Metaphysics as the ground of all sciences and as the unifying force of all sciences still holds, whatever pretentious claims a few individual scientists may put up against the legitimacy of metaphysics. Such scientists need to be reminded that there is no science which has not emerged out of philosophy and which has not been founded by a philosopher, whether it be mathematics or physics, chemistry or biology, economics or politics, psychology or sociology. When the protagonists of these new sciences are anxious to repudiate their paternity and look upon philosophy as an unwanted parent, their very excesses lead them back to philosophy, for only philosophy can make them conscious of their inner contradictions and bring them round to a sober outlook. . . .

If philosophy is something more than an effect of mere climatic and geographical conditions and if it is fundamentally a search for Truth, the East and the West must meet at some point and cannot be always confronting each other like two hostile armies. This can never happen so long as Indian philosophy claims to be supra-rational and Truth is something to be found only in the depths of Silence with a capital S.

Protagonists of Indian philosophy do not adequately appreciate that even within the four walls of Indian spiritual experience there have been marked differences between the different schools of Vedanta, all based on intuition, and these differences can never be solved so long as we stick to mere intuitions and do not have these differences threshed out in the open forum of reason in spite of all its limitations. Vedanta claims to be nothing if not logical, and so the challenge of the West can be safely accepted and the palpable lacunae of Western philosophy can be logically filled up. Mere assertions about the superiority of Indian philosophy will cut no ice and Westerners will continue to talk of there being no philosophy in India—at least in the Western sense of the term— or they will continue to look upon it as mere theology.

But apart from what Westerners may choose to think of our philosophy it is very vital for our national existence to show what philosophy can do for the regeneration of our life. This we can hope to do only if we keep it clear of its religious trappings and make it a live instrument of thought for the problems which face us to-day. If philosophy is not only metaphysics dealing with the Ultimate Reality, but also an over-lord whose function it is to co-ordinate the different sciences, it has a vital bearing on ethical and social problems as well. If we say that these problems are all a part of *maya*, having nothing to do with philosophy, we shall have no reason to quarrel with those of our countrymen who openly say that philosophy is of no use, nay, that it is positively harmful, for it just offers a sort of defence mechanism to escape the living problems of life.

Assuming that India with the rest of Asia has definitely turned her back on the old feudal middle ages and seeks to transform herself into a modern state wedded to industrialism and socialism of one brand or another, the need for philosophy is no less acute. It will not do just to speak of Western civilization as merely materialistic. Rather we shall have to purge our own religious practices of the materialism latent in them, develop a new democratic outlook, for democracies are not created by paper constitutions, but only by the birth of a new sense of human dignity and by a fresh valuation of human life. If the West is apt to over-emphasize the pleasures of material life, it will be for India to remind the world that behind matter and sustaining it there is spirit.

There is yet one other important role that philosophy has to play in modern society. Very fortunately old religious acerbities have almost disappeared from civilized societies, but something equally ugly and unhealthy has taken their place in the form of racialism and nationalism. Philosophy with its capacity to view things as a whole and in their totality has to show up the spiritual poverty of racialism and nationalism just as it has so successfully shown the futility of one religion claiming to be superior to another.

In this respect China has been a wonderful world-teacher. The Chinese can bow with equal reverence before a Confucian and a Buddhist temple. One can note with pleasure that this spirit has entered even Japan in spite of her more limited insular vision. There is a Japanese Rotarian who sits at the feet of Buddha for four hours each morning and yet he gave to his Christian wife funds for the building of a Y.W.C.A. In such a catholic attitude there is more philosophy than in books on philosophy, and the aim of philosophy should be to make us better men and women: more cultured, more tolerant of others' shortcomings—*tout comprendre c'est tout pardonner*—more appreciative of the good in others.

To sum up: the philosopher has still to play a vital part in our modern society. He can make full use of all the wealth of scientific discoveries and yet be conscious of their limitations. He can bring a philosophic outlook to bear on the problems of life not just to escape the ills of life as an unreal manifestation of our ignorance, but to face them and transform them into good. He can help his generation to become conscious of its social problems and to solve them. Lastly he can bring to light the inner source of life which runs through the inorganic to the organic, through the organic to the mental, through the mental to the spiritual. Above all he will have to show that the Ultimate is not something far removed from us, rather that it is *here* and *now* with us. The Vedantic *tat tvam asi* finds its echo in Christ's pregnant saying: The kingdom of God is within ye.

BIBLIOGRAPHY

LISTED HERE ARE (A) THE SOURCES FROM WHICH THE SELECTIONS printed in this volume were taken, and (b) additional sources pertinent to the respective chapters and parts of chapters. Under the first heading are listed works which cover the entire course, or the course of several periods, of Indian philosophy.

Introduction: *The Currents and Course of Indian Philosophy*

The following source book covering the entire course of Indian philosophy contains, in literal translations, somewhat longer selections from some of the works represented in the present volume than are given here (and shorter selections from others), plus a few specialized works not included here (while omitting a number of the items which the present volume includes):

Radhakrishnan, Sir Sarvepalli; and Charles A. Moore (editors). *A Source Book in Indian Philosophy.* Princeton: Princeton University Press, 1957. 683 pp.

General historical treatments of Indian philosophy as a whole, which have been published in recent years, and older works which are standard, include the following:

Chatterjee, S. C.; and D. M. Datta. *An Introduction to Indian Philosophy.* Fifth edition. Calcutta: University of Calcutta, 1954. 443 pp.

The Cultural Heritage of India, by about 100 Indian scholars. With an introduction by Sarvepalli Radhakrishnan. Second edition. Calcutta: Ramakrishna Mission Institute of Culture, 1953–1962. 4 volumes. (Volume I covers the Vedas, the Upanishads, Buddhism, and Jainism; Volume II, the two epics, the *Bhagavad*

Gita, the laws of Manu, and other relevant materials; Volume III, the six systems and related topics; and Volume IV, Shaivism, Vaishnavism, Shaktism, Sikhism, Ramakrishna, and related topics.)

Dasgupta, S. N. *A History of Indian Philosophy.* Cambridge (England): University Press, 1922–1955. 5 volumes. (Covers the ancient and medieval periods.)

Prabhavananda, Swami; with the assistance of Frederick Manchester. *The Spiritual Heritage of India.* London: George Allen & Unwin, 1962. 374 pp. (Covers the ancient and medieval periods plus three thinkers since 1500.)

Radhakrishnan, Sir Sarvepalli. *Indian Philosophy.* Second edition. London: George Allen & Unwin, 1931 (reprinted 1941). 2 volumes. (Covers the ancient and medieval periods.)

Schweitzer, Albert. *Indian Thought and Its Development.* Translated from the German by Mrs. Charles E. B. Russell. New York: Henry Holt & Co., 1936. 272 pp.

Sinha, Jadunath. *A History of Indian Philosophy.* Calcutta: Sinha Publishing House, 1952–1956. 2 volumes.

The following is a useful history of Indian philosophy in the nineteenth and twentieth centuries:

Naravane, V. S. *Modern Indian Thought; A Philosophical Survey.* Bombay: Asia Publishing House, 1964. 310 pp.

Among the significant books on Indian philosophy as a whole in which the exposition is primarily analytical rather than historical are the following:

Chatterjee, Satischandra; and Datta Dhirendramohan. *An Introduction to Indian Philosophy.* Fifth edition. Calcutta: University of Calcutta, 1954. 443 pp.

Gokhale, B. G. *Indian Thought Through the Ages; A Study of Some Dominant Concepts.* Bombay: Asia Publishing House, 1961. 236 pp.

Heimann, Betty. *Facets of Indian Thought.* New York: Schocken Books, 1964. 177 pp.

Potter, Karl H. *Presuppositions of India's Philosophies.* Englewood Cliffs, N.J.: Prentice-Hall, 1963. 276 pp.

Sharma, Chandradhar. *Indian Philosophy; A Critical Survey.* New York: Barnes and Noble, 1962. 405 pp.

Sinha, Jadunath. *Outlines of Indian Philosophy.* Calcutta: Sinha Publishing House Private, 1963. 444 pp.

Smart, Ninian. *Doctrine and Argument in Indian Philosophy.* London: George Allen & Unwin, 1964. 255 pp.

Zimmer, Heinrich R. *Philosophies of India.* Edited by Joseph Campbell. New York: Pantheon Books, 1951. 687 pp. (Reprinted in 1956 by Meridian Books.)

Indian philosophy as a whole is covered as part of a larger topic in such works as the following, one of which is documentary, one narrative, and one analytical:

Müller, F. Max (editor). *Sacred Books of the East.* Oxford: Clarendon Press, 1879–1910. 50 volumes. (Classics of Indian philosophy and religion, in scholarly translations, are presented in 32 of the volumes. Individual volumes in the series have been reprinted in recent years, in paperback editions, by Dover Publications, New York.)

Radhakrishnan, Sir Sarvepalli (principal editor). *History of Philosophy, Eastern and Western.* London: George Allen & Unwin, 1952–1953. 2 volumes. (Indian philosophy is dealt with in the first 20 of the 25 chapters of Volume I.)

Raju, P. T. *Introduction to Comparative Philosophy.* Lincoln (Nebraska): University of Nebraska Press, 1962. 364 pp. (Part 3 of the 4 parts gives an illuminating interpretive account of the development of Indian philosophy.)

I. *"That Art Thou"*: Ancient Vedantism

GENERAL

The passages included in the introduction to Chapter I were taken from (1) the Monier-Williams work cited on p. 242; (2) *Prayers, Praises and Psalms,* translated by V. Raghavan (Madras: G. A. Natesan and Co., 1938; 512 pp.); and (3) *Srimad Bhagavatam; The Wisdom of God,* translated by Swami Prabhavananda (Mylapore: Sri Ramakrishna Math, second edition, 1947; 320 pp.).

An analysis of the main ideas in the Vedic hymns, as well as in the Upanishads (and other appendixes to the collections of Vedic hymns), will be found in:

Keith, A. B. *The Religion and Philosophy of the Veda and Upanishads.* Cambridge (Mass.): Harvard University Press, 1925. 2 volumes.

New scholarly translations of the Vedantic classics will be found in:

The Beginnings of Indian Philosophy; Selections from the Rig Veda, Atharva Veda, Upanishads and Mahabharata. Translated by Franklin Edgerton. Cambridge (Mass.): Harvard University Press, 1965. 362 pp.

VEDIC HYMNS

The Vedic hymns included in the present volume were taken from the following sources:

Monier-Williams, Sir Monier. *Indian Wisdom.* Fourth edition. London: Luzac and Co., 1893. 575 pp. (A new printing, designated as the "Second Edition," was published at Varanasi by the Chowkhamba Sanskrit Series Office in 1963, in 542 pp.)

Muir, John. *Metrical Translations from Sanskrit Writers.* London: Trübner & Co., 1879. 376 pp.

The four historic collections of Vedic hymns—the Atharva, Rig, Sama, and Yajur Vedas—have been translated in their entirety into English, the Rig Veda and the "white" edition of the Yajur Veda having been translated twice, as follows:

The Hymns of the Atharva-Veda. Translated, with a commentary, by Ralph T. H. Griffith. Banaras: E. J. Lazarus & Co., 1895–1896. 2 volumes.

The Hymns of the Rigveda. Translated by Ralph T. H. Griffith. Fourth edition. Varanasi: Chowkhamba Sanskrit Series Office, 1963. 2 volumes.

Rig-Veda-Sanhita; A Collection of Ancient Hindu Hymns. Translated by H. H. Wilson. London: W. H. Allen & Co., 1850–1888. 6 volumes.

The Hymns of the Samaveda. Translated by Ralph T. H. Griffith. Fourth edition. Varanasi: Chowkhamba Sanskrit Series Office, 1963. 338 pp.

The Yajur Veda. Translated by Devi Chand. Hoshiarpur: Published by the translator, 1959. 354 pp. (A translation of the White Yajur Veda.)

The Texts of the White Yajurveda. Translated, with a commentary, by Ralph T. H. Griffith. Banaras: E. J. Lazarus & Co., 1899. 344 pp.

The Veda of the Black Yajus School. Translated by A. B. Keith. Cambridge (Mass.): Harvard University Press, 1914. 2 volumes.

UPANISHADS

The Upanishads printed in the present volume were taken from:

The Ten Principal Upanishads. Translated by Shree Purohit Swami and W. B. Yeats. London: Faber & Faber (New York: The Macmillan Co.), 1937. 158 pp.

Other significant translations of a few or more of the Upanishads include:

The Principal Upanishads. Edited and translated by Sir Sarvepalli Radhakrishnan. London: George Allen & Unwin, 1953. 958 pp.

The Thirteen Principal Upanishads. Translated by R. E. Hume. Second edition. Madras: Oxford University Press, 1949. 587 pp.

The Upanishads. Translated, with explanations, by Swami Nikhilananda. New York: Harper & Brothers, 1949–1959. 4 volumes.

The Upanishads, Breath of the Eternal. Translated by Swami Prabhavananda and Frederick Manchester. Hollywood (Calif.): Vedanta Press, 1948. 210 pp. (Later printings include a paperback edition.)

The Upanishads; Selections from the 108 Upanishads. With an English translation by T. M. P. Mahadevan. Madras: G. A. Natesan & Co., 1940. 400 pp.

The following are useful analytical studies of the ideas expounded in the Upanishads:

Deussen, Paul. *The Philosophy of the Upanishads.* Translated from the German by Rev. A. S. Geden. Edinburgh: T. & T. Clark, 1908. 429 pp. (Paperback reprint issued at New York by Dover Publications, 1966.)

Radhakrishnan, Sir Sarvepalli. *The Philosophy of the Upanishads.* With a foreword by Rabindranath Tagore. London: George Allen & Unwin (New York: The Macmillan Co.), 1935. 143 pp.

II. *The Road to Nirvana: Ancient Buddhism*

GENERAL

The following are among the compilations of excerpts from the basic texts and the later discourses of Buddhism, in English translations:

The Buddha's Philosophy; Selections from the Pali Canon. Translated by George F. Allen. New York: The Macmillan Co., 1959. 194 pp.

Buddhism, A Religion of Infinite Compassion. Edited by Clarence H. Hamilton. New York: Liberal Arts Press, 1953. 189 pp.

A Buddhist Bible. Edited by Dwight Goddard. Revised and enlarged edition. New York: E. P. Dutton & Co., 1952. 677 pp.

Buddhist Scriptures. Translated by Edward Conze. Harmondsworth, Middlesex, England: Penguin Books, 1959. 250 pp.

The Teachings of the Compassionate Buddha. Edited by E. A. Burtt. New York: New American Library, 1955. 247 pp.

The Wisdom of Buddhism. Edited by Christmas Humphreys. New York: Random House, 1961. 280 pp.

Analytical or historical studies, and studies written with both purposes, include:

Bahm, Archie J. *Philosophy of the Buddha.* New York: Harper & Brothers, 1959. 175 pp.

Bapat, P. V. (editor). *2500 Years of Buddhism.* With a foreword by Sir Sarvepalli Radhakrishnan. Delhi: Ministry of Information and Broadcasting, 1956. 503 pp.

Conze, Edward. *Buddhism; Its Essence and Development.* With a preface by Arthur Waley. New York: Harper & Brothers, 1959. 212 pp.

Coomaraswamy, A. K. *Buddha and the Gospel of Buddhism.* Bombay: Asia Publishing House, 1956. 370 pp. (Reprinted at New Hyde Park, N.Y., by University Books in 1964.)

Gard, Richard A. (editor). *Buddhism.* New York: George Braziller, 1961. 256 pp. (Contains extracts in English from basic Buddhist texts and from present-day monographic studies.)

Sangharakshita, Bhikshu. *A Survey of Buddhism.* Bangalore: Indian Institute of World Culture, 1957. 500 pp. (The bhikshu—devotee—is a London-born Englishman who was converted to Buddhism and went to India.)

Thomas, Edward J. *The History of Buddhist Thought.* Second edition. New York: Barnes & Noble, 1951. 316 pp.

BASIC TEXTS

The Sermons, by Buddha, printed in the present volume, were taken from the following source:

Some Sayings of the Buddha, According to the Pali Canon. Translated by Francis L. Woodward. London and New York: Oxford University Press, 1939 (reprinted 1942). 356 pp. (Originally published in another format in 1925.)

For further discussions of Buddha's contribution to Indian philosophy, see:

Davids, Mrs. Rhys. *Gotama the Man.* London: Luzac & Co., 1928. 302 pp.

Radhakrishnan, Sir Sarvepalli. *Gautama the Buddha.* Bombay: Hind Kitabs, 1945. 65 pp.

The excerpts from the *Dhammapada* presented here were taken from:

The Dhammapada. Translated, with an essay on Buddha and the Occident, by Irving Babbitt. New York and London: Oxford University Press, 1936. 123 pp.

Readers especially interested in this classic should see also:

The Dhammapada. With introductory essays, the Pali text, an English translation, and notes. By Sir Sarvepalli Radhakrishnan. London and New York: Oxford University Press, 1950. 194 pp. (Paperback edition printed at New York by the New Directions Publishing Corporation, 1965.)

Of the basic texts of the Buddhist canon, two other works, besides the *Dhammapada,* have been translated in their entirety into English, namely, the *Digha-Nikaya* and the *Majjhima-Nikaya*:

Dialogues of the Buddha. Translated by T. W. Rhys Davids. London: Oxford University Press, 1899–1921. 3 volumes. (The *Digha-Nikaya.*)

The Collection of the Middle Length Sayings (Majjhima-Nikaya). Translated by I. B. Horner. London: Luzac & Co., 1954–1959. 3 volumes. (An earlier translation, in 2 volumes, by Lord Chalmers, was published by the Oxford University Press in 1926–1927.)

LATER DISCOURSES

The excerpts printed in the present volume from the Theravada (Hinayana) work entitled *Questions of King Milinda* were taken from the *Buddhist Scriptures* mentioned above. For a complete translation of the work and a study of its significance, see:

The Questions of King Milinda. Translated by T. W. Rhys Davids. Volumes 35 and 36 of *The Sacred Books of the East,* mentioned above.

Davids, Mrs. C. A. Rhys. *The Milinda-Questions; An Inquiry into Its Place in the History of Buddhism.* London: G. Routledge and Sons, 1930. 168 pp.

Other studies bearing especially on Theravada Buddhism include:

Bhagvat, Miss Durga N. *Early Buddhist Jurisprudence (Theravada Vinaya-Laws).* Poona: Oriental Book Agency, 1939. 204 pp.

Walters, John. *Mind Unshaken; A Modern Approach to Buddhism.* London: Rider and Co., 1961. 127 pp.

The excerpts from the Mahayana work entitled *Lankavatara Sutra* were taken from the *Buddhist Bible* mentioned above. For a complete translation of this work and a detailed discussion of it, see:

The Lankavatara Sutra; A Mahayana Text. Translated by D. T. Suzuki. London: Routledge and Kegan Paul, 1932; reissued 1956. 300 pp.

Suzuki, D. T. *Studies in the Lankavatara Sutra.* London: G. Routledge and Sons, 1930. 464 pp.

Other studies or compilations bearing especially on Mahayana Buddhism include:

Buddhist Mahayana Texts. Translated by various hands. Volume 49 of *The Sacred Books of the East.*

Suzuki, D. T. *Outlines of Mahayana Buddhism.* London: Luzac and Co., 1907. 420 pp.

III. *Reverence for Life: Ancient Jainism*

GENERAL

For general treatments of Jainism as a philosophy and as a religion, see:

Jagmandar-lal Jaini. *Outlines of Jainism.* Second edition. Cambridge (England): University Press, 1940. 159 pp.

Mehta, Mohan Lai. *Outlines of Jaina Philosophy.* Bangalore: Jain Mission Society, 1954. 168 pp.

BASIC TEXTS

The *Discourse of Performed Precepts* and the *Higher Meditation* were taken from Volume 45 of *The Sacred Books of the East.*

LATER DISCOURSES

The *Discourse to the Soul* and the *Essence of the Scripture* were taken, respectively, from:

Guna-Bhadra. *Atmanushasana (Discourse to the Soul).* Translated by B. J. L. Jaini. Ajitashram: Central Jaina Publishing House, 1928. 75 pp.

Kundakunda. *The Pravacana-sara . . . together with the Commentary Tattva-Dipika.* Translated by Barend Faddegon. Cambridge (England): University Press, 1935. 227 pp.

Other works by Kundakunda available in English are:
The Building of the Cosmos, or Panchastikayasara. Edited and translated by A. Chakravartinayanar. Arrah: Kumar Devendra Prasada, 1920. 174 pp.
Niyamsara (The Perfect Law). Edited and translated by Uggar Sain, with the assistance of B. S. P. Ji. Ajitashram: Central Jaina Publishing House, 1931. 78 pp.
Samayasara (The Soul-Essence). Edited and translated by B. J. L. Jaini, with the assistance of B. S. P. Ji. Ajitashram: Central Jaina Publishing House, 1930. 214 pp.

IV. Ancient and Medieval Epitomes and Commentaries

FATALISM AND HEDONISM

The excerpts from the *Bhagavad Gita* and from Madhava's epitome of hedonism were taken, respectively, from:
The Song Celestial, or Bhagavad-Gita. Translated by Sir Edwin Arnold. Boston: Roberts Brothers, 1885. 185 pp.
Madhava. *Sarva-Darsana-Samgraha*. Translated by E. B. Cowell and A. E. Gough. Fourth edition. London: Kegan Paul, Trench, Trübner & Co., 1914. 281 pp.

Other translations of the *Bhagavad Gita* abound. Two which are perhaps worthy of special mention are:
The Bhagavad Gita. With an introductory essay, Sanskrit text, English translation, and notes, by Sir Sarvepalli Radhakrishnan. London: George Allen and Unwin (New York: Harper & Brothers), 1948. 388 pp.
The Gospel of Selfless Action, or The Gita According to Gandhi. By Mahadev Desai. Ahmedabad: Navajivan Publishing House, 1948. 390 pp. (A translation into English of M. K. Gandhi's translation of the *Bhagavad Gita* into Gujarati, with Gandhi's introduction, some notes by Gandhi, and an introduction and notes by Desai.)

Noteworthy discussions of the significance of the *Bhagavad Gita* include the following:
Bhave, Vinoba. *Talks on the Gita*. New York: The Macmillan Co., 1960. 267 pp.
Ghose, Aurobindo. *Essays on the Gita*. New York: Sri Aurobindo Library, 1950 (reissued 1953). 580 pp.

THE SIX SYSTEMS

The sutras of the six systems—Nyaya and Vaishesika, Sankhya and Yoga, and Mimamsa and Vedanta (Brahma)—were taken from the following sources, respectively:

Gautama. *The Aphorisms of the Nyaya Philosophy.* Translated by J. R. B. Allahabad: Presbyterian Mission Press, 1850. 56 pp.

Kanada. *The Vaishesika Aphorisms of Kanada, with Comments from the Upaskara of San-kara-Misra and the Vivritti of Jaya-narayana-Tarkapanchanava.* Translated by A. E. Gough. Banaras: E. J. Lazarus & Co., 1873. 310 pp.

The Sankhya Karika of Iswara Krishna; An Exposition of the System of Kapila. Translated by John Davies. Second edition. Calcutta: Susil Gupta, 1957. 86 pp.

Patanjali. *Aphorisms of Yoga.* Translated by Shree Purohit Swami, with an introduction by W. B. Yeats. London: Faber & Faber, 1938. 94 pp.

Jaimini. *Mimamsa; The Secret of the Sacred Books of the Hindus.* Translated by N. V. Thadani. Delhi: Bharati Research Institute, 1952. 570 pp.

Badarayana. *Vedanta-Sutras, With the Commentary by Sankarakarya.* Translated by George Thibaut. Volume 34 of *The Sacred Books of the East.*

The additional selections pertinent to the Brahma (Vedanta) Sutras were taken from the following sources:

Madhva, Anandatirtha. *Srimad Visnu-Tattva-Vinirvana.* Translated by S. S. Raghavachar. Mangalore: Sri Ramakrishna Ashrama, 1959. 98 pp.

Ramanuja. *Vedarthasamgraha.* Edited and translated by J. A. B. van Buitenen. Poona: Deccan College, Postgraduate and Research Institute, 1956. 316 pp.

Wood, Ernest E. *The Glorious Presence.* New York: E. P. Dutton & Co., 1951. (Contains the selection from Shankara.)

Three noteworthy new translations of the Yoga Sutras have been published in recent years:

How to Know God; The Yoga Aphorisms of Patanjali. Translated by Swami Prabhavananda and Christopher Isherwood. New York: Harper & Brothers, 1953. 224 pp.

The Textbook of Yoga Psychology; A New Translation and Interpretation of Patanjali's Yoga Sutras. By Rammurti S. Mishra. New York: Julian Press, 1963. 401 pp.

Yoga, Union with the Ultimate; A New Version of the Ancient

Yoga Sutras of Patanjali. By Archie J. Bahm. New York: Frederick Ungar Publishing Co., 1961. 162 pp.

The following are special treatments of Shankara, Ramanuja, and Madhva, including one of the available anthologies of Shankara's writings:

Kumarappa, Bharatan. *The Hindu Conception of the Diety as Culminating in Ramanuja.* London: Luzac & Co., 1934. 356 pp.

Menon, Y. K.; and Richard Allen. *The Pure Principle; An Introduction of the Philosophy of Shankara.* East Lansing (Mich.): Michigan State University Press, 1960. 127 pp.

Radhakrishnan, Sir Sarvepalli. *The Vedanta According to Samkara and Ramanuja.* London: George Allen and Unwin, 1928. 287 pp. (A separate printing of two chapters of Radhakrishnan's *Indian Philosophy.*)

Sarma, R. N. R. *Reign of Realism in Indian Philosophy.* Madras: National Press, 1937. 695 pp. (Deals with the philosophy of Madhva.)

Select Works of Sri Sankaracharya. Edited and translated by S. Venkataramanan. Third edition. Madras: G. A. Natesan & Co., 1944. 256 pp.

Varadachari, K. C. *Sri Ramanuja's Theory of Knowledge; A Study.* Tirupati: T.-T. Devasthanams Press, 1943. 239 pp.

Venkatarama Iyer, M. K. *Advaita Vedanta According to Samkara.* New York: Asia Publishing House, 1964. 213 pp.

The following older work was recently reprinted because of its continued usefulness:

Müller, Max. *The Six Systems of Indian Philosophy.* London: Longmans, Green and Co., 1899. 478 pp. (Reprinted in 1903, 1912, 1916, 1919, 1928; reprinted again at Varanasi in 1963 by the Chowkhamba Sanskrit Series Office.)

LAWS, PROVERBS, AND RHAPSODIES

The excerpts from Yajnavalkya's and Manu's Codes were taken, respectively, from:

Nilakantha Mimamsakabhatta (son of Shankara). *Vyahavara Mayukha . . . Also the Yajnavalkya Smriti.* Translated, with notes, by V. N. Mandlik. Bombay: Education Society's Press, 1880. 2 volumes.

Monier-Williams, Sir Monier. *Indian Wisdom.* Cited on p. 242.

Additional material from the law codes and political philosophies of India, including a quasi-Machiavellian political treatise which is embedded in the *Mahabharata,* will be found in D. Mackenzie Brown (editor), *The White Umbrella; Indian Political Thought from Manu to Gandhi* (Berkeley: University of California Press, 1953; paperbound edition, 1959; 204 pp.).

The excerpts from the *Kural* were taken from the following translation:

> *The Kural, or the Maxims of Tiruvalluvar.* Translated by V. V. S. Aiyar. Tiruchirapalli: Dr. V. V. S. Krishnamurthy, 1952. 287 pp. (Aiyar translated the *Kural* while under detention and awaiting deportation from India as a revolutionary in 1914–1915. The translation was published by his son.)

The excerpts printed here from the Great Liberation Tantra were taken from:

> *The Great Liberation (Mahanirvana Tantra).* Translated by Arthur Avalon, i.e., Sir John G. Woodroffe. Second edition. Madras: Ganesh & Co., 1927. 461 pp.

Reference may also be made to the following:

> *The Serpent Power* (translation of two Tantrik texts). By Sir John G. Woodroffe. Fifth edition. Madras: Ganesh and Co., 1953. 2 vols. in 1.

> Woodroffe, Sir John G. *Shakti and Shakta; Essays and Addresses on the Shakta Tantashastra.* Third edition. Madras: Ganesh and Co., 1929. 724 pp.

V. *"The Life Divine"*: Modern Mysticism

GENERAL

With regard to Lal Ded and Kabir, who are mentioned in the introduction to Chapter V, reference may be made to the following sources, in addition to the Kabir translation by Tagore which is mentioned in Chapter V:

> Keay, Rev. F. E. *Kabir and His Followers.* Calcutta: Association Press, 1931, 186 pp.

> *Lalla-Vakyani, or the Wise Sayings of Lal Ded, a Mystic Poetess of Ancient Kashmir.* Edited and translated by Sir George Grierson and L. D. Barnett. London: Royal Asiatic Society, 1920. 225 pp.

> *The Word of Lalla the Prophetess.* Translated by Sir Richard C. Temple. Cambridge (England): University Press, 1924. 292 pp.

EARLY SIKHISM

The selections printed herein from the writings of Nanak were taken from:

The Jap Ji, the Message of Guru Nanak. Translated by Kirpal Singh. Delhi: Ruhani Satsang, Sawan Ashram, 1959. 182 pp.

Macauliffe, Max A. *The Sikh Religion; Its Gurus, Sacred Writings and Authors*. Oxford: Clarendon Press, 1909. 6 volumes.

The excerpt from the writings of Arjun was taken from:

The Psalm of Peace, an English Translation of Guru Arjun's Sukhmani. By Teja Singh. Bombay: Oxford University Press, 1950. 122 pp.

Other recent works on Sikhism include the following:

Sri Guru-Granth Sahib; English Version. Translated and annotated by Gopal Singh. New Delhi, Gur Das Kapur, 1962. 4 volumes. (Reprinted at New York by the Taplinger Publishing Co. in 1965 in a limited edition, 4 volumes, under the title *Guru-Granth Sahib; The Holy Books of the Sikhs*.)

Narang, Sir Gokul C. *Transformation of Sikhism*. Fifth edition. New Delhi: New Book Society of India, 1960. 268 pp.

Selections from the Sacred Writings of the Sikhs. Translated by Trilochan Singh and others. With an introduction by Sir Sarvepalli Radhakrishnan and a foreword by Arnold Toynbee. New York: The Macmillan Co., 1960. 288 pp.

NINETEENTH CENTURY

The passages printed here in excerpts may be found in full in the following compilations:

The Gospel of Ramakrishna. With a foreword by Christopher Isherwood. New York: Vedanta Society, 1947. 436 pp.

The Complete Works of Swami Vivekananda. Mayavati: Advaita Ashrama, 1924–1932. 7 volumes plus an unnumbered index volume.

Regarding the general resurgence of mysticism in India in the nineteenth century, see:

Parekh, Manilal C. *The Brahma Samaj, A Short History*. Rajkot: Oriental Christ House, 1929. 287 pp.

The Theosophical Movement, 1875–1925; A History and Survey. New York: E. P. Dutton & Co., 1925. 705 pp. (An edition of this work which, although shorter, carries the history down to 1950, was published by the Cunningham Press, Los Angeles, in 1951, in 351 pp.)

For combined studies of both Ramakrishna and his pupil Vive-
kananda, see:
    Isherwood, Christopher. *Ramakrishna and His Disciples*. New
York: Simon and Schuster, 1965. 348 pp.
    Nehru, Jawaharlal. *Sri Ramakrishna and Swami Vivekananda*.
Mayavati: Advaita Ashrama, 1949. 14 pp.
    Rolland, Romain. *Ramakrishna . . . and the Universal Gospel
of Vivekananda*. Translated from French by E. F. Malcolm-
Smith. Mayavati: Advaita Ashrama, 1931. 2 volumes.
On Ramakrishna in particular, see:
    Life of Ramakrishna. Sixth edition. Mayavati: Advaita Ash-
rama, 1948. 620 pp.
    Mukerji, Dhan Gopal. *The Face of Silence*. New York: E. P.
Dutton & Co., 1926. 255 pp.
    Müller, F. Max. *Ramakrishna; His Life and Sayings*. London:
Longmans, Green & Co., 1898 (reissued 1901). 200 pp.
On Vivekananda in particular, see:
    Datta, Bhupendranath. *Swami Vivekananda, A Patriot-
Prophet; A Study*. Calcutta: Nababharat Publishers, 1954.
428 pp.
    The Life of Swami Vivekananda. By his Eastern and Western
disciples. Third edition. Mayavati: Advaita Ashrama, 1944. 2
volumes.
    Nikhilananda, Swami. *Vivekananda; A Biography*. New York:
Ramakrishna-Vivekananda Center, 1953. 216 pp.
    Reminiscences of Swami Vivekananda. By his Eastern admirers.
Calcutta: Advaita Ashrama, 1961. 404 pp.
    "Vivekananda Centenary Number," *Vedanta and the West*
(Hollywood, Calif.), November–December 1962.

TWENTIETH CENTURY

The passages included here were taken from the following sources:
    Ghose, Aurobindo. *Last Poems*. Pondicherry: Sri Aurobindo
Ashram, 1952. 48 pp.
    Krishnamurti, Jiddu. *The Pool of Wisdom . . . and Three
Poems*. Eerde (Netherlands): The Star Publishing Trust, 1928.
100 pp.

As to Aurobindo Ghose, his voluminous writings include poems and
plays (collected and published in two volumes at Pondicherry in 1942);
letters (collected and published in several series at Bombay in 1947
to 1951); speeches (third edition of a collection of them, published

at Pondicherry in 1952); translations of works ancient, medieval, and modern (published in separate volumes at Pondicherry and Madras); and—most important of all—essays. Of the volumes of essays, the most popular is *The Life Divine*, first published in two volumes at Calcutta and reprinted twice at New York in one volume some years later.

The main works of recent years dealing with the life and thought of Aurobindo Ghose are:

Chaudhuri, Haridas; and Frederic Spiegelberg (editors). *The Integral Philosophy of Sri Aurobindo; A Commemorative Symposium*. London: George Allen & Unwin, 1960. 350 pp.

Donnelly, Morwenna. *Founding the Life Divine; An Introduction to the Integral Yoga of Sri Aurobindo*. New York: Hawthorn Books, 1956. 246 pp.

Purani, A. B. *The Life of Sri Aurobindo*. Second edition. Pondicherry: Sri Aurobindo Ashram, 1960. 372 pp.

Srinivasa Iyengar, K. R. *Sri Aurobindo*. Second edition. Calcutta: Ayra Publishing House, 1950. 404 pp.

Varma, V. P. *The Political Philosophy of Sri Aurobindo*. New York: Asia Publishing House, 1961. 471 pp.

Krishnamurti's writings may be grouped in three series: (a) transcripts of his talks (about 20 volumes and pamphlets), (b) essays (about 10 volumes), and (c) poems (3 booklets). A number of these works have been translated into foreign languages, including (in recent years) translations into German in 1961 and into Spanish in 1962. Of the books written about Krishnamurti, aside from those in French, German, and Italian (two of the French works, by Ludowic Rehault and Carlo Suares, having been translated into English), reference may be made to two books by Lilly Heber: *Krishnamurti, The Man and His Message* (London: George Allen & Unwin, 1931; 254 pp.); and *Krishnamurti and the World Crisis* (same publisher, 1935; 291 pp.).

VI. *"The Men of the Great Soul"*: Twentieth-Century Popular Philosophy

SOUL FORCE AND REALITY

The passages from Tagore were taken from the following books written by him:

Sadhana, The Realisation of Life. New York: The Macmillan Co., 1913. 164 pp. (Reissued 1916. Translated into French and Spanish in the 1940s.)

The Religion of Man, Being the Hibbert Lectures for 1930.
New York: The Macmillan Co., 1931. 244 pp. (Reissued at
London by Unwin Books, 1961; 128 pp. A French translation,
described as the sixth edition, was published in 1933 and a German translation in 1962.)

Other writings by Tagore are indicated in the introductory remarks
preceding the two selections from him in Chapter VI. Writings about
the philosophy of Tagore include the following:

Naravane, V. S. *Rabindranath Tagore; A Philosophical Study.*
Allahabad: Central Book Depot, no date (late 1940s or 1950s).
238 pp.

Radhakrishnan, Sir Sarvepalli. *The Philosophy of Rabindranath
Tagore.* London: Macmillan and Co., 1918. 294 pp. (Reissued
at Baroda by Good Companions in 1961; 180 pp.)

Ray, B. G. *The Philosophy of Rabindranath Tagore.* Bombay:
Hind Kitabs, 1949. 155 pp.

Sen Sachin. *The Political Thought of Tagore.* Calcutta: General Printers and Publishers, 1947. 360 pp.

Sinha, Sasadha. *Social Thinking of Rabindranath Tagore.* New
York: Asia Publishing House, 1962. 198 pp.

SOUL FORCE AND CONDUCT

The selections from Gandhi's essays in *Young India* were reprinted in the present volume from:

Hindu Dharma (a collection of writings by M. K. Gandhi).
Edited by Bharatan Kumarappa. Ahmedabad: Navajivan Publishing House, 1950. 443 pp.

Gandhi's chief published writings are mentioned in the introductory
remarks preceding the selections from him presented in Chapter VI.
An edition of his *Collected Works* began to be issued by the Indian
Ministry of Information and Broadcasting in 1958. Writings about
Gandhi's philosophy include:

Bondurant, Joan V. *Conquest of Violence; The Gandhian
Philosophy of Conflict.* Princeton: Princeton University Press,
1958. 269 pp.

Datta, D. M. *The Philosophy of Mahatma Gandhi.* Madison:
University of Wisconsin Press, 1953. 155 pp.

Dhawan, G. N. *The Political Philosophy of Mahatma Gandhi.*
Second edition. Ahmedabad: Navajivan Publishing House, 1951.
407 pp.

Patel, M. S. *The Educational Philosophy of Mahatma Gandhi.*
Ahmedabad: Navajivan Publishing House, 1953. 288 pp.

VII. *Twentieth-Century Theories of Value, the Self, and God*

GOD AND THE SELF

The selection from Radhakrishnan printed here was taken from his book *An Idealist Theory of Life, Being the Hibbert Lectures for* 1929 (London: George Allen & Unwin, 1932; revised 1937; reprinted at New York by Barnes and Noble in a paperback edition, 1964; 351 pp.; reissued 1961 in a print of 279 pp.). The selections from Datta and Chatterjee were taken from:

Radhakrishnan, Sir Sarvepalli, and others (editors). A. R. Wadia; Essays in Philosophy Presented in His Honour. Bangalore: N. A. Nikam, 1954. 364 pp.

Other significant writings by Radhakrishnan, Datta, and Chatterjee (and the 1952 collection of essays on Radhakrishnan's philosophy) are mentioned in the introductory passages preceding the selections from the three thinkers in Chapter VII. Reference may also be made to J. S. Samartha's *Introduction to Radhakrishnan; The Man and His Thought* (New York: Association Press, 1964; 127 pp.).

VALUES

The selection from Hiriyanna presented in this volume was taken from his book *The Quest After Perfection* (Mysore: Kavyalaya Publishers, 1952; 112 pp.); the selection from Coomaraswamy, from his book *Figures of Speech or Figures of Thought* (London: Luzac & Co., 1946; 256 pp.); and the selection from Wadia, from his book *The Philosophy of Mahatma Gandhi, and Other Essays* (Mysore: University of Mysore, 1958; 745 pp.).

Other significant writings by Hiriyanna, Coomaraswamy, and Wadia are mentioned in the introductory passages preceding the selections from them in Chapter VII.

OTHER CONTEMPORARY LEADERS

Leading contemporary thinkers of India besides those represented in this volume include (1) B. K. Bhattacharya, author of *Logic, Value and Reality* (Calcutta: University of Calcutta Press, 1961; 285 pp.), which has a foreword by Sir Sarvepalli Radhakrishnan; (2) H. M. Bhattacharyya, author of *The Principles of Philosophy* (Calcutta: University of Calcutta Press, 1944; 437 pp.); (3) Kalidas Bhattacharyya, author of *Alternative Standpoints in Philosophy* (Calcutta: Das Gupta, 1953; 366 pp.); (4) T. M. P. Mahadevan, author of

The Philosophy of Advaita (London: Luzac & Co., 1938; 284 pp.) and *Outlines of Hinduism* (Bombay: Chetana, 1956; 312 pp.), each of these two works containing a foreword by Sir Sarvepalli Radhakrishnan); and (5) P. T. Raju, author of *Idealistic Thought of India* (London: George Allen & Unwin, 1953; 454 pp.) and *Introduction to Comparative Philosophy* (Lincoln: University of Nebraska Press, 1962; 364 pp.) and co-editor, with Sir Sarvepalli Radhakrishnan, of *The Concept of Man; A Study in Comparative Philosophy* (Lincoln: Johnsen Publishing Co., 1960; 383 pp.).

The reader is referred also to the following basic sources of philosophical thought of the present day in India:

Philosophical Quarterly. Calcutta (later Amalner): 1925—. (Organ of the Indian Institute of Philosophy and the Indian Philosophical Congress.)

Radhakrishnan, Sir Sarvepalli (editor). *Contemporary Indian Philosophy.* Second edition. London: George Allen & Unwin, 1952. 648 pp. (Contains chapters on their own philosophies by Kalidas Bhattacharyya, Coomaraswamy, Datta, Gandhi, Hiriyanna, Radhakrishnan, Raju, Wadia, and others.)

The Mind of India presents, in historical sequence, fifty great works of Indian thought in English translations of high literary quality. Included are the most poignant and brilliant passages of the classics—the Vedic hymns, the Upanishads, the Buddhist and Jain discourses, the *Bhagavad Gita*, the "Sentences" of the six systems, the laws of Manu, the Sikh psalms, and the spiritual teachings of Ramakrishna—and a generous representation of modern Hindu philosophical writings by such thinkers as Gandhi, Tagore, Radhakrishnan, Krishnamurti, and Coomaraswamy.

In the introduction, Dr. Gerber has distilled the principal components of Indian thought in terms of eighteen basic theses. Headnotes place each selection in historical perspective, defining the Indian interpretation of such concepts as nirvana, good and evil, salvation, and illusion and reality, and drawing attention to analogous insights in Occidental thought.

The translations, by William Butler Yeats and Irving Babbitt, among others, have been selected for their readability and faithful rendering. A descriptive bibliography is provided, and pronunciation aids for difficult Indian names are given. *The Mind of India* is a selective, yet comprehensive, historical introduction to Indian thought, both in its perennial concerns and in its evolving interests, from 2000 B.C. to the present.